The Politics of Latin Literature

The Politics of Latin Literature

WRITING, IDENTITY, AND EMPIRE IN ANCIENT ROME

Thomas N. Habinek

PRINCETON UNIVERSITY PRESS

PRINCETON, NEW JERSEY

Copyright © 1998 by Princeton University Press
Published by Princeton University Press, 41 William Street,
Princeton, New Jersey 08540
In the United Kingdom: Princeton University Press,
Chichester, West Sussex

All Rights Reserved

Library of Congress Cataloging-in-Publication Data

Habinek, Thomas N., 1953–
The politics of Latin literature : writing, identity, and empire in ancient
Rome / Thomas N. Habinek.
p. cm.
Includes bibliographical references and index.

ISBN: 0-691-06827-5 (cl : alk. paper)
1. Latin literature—History and criticism.   2. Authorship—Political
aspects—Rome.   3. Politics and literature—Rome.   4. Group identity in literature.   5. Imperialism in literature. I. Title.
PA6029.P64H33   1998
870.9′001   dc21   97-40074 CIP

This book has been composed in Sabon

Princeton University Press books are printed
on acid-free paper and meet the guidelines
for permanence and durability of the Committee
on Production Guidelines for Book Longevity
of the Council on Library Resources

http://pup.princeton.edu

Printed in the United States of America

1   3   5   7   9   10   8   6   4   2

NMH & JKH

CONTENTS

ACKNOWLEDGMENTS

THIS BOOK had its origin in a conversation many years ago with Joanna Hitchcock, who urged me to present my ideas about the political and social dimensions of Latin literature through examination of a set of interrelated episodes. Since that time more scholars and friends than I can adequately thank have provided valuable advice and encouragement. Here I would like to record special debts to Martin Bloomer and Leslie Kurke, who served as sounding boards for many of the ideas contained within this study; to Erik Gunderson, who did double duty as critic and research assistant; to Carolyn Dewald, Page duBois, and Stephen Hinds, who responded thoughtfully to oral or written presentations of some or all of the chapters published here; to Victoria Wohl for assistance at an early stage; to Mark Griffith and William Fitzgerald for their expressions of confidence; to the anonymous referees, who helped me to articulate the unifying themes of the book; to Brigitta van Rheinberg, who both shepherded the manuscript through the publication process and provided her own helpful comments on a penultimate draft; and to Timothy Foy who provided much-needed support as my work on this project drew to a close. I am also happy to acknowledge the assistance provided by the Doreen B. Townsend Center for the Humanities at the University of California at Berkeley, and especially by its former director Paul Alpers, who facilitated a number of wide-ranging and stimulating conversations with scholars outside of classical studies. In addition, a grant from the Hewlett Fund administered by the Office of the Provost at the University of Southern California aided in the preparation of the final manuscript. Finally, as small recompense for their patience and love, I dedicate this book to my children, Nadja and Jacob.

The Politics of Latin Literature

INTRODUCTION

RECENT YEARS have seen a renewed interest in the relationship between Latin literature and its historical context. Without abandoning earlier study of language, form, and literary tradition, scholars have begun to consider as well the means through which literature was produced and circulated, the relationship between artist and patron, and ideological aspects of the production, consumption, and interpretation of classical literary texts. The present study continues this interest in texts and contexts, but with a crucial shift of emphasis. Instead of viewing texts as chiefly illustrative of or reactive to social, political, and economic practices, it regards literature as a medium through which competing sectors of Roman society sought to advance their interests over and against other sources of social and political authority. In other words, literature is here studied not only as a representation of society, but as an intervention in it as well.

The social milieu from which Latin literature emerged and in the interests of which it intervened was that of the elite sector of a traditional aristocratic empire. Many of the characteristics of Latin literature can be attributed to its production by and for an elite that sought to maintain and expand its dominance over other sectors of the population through reference to an authorizing past. While the precise social function of literature varies among texts, genres, and historical eras, taken collectively as an institution involving production, consumption, and interpretation, Latin literature of the classical period advances the interests of Rome's elites in the following ways: by fostering the development and promulgation of a prestige dialect; by providing a means of recruitment and acculturation for members of the imperial elites; by negotiating potentially explosive conflicts over value and authority; by augmenting the symbolic capital of the Roman state through expropriation of the cultural resources of recently colonized communities; and, eventually, by constructing the Roman reader as the quiescent subject of an imperial regime. In these multiple capacities, the literature of ancient Rome draws upon and enhances other forms of social authority, such as patriarchy, religious ritual, cultural identity, and the aristocratic procedure of self-scrutiny, or *existimatio*. Even the choice of technologies through which literature is circulated can be seen to work to the advantage of elite performers of literary texts.

The chapters that constitute this book present a set of scenarios for relating the literature of ancient Rome to its social, economic, and cultural contexts. This arrangement, rather than a continuous narrative, has seemed the best way to allay anxieties about compressing a multiplicity of issues and concerns into a single governing structure while at the same time communicating a point of view sufficiently coherent to permit assent, demurral, or constructive engagement. In a sense, each chapter presents a scenario for understanding a particular period, problem, or text, while the book as a whole presents an overarching scenario for assessing the social function of literature within a traditional aristocratic empire. Perhaps the closest analogy to the style of presentation adopted here, both chapter by chapter and in toto, is the practice in the ancient schools of rhetoric of choosing a *color*, that is, a light in which to cast a case or an angle from which to present it. In other words, while I have not knowingly suppressed evidence that runs counter to the constructive claims made here, neither have I considered it possible or advisable to retail every alternative assessment of the issues under examination. In placing emphasis on the aristocratic dimension of Roman literature, I seek to construct one possible scenario for understanding the developments in question, a scenario that in my view has received insufficient attention in earlier scholarship. To withhold from developing and arguing for such a scenario, either out of a positivistic obsession with covering all of the evidence or—as is increasingly the case among younger scholars—out of a postmodern suspicion of generalities, strikes me as showing little faith in the reader's ability to bring his or her own knowledge to bear on the arguments developed here or to adjudicate between my presentation and alternative accounts. To revert to the forensic model: juries, we are told, mostly decide cases by assessing which scenario (guilt or innocence) makes fullest use of the evidence at hand in light of their own experiences and expectations. Readers seem to engage in a similar process of deliberation, whether they expressly articulate it as such or not.

Beyond adjudication there is also pleasure. When thinking historically, we tend to ask ourselves which narrative is truer or, as I would contend, which scenario is more plausible. When reading what has come to be called literature, pleasure is an important dimension of the experience and a privileged criterion of evaluation. To the ancient Romans as well as to most contemporary readers, encounters with literature can be ludic experiences: playful, fragmented, at ease, improvisational, even escapist.[1] To be sure, categories of the ludic or the aesthetic are themselves historical constructs with specific political connotations, and the pleasures of reading are hardly un-ideological. Indeed, the chief aim of this book, as the title makes clear, is to politicize and historicize the reading of texts of classical Latin literature that are still too frequently regarded in purely formalistic or aesthetic terms. But for all that literature is part of history, it seems important to recognize that history can be part of the pleasure of literature. In bringing economic, scientific, and religious intertexts to bear on the reading of Latin poetry and prose, I seek not to foreclose or regulate the experience of reading, but to expand and enrich it. Thus it is my hope that even those readers who are not fully convinced of the plausibility of the historical scenarios I have constructed will find their experience of the texts I analyze enriched by the new connections and combinations that a more historically engaged mode of reading makes possible.

In combining a materialist interpetation of literature as ideological discourse and social institution with a playful or ludic approach to the process of reading, I reveal my own commitment to the cultural-materialist branch of literary studies. That is to say I share with a critic like Raymond Williams an abiding interest in the cultural production of meaning and values, past and present, and in the use of language as a material form that relies on specific technologies and structures of communication.[2] At the same time, I acknowledge, or, perhaps better, hope that an unsentimental assessment of the political and ideological mystifications of past literature can make us more alert to the mystifications of our own day and age, including most particularly those in which we ourselves otherwise unwittingly engage. Indeed, it is worth remembering in this context that the Latin word *ludus*, interpreted above as referring to play or relaxation, also means "school." The ludic experience of literature has an educative function potentially more meaningful and more progressive than does indoctrination in any canon, regardless of who constructs it. Thus, while some feminist classicists, for example, have expressed anxiety over their involvement in the transmission of a largely misogynistic tradition, I feel no such compunction with respect to my study of a tradition that can also be legitimately described as imperialistic and obsessed with status. For it is not the tradition itself that defines our politics or our morality, but the use we make of it. Like Walter Benn Michaels, I am puzzled by the tendency in some branches of contemporary scholarly and critical discourse "to conflate people's views of what happened in the past with their desires about what will happen in the future."[3] And so I trust the reader will understand that in describing classical Latin literature as instrumental to the maintenance of aristocratic cultural hegemony and Roman political dominance, I am not recommending that contemporary poets, artists, and other culture workers emulate their esteemed predecessors.

Edward Said has described beginnings not as fresh starts but as disruptions of what went before.[4] He reminds us as well that such disruptions, or beginnings, are constituted out of the old way of doing things: God used the ark and its passengers to make the world anew. In abandoning narrative for scenario construction and in insisting on an unsentimental-ized account of the political and social function of treasured classical texts, I have perhaps already hinted at the disruptive potential of the present study. But what are the resources and tools out of which a new account is to be fashioned? What of the old is to be preserved in the creation of the new?

First and foremost is philology, the art of reading slowly and the science of studying language as it is and has been used. Most of the essays gathered in this volume began as questions about the meaning and usage of specific Latin words and phrases in specific discursive contexts. How did terms from economics, such as *aestimatio* and *exemplum*, come to assume such centrality in Roman moral and literary discourse? What residue of their economic origin persists in their non-economic uses? Why does Cicero repeatedly call Catiline a *latro*, or bandit, as opposed to any of the other possibilities the rich vocabulary of Roman insult made available to him? How is it that a *puella* can be *docta* yet still not merit the same degree of respect accorded to the *doctus poeta*? Is there something about "doctitude" that conflicts with female status? Or are there dimensions of meaning to the term *doctus* that are lost in the translation "learned"? How carefully do Horace and other authors use terms of geographical reference? Is it important that Augustus is said to tend to *res Italae* as opposed to *res Romanae*, that Nepos is described by Catullus as *unus Italorum*, that Aeneas and his followers seek Italy but found Rome? In pondering such matters, we would do well to recall Duncan Kennedy's observation that "[w]ords are the principal medium through which meaning acts to develop, enact, and sustain relationships of power."[5] If such is the case, then exploring the meaning of individual words, especially ones as highly charged as those listed here, inevitably takes us into the realm of political history and political interpretation.

In moving from the politics of words to the politics of texts and of systems of texts, I have been aided in my thinking by a large body of work on the discursive construction of political identity, especially writings by the political scientists Anthony Giddens and Ernst Gellner, the historian Eric Hobsbawm, and the anthropologist Benedict Anderson. While their work chiefly pertains to the construction of national identity and nationhood as discursive phenomena, the underlying interest in language and literature as constitutive of identity can and has been applied to racial, sexual, class, and ethnic identity as well. But national identity is what concerns us most here, since one reason the Roman empire succeeded as well as it did—success being measured by size and duration—is that it created, in large part through its literary system, a Roman nation that served as a unifying focus for an otherwise disparate and farflung empire. For reasons discussed in chapter 2, Latin literature, despite its youth and poverty with respect to Greek, had a more significant part to play in the spread of Roman power than did Greek literature and culture in the aftermath of Alexander's imperial conquests. In describing the political need that prompted the emergence of Latin literature and the political use to which that literature was put, I have sought to supplement the recent studies of the ancient historian Erich Gruen by drawing on Anderson's description of how literature functions to create an "imagined community" of readers and writers in the development of modern nationalisms. At the same time, I have tried never to lose sight of the vast gulf that separates ancient Rome from contemporary nation-states. To do so, I have balanced my use of Giddens, Gellner, and Anderson with the work of other political scientists, such as Kautsky and Powis, who focus on the political and social dimensions of traditional aristocratic empires. Indeed, one way of regarding this book is as a case study of the relationship between formalized language and social authority in traditional societies. To this end, it has also been useful to draw on a wide range of material concerning literacy in other premodern contexts ranging from Meso-America to archaic Greece. Among the numerous fine works recently published in this area of particular value to the classicist is Deborah Steiner's study of myths of writing in archaic Greece, the title of which, *The Tyrant's Writ*, itself indicates an awareness of the complicated and in some ways counterintuitive political ramifications of the early spread of literacy.

If philology supplies the raw material and studies of nation-building construct a framework for comparative analysis, economic history, especially the writings of Karl Polanyi, helps to articulate some key observations about the differences between ancient Rome and contemporary society, particularly with respect to issues of language and power.[6] One important difference consists in the greater tendency in antiquity to recognize and take advantage of the interconvertibility of what to us are different categories of resources, such as the ownership of property, political office, social status, the power to command others, erudition, renown, religious authority, and artistic achievement. In ancient Rome generals and politicans compete for literary glory, professors of rhetoric and philosophy receive handsome endowments, an ancestor's literary achievement propels a family up the social hierarchy. Whereas in the modern world achievement in one realm is convertible to achievement in another realm chiefly through the operation of the marketplace, in the ancient world convertibility is often a more direct matter, although the rate of exchange between various sorts of "capital" is under intense negotiation at all times.

Closely connected to the issue of interconvertibility is the tendency for economic power, to which modern students of power and authority tend to give the greatest weight, to be embedded in, and therefore only with difficulty separable from, other forms of social connection. In Rome this embeddedness of wealth is reflected, for example, in the potlatch strategies articulated in inheritance regulations, "reckless" (from our standpoint) spending and borrowing on the part of the elites, and sumptuary laws, that is, procedures whereby the collective wealth, or *res*, of the ruling class is protected and enhanced without particular regard to the separable property of individual owners or their families.[7] Together these two features of ancient Roman society, the interconvertibility of forms of power and the embeddedness of economic power in other social relations, apart from illuminating numerous passages of Latin literature, serve to explain why the stakes involved in literary discourse were greater in ancient Rome than in the modern world. Literature becomes for the Romans a medium of exchange between different forms of capital. More than just a common discourse through which issues can be discussed and values negotiated, although it is that as well, Latin literature constitutes a crucial site of contest over the distribution of power in the Roman world as well as a social practice with real historical consequences of its own.

A final resource of which I have availed myself is perhaps best described as the deconstructive spirit of recent and contemporary literary criticism. By this I refer in the loosest and most general terms to the recognition that there is no one-to-one correspondence between language and external reality, that writing inevitably involves a certain degree of bad faith, that texts work to construct versions of reality which the reader can deconstruct through close attention to what is unspoken or suppressed, to oppositions and hierarchies left implicit, to tensions or oppositions glossed over by the use of language that consolidates and naturalizes the particularities of experiences and phenomena. In its most general sense this spirit of reading characterizes a wide range of schools of thought, from feminism, with its attention to implied and expressed gender hierarchies, through Marxism, with its interest in exposing and demystifying false consciousness and elite ideologies, to the efforts by figures as diverse as McLuhan and Foucault to understand how the human agent is constructed as the subject of discourse. Of all these diverse and conflicting schools of thought, perhaps only feminism has effected widespread changes in the study of Latin literature; even then it tends to be a type of feminism that is more interested in recovering women's history than in exploring the rhetoricity of the texts that preserve the "information" that serves as the basis of that history.[8]

Perhaps another way of describing the style of reading I employ here is to say that I am inclined to accept Lyotard's collapse of the performative and the constative categories of speech acts: as far as Lyotard is concerned, all utterance is to some degree strategic.[9] As a result, what interests me at first glance about a literary utterance is not its truth value or its formal features so much as the question *cui bono*? That is, in whose interest is this statement made, this god invoked, this genre revised, and so on. Ultimately, I believe that a study of the interestedness of particular utterances can lead to certain constructive claims about the function of a text, its historical and political dynamics, and so on; hence the scenarios that form the body of this book. But it is, I believe, in its emphasis on interestedness, on the strategic function of the various machinations that go to make up a text, that the style of reading adopted here differs from another that has gained some ascendancy in Latin literary studies in recent years, namely the semiotic approach that has generated extensive discussion of codes and intertexts and allusions. While we as readers stand to learn a great deal from the skillful unpacking of a phrase or text that characterizes the work of scholars such as Barchiesi or Conte, without attention to the strategic positioning of the phrase or text and without a sociology rigorous enough to relate the ideology of the text to the material circumstances of ancient society, we are still left with an essentially formalist and idealist approach to literature. Barchiesi is surely right, in his recent study, *Il poeta e il principe*, to call attention to the modern imposition upon ancient poetry of a sharp divide between the aesthetic and the political. While his work seeks by and large to bridge the gap by aestheticizing the political—for example, by assessing Augustus as a literary challenge—I take the approach of politicizing the aesthetic.

From materials we proceed to a blueprint. As a set of scenarios, the chapters in this book need not be read in the order printed. I have made some attempt to relate each to its predecessor and successor, but by and large the chapters were composed as and remain freestanding units. Nonetheless there is an implicit narrative in this as in any sequence, and it may help the reader to have it summarized here. To begin with, if we are being asked to make a significant change in our way of approaching Latin literature and of relating it to Roman culture, we may well ask what is wrong with the old way. This question is the focus of chapter 1, Latin Literature and the Problem of Rome. Through brief consideration of one of the founding figures of modern classical philology, Basil Gildersleeve, first tenant of the chair of Greek at The Johns Hopkins University and first president of the American Philological Association, I hope to bring to light, by way of representative anecdote, some of the ideological anxieties that characterize classical studies, especially in the United States, well into the latter part of the twentieth century. In contrast, I show how other models of classics were available in Gildersleeve's time, here by examining the work of the French scholar Jules Michelet and the Polish poet-professor Adam Mickiewicz. I do this partly to elucidate the choices involved in the construction of classical studies in such a way as to isolate

Latin literature from its cultural context, partly to claim some historical pedigree for my own approach, and partly to call attention to the inevitable interestedness of all readings, past and present. As the chapter in question seeks to demonstrate, the suppression of Rome in preference for an idealized version of Greece and the isolation of Latin literature from Roman culture have served historically as mutually reinforcing strategies for protecting scholar/critics from the social implications of their own practice and for advancing the interests of the sector(s) of society with which they identify.

Having acknowledged the historical and institutional pressures that work against an overtly political and social reading of Latin literature, we may begin to construct precisely such a reading by examining the so-called origins of Latin literature. In opposition to the conventional account, which has Latin literature emerge in the late third and early second century B.C.E. virtually ex nihilo, chapter 2, Why Was Latin Literature Invented? argues for its creation as a means of defeating or containing other sources of social authority, such as the preliterature polis culture postulated by Zorzetti and others for early Rome, the Greek heritage of an increasingly significant sector of the Italian population, and the claims to hegemony by Rome's former Italian allies in the struggle against Hannibal. Any institution that enjoys the immediate and persistent success of Latin literature is likely to be overdetermined in its social function, and I acknowledge several bases for literature's success: it provides a means of unifying a geographically dispersed imperial elite; the flexibility of language, especially when shared by an identifiable elite, provides a context for negotiating conflicts over value; literature's formal distance from the language of everyday Romans makes of it a mark of status to be deployed accordingly in an increasingly stratified society; and its newness as a social habitus allows it to incorporate the symbolic treasures of newly occupied territories, especially but not exclusively those of the Greek-speaking world. While the past is always a product of the present, it is nonetheless the case that much of the past is transmitted to successor generations through inattention or apathy on the part of the latter. Like all traditional cultures, and many modern ones as well, the Romans battle energetically throughout their history over ownership and interpretation of their past. But in the literary sphere, the primal scene of literature's origin, as represented by the relationship of the *amicus minor* to the *amicus maior* in Ennius, Polybius, and Cato, remains an important governing trope for the social function of literature in later generations.

From primal scene we move to virtuoso performance in a chapter entitled Cicero and the Bandits. Cicero is the supreme exemplar of the elite Roman's ability to deploy linguistic resources in tandem with political authority, religious ritual, and an impresario's flair for the dramatic to effect concrete political goals. His performance genre—political oratory—gives him distinct advantages over poets, playwrights and philosophers in the competition for social authority and thus makes of him something of an unfair choice as an example of literature's power. And yet it is precisely the transparency of Cicero's devices that makes him useful for a study of this sort; for he accomplishes openly and in an easily analyzable way what all other writers in the Roman tradition tacitly aspire to; namely, to intervene in the distribution of power in their social context. Indeed, much of the resistance to serious study of Cicero seems to derive from precisely this uncomfortable recognition on the part of contemporary scholars. What is more, the fact that even Cicero's embeddedness in the wide variety of discourses—legal, religious, artistic, historical, and cosmological—that constitute his social environment has been neglected by modern scholars until quite recently serves as reminder of how much work remains to be done in investigating the implication of other authors and other texts in Roman culture.

Chapter 4, Culture Wars in the First Century B.C.E., picks up one of the threads of the discussion of archaic Latin literature as it unraveled during the century in question. The thread is literature's involvement in the rivalry between Rome and Italy, and the texts whose fabrics it interweaves include Catullus' *libellus*, Cicero's *Brutus*, Vergil's *Aeneid*, and the *Odes* and *Epistles* of Horace. Between the era of Ennius and Cato and the two generations spanning Catullus and the late years of Horace, Italy had exploded in civil conflict, most disastrously in the Social Wars of the 90s B.C.E., which led to the forced coalescence of Roman and Italian elites. The conflict of the 90s no more ended the struggle between Rome and other sectors of Italian society than the Thirty Years' War resolved the dispute between Protestants and Catholics or the First World War ended Europe's crisis of modernity; indeed, the civil wars that led to the establishment of the Augustan principate in 27 B.C.E. can also be regarded as another act of the Social Wars. In view of this historical context, it is somewhat surprising to note that critics of Latin literature make little of the elaborate discourse of Romanness vs. Italianness that preoccupies the writers listed above as well as others who have by and large been disappeared from the historical record. And so this chapter traces the discourse of Roman particularism in late republican and Augustan poetry while simultaneously attempting to recover the Italian half of the dialectic that the canonical tradition almost manages to suppress. The contrast between Rome and Italy intersects with the tension between performance and writing—if you are going to govern Italy from Rome, you need to write—and tests the limits of the imagined community of Latin speakers. The resolution of the ethnic and cultural conflicts depends upon the reinforcement of the boundary between performance and text, with the result that Roman literature becomes decentered from performance and from Rome. What later scholars interpet as a post-Augustan decline can also be taken as an array of strategies, mostly neurotic, for coping with this cultural trauma.

In arguing for the privileging of written text over spectacular performance, Horace, in the *Letter to Augustus*, brings to light one of the tensions in the aristocratic project of Latin literature that had been sucessfully finessed by preceding generations. As an aristocratic enterprise, Latin literature draws on the implied or real presence of the authorial voice for its social authority; yet as the glue that holds together an imperial elite, literature needs to be written, and hence portable. In later periods of history, the portability of literature makes of it both a potential commodity and a potential agent of personal freedom. During the Roman principate, these potentialities are constantly reined in by authors who persist in emphasizing the speakability of literary texts. They characterize writing less as a means of disseminating an author's ideas than as a strategy for widening the circle of his admirers. How Latin literature managed the contradiction between the privileging of authorial presence and the reality of textual dissemination is the subject of chapter 5, Writing as Social Performance. Strategies examined include both external or institutional arrangements, such as restriction of access to texts and manipulation of the school curriculum, and internal or textual devices, such as insistence on authorial charisma and assimilation of portable media (paper, parchment) to the immovability of stone and bronze.

One such internal strategy, namely, the differential definition of the adjective *doctus/a* when applied to women as opposed to men, receives separate treatment in the sixth chapter, entitled Roman Women's Useless Knowledge. The exclusion of women from the performance space of literary production is one of the enigmas of the Roman tradition, since, in contrast to Athenian women, Roman women, especially of the late republic and early to middle empire, appear to have been better educated, more mobile, and more likely to have been literate. While broader social pressures surely account for the relative paucity of writing by Roman women, the interventionist role of the literary tradition itself should not be overlooked. The adjective *doctus*—a keyword of the Latin tradition if ever there was one—carries with it traces of the primal scene of literary production—that is, friend evaluating friend in preparation for evaluation by a wider circle of friends—since it implies the coexistence of knowledge, discernment, and skill at performance. Tracing its history from the republic through the early empire thus illustrates Latin literature's continual return to its own authorizing scenario. But it also exemplifies literature's success as an institution of containment, since in this matter in particular the real impact of literary subtleties becomes apparent in the historical record. Their knowledge defined as useless by successive male performers of literature, Roman women are indeed, albeit with rare exceptions, denied the opportunity to use it, as their male counterparts would have, to produce and transmit their own literary texts.

If Cicero in his political oratory is a virtuoso of the oral production of Latin literature, Seneca, whose prose treatises and epistles constitute the subject matter of chapter 7, An Aristocracy of Virtue, is a virtuoso of text as script. In expressly seeking to replace Cicero as culture hero and pedagogical resource, Seneca acknowledges the continuing and even increasing social role of literature under the Roman Empire. For both Cicero and Seneca, literature is politics by other means. While Cicero sought to legitimize the traditional aristocracy either through contrast with its alleged subverters—Catiline, Clodius, Antony—or through manufacture of a past that would authorize arrangements in its present interest (and this I take it to be the chief social function of Ciceronian "philosophy"), Seneca needs to develop an ideology that acknowledges the subordination of the aristocrat vis-à-vis the emperor while still advancing his interests over and against other claimants to social authority—for example, women, freedmen, provincials, businesspeople, soldiers, non-Stoic philosophers. He meets this need through the invention of an aristocracy of virtue, one suspiciously similar to the aristocracy of birth it is intended to supplant. Writing becomes an important indicator and agent of this aristocracy's privileged position not only because of the constriction of opportunity for public political performance resulting from the ascendancy of the emperor, but also because of the advantages to be obtained through the maintenance of long-distance networks of elite acquaintances and supporters. It is an enabling strategy for the reproduction of aristocratic hegemony under changed material conditions that virtue, the public performance of which had legitimized the traditional republican aristocracy, can now be demonstrated through writing.

If, in historical terms, at least according to the arguments advanced in this book, it is Seneca who epitomizes the conditions of authorship under the Roman Empire, it is Ovid the exile who has captured the imagination of more recent readers and writers. The poet's removal from Rome to the "periphery of the universe" (*in margine mundi*) fits contemporary notions of the powerlessness of literature against tyranny, ancient or modern. But Ovid's exile, which is known to us only through his writings, is a more complicated political phenomenon than is generally acknowledged. As the eighth and final chapter, entitled *Pannonia Domanda Est*: The Construction of the Imperial Subject through Ovid's Poetry from Exile, reminds us, the boundary between exile and colonization was not always clearly demarcated in ancient societies. Ovid's laments from exile simultaneously deprecate his physical and cultural surroundings while enhancing the authority of the dominant culture that sustains his relatively privileged position in Tomis. He invites the metropolitan subject of Roman imperialism to condition himself or herself to the laborious process of pacification of the unruly forces the empire has taken under its control. The costs of this endeavor, as Ovid intimates, will be enormous, entailing isolation from family and friends, sterile intercourse with uncooperative natives, and negotiation with cultures long deemed inferior. As the Roman Empire is transformed from what Joseph Conrad called "merely a squeeze" to a system of domination backed up by an idea, poets, historians, novelists, and other artists become implicated in the process of constructing, refining, and promulgating the discourse that situates not just the dominated subject but the dominators as well. In failing to take stock of Ovid's contribution to the project of Roman colonialism, contemporary readers run the risk of reenacting the scenario performed by Gildersleeve and other second-generation Romantics who avoided the historical reality of Rome in order to actualize their own fantasies of the apolitical innocence of literature and literary studies. In concluding with Ovid, then, I seek to supplement the account of the primal scene of literary production with a return to what I regard as the primal scene of the reception of Latin literature: namely, the reader/critic's identification with and replication of the sorrows of the beleaguered exile.

Chapter 1

LATIN LITERATURE AND THE
PROBLEM OF ROME

THE FIRST VOLUME of Martin Bernal's *Black Athena* reminds us that the invention of modern notions of classical history and culture by late eighteenth- and early nineteenth-century German Romanticism was a process of exclusion and suppression as much as it was one of discovery and articulation.[1] Even those who seek to discredit Bernal agree with this general observation, acknowledging, as one of his critics has put it, "that towards the end of the eighteenth century and then thereafter, many aspects of the German attitude toward Greece were unquestionably based on nationalistic and chauvinistic prejudice."[2] Bernal's concern in his study is chiefly with the exclusion of Semitic and Egyptian or African contributions to ancient Mediterranean civilization, but he notes in passing the concomitant tendency toward the suppression of Rome. Winckelmann, who must figure prominently in any account of neo-Hellenism, went to Rome in more ways than one, converting to Catholicism and serving as librarian to Cardinal Albani; but he did so in order to have access to the treasures of his beloved Hellas. Winckelmann's privileging of classicism and of a distinctively Greek artistic genius stands in marked contrast to the views implied in the work of Montfauçon, who just a generation earlier (1719–24 versus 1764) could present all of European art from antiquity through the Renaissance as part of a coherent generic and symbolic system.[3] As Bernal rightly observes, Winckelmann and others like him were concerned with "the threat to Germany . . . from Paris, a 'new Rome,' and from French, a Romance language."[4] Germany, it was felt, "had the potential to be a major cultural centre," but lacked the political and military strength of France. "[W]hile Germany could not become a new Rome, she could be the new Hellas."[5]

A privileging of Greece at the expense of Rome is deeply embedded in the literary and scholarly output of the German Romantic period, much of it, at least on superficial inspection, unconcerned with issues of national identity. We encounter the subtle yet pervasive influence of anti-Romanism in one of the central texts of the high Romantic period, Friedrich Schiller's essay "On Naive and Sentimental Poetry."[6] There we are told, among many other things, that "even Rome in all its splendour, except it be transfigured by the imagination, is a limited greatness, and

therefore a subject unworthy of poetry, which, raised above every trace of
the actual, ought only to mourn over what is infinite."[7] Schiller's criticism
is aimed at Ovid's exile poetry, and there is a specific point being made
about the transcendent power of the imagination; but it is characteristic
of Schiller's rhetoric that the negative example is drawn from Latin literature, and not from the writing of the Greeks, whose "impatient imagination," he reports, "only traverses nature to pass beyond it to the drama of
human life. It [this Greek imagination] only takes pleasure in the spectacle
of what is living and free."[8] Indeed, Schiller suggests in a letter to Wilhelm
von Humboldt that the essay "Naive and Sentimental" was prompted by
anxiety over his own inevitable separation from the Greek ideal. "Given
my distance from the spirit of Greek literature, to what extent can I still
be a poet and indeed a better poet than the extent of that distance seems
to allow?"[9] Schiller's answer, as elaborated in the essay, is that through
sentimentality he can reconstruct the lost naivete. As recent commentators have suggested, this pattern is precisely the one Schiller ascribes to
Goethe when he writes, "Had you been born a Greek, even only an Italian . . . then perhaps your path would have been shortened immeasura-
bly. . . . But, since you were born a German, since your Grecian spirit was
thrown into this Northern world, so there was no other choice open to
you except either to become a Northern artist yourself, or, with the assistance of the power of thought, to supply your imagination with that
which reality denied to it and thus as it were from within and by rational
means to give birth to your own Greece."[10]

Recent scholarship has documented the persistence and vitality of
Schiller's formulations in the criticism of pastoral poetry.[11] We can carry
this analysis a step further and trace the survival of Schiller's categories
and hierarchies in criticism of Latin literature more generally. To take but
one example, a major work on Vergil's *Georgics*, by a scholar who has
himself taken issue with the Romantic tendency in Latin literary criticism,
begins with an apologia constructed around a set of oppositions characteristic of Schiller's text:

> Virgil is by no means an easy poet. The *Odyssey* is read by school children,
> and the *Iliad* can be understood by the average college student more easily
> and (I think) more accurately than any other work of classical literature
> likely to be encountered in survey courses. The *Aeneid*, however, often
> seems tedious and mechanical to these same students and more often than
> not frustrates the lecturer who tries to convey to a general audience some
> idea of the depth and beauty of Virgil's verse and the poem's profound
> power over mind and emotions.[12]

Even as the modern scholar seeks to defend the study of Vergil against
a Romantic longing for the simple and heroic, he reinforces Schiller's op-

positions between childhood and adulthood, Greek and Roman, imagination and analysis, the special soul and the run-of-the-mill general public, with their implicit privileging of the former over the latter in each pair. The tedious and mechanical nature of the *Aeneid*, we learn, is a matter of appearances, the implication being that in reality the poem merits some such Schillerian laudatory epithet as "vital" or "organic." The momentary belittlement of the Greek epics as fit for children, or at best college students, turns out to be an expression of the writer's failed ambition to make the Latin poem available to precisely such readers. Even the tone of frustrated melancholy that pervades the passage evokes Schiller's opposition, replete with erotic connotations, between the "scholastic spirit" that "enervates and blunts thought in order not to wound the reader" and "genius . . . wherein expression gushes forth spontaneously from the idea" and "the spirit appears as if disclosed in a nude state."[13] The modern-day interpreter of Vergil presents himself as doomed to an enervated scholasticism while longing for the joyous escapism attributed to the Greeks. Yet what he hopes to escape to is not a transcendent world soul, or even Greece, but the authentic experience of Vergil. The scholar, consigned to lecturing to the uncomprehending masses, finds himself cast out of paradise, foiled in his efforts to return. His position is exactly that of the second generation of Romantic writers, who found themselves, in Nemoianu's terms, burdened with "limited versions of Eden"[14] and therefore undertook the "task of restoring and compromising without entirely relinquishing paradise."[15]

In the historical evolution of Romanticism, the task of "compromising paradise" by attempting to create "limited versions of Eden" was taken up by the inventors of the research university. Not surprisingly, the Edens reconstructed by these early professors tended to resemble idealized Greece rather than hopelessly problematic Rome. Barthold Niebuhr, who was appointed to the post of Roman history at Wilhelm von Humboldt's newly established University of Berlin in 1810, sought in Rome precisely the characteristics of youth and liberty associated with Greece by Winckelmann and Schiller. As a result, he turned not to the Rome of the late republic or high empire, but to pre-historic, Edenic Rome with its folksongs and *ager publicus*, its tribunes speaking in defense of a free and loyal peasantry—prototypes of Niebuhr's Danish contemporaries—and its nonviolent resolution of social conflict. Niebuhr seeks in Rome a politically stable version of the lost Hellenic paradise.[16]

Along with Niebuhr's evasion of historical Rome comes an additional and, for the student of Latin literature, more troubling evasion of the texts that survive from Roman antiquity. In a curious passage from the preface to the second edition of his *History of Rome*, printed posthumously in 1832, Niebuhr notes the transition in scholarly interest from

"Greek literature" to "Roman history"—as if Greece had no history and Rome had no literature.[17] In the same text he proclaims the advances in the understanding of Roman history made possible by philological elucidation of "Lydus, Gaius, and Cicero's *Republic*"[18] and eulogizes philology for recognizing "its calling, to be the transmitter of eternity thus affording us the enjoyment of unbroken identity, across thousands of years, with the noblest and greatest peoples of antiquity; to make us as familiar with their spiritual creations and their history as if no gulf separated us."[19] While philology receives effusive praise, the "mere words" in which it deals are scorned. Niebuhr's misguided predecessors, we are told, had confused "the writings of the ancient historians" with the "objects they represented."[20] In other words, the writings are of value not in themselves but as transmitters of objective reality. Yet this objective reality turns out, both in theory and in practice, to be the world as Niebuhr experiences it. No writer can entirely escape the constraints and biases of his or her own time and place; but Niebuhr here makes a virtue of necessity, treating history as self-study and philology, together with the texts it studies, as a mere means to that end.

The later Romantic writers' project of recovering a lost paradise through their elevation of Greece and evasion of Rome was carried to the Americas by one of their most successful and influential students, Basil Lanneau Gildersleeve. Gildersleeve, who studied at Berlin, Bonn, and Göttingen in the early 1850s, returned to the United States where he taught at the University of Virginia, served in the Confederate armed forces during the Civil War, and went on to hold the first chair of Greek at The Johns Hopkins University.[21] If, as Bernal has suggested, the "Romantics longed for small, virtuous, and 'pure' communities in remote and cold places: Switzerland, North Germany, and Scotland,"[22] and through their longing managed to transform Greece, with its hot climate and seaward orientation into an early version of Switzerland, then Gildersleeve performed an even more remarkable feat of geographical legerdemain, for he found in the ancient Greeks kindred spirits to his beloved antebellum Southerners and eventually to all Americans who resisted what he regarded as the homogenization and mongrelization of their society. In an essay entitled "A Southerner in the Peloponnesian War," Gildersleeve manages to ascribe to the Confederacy the best qualities of both the Spartans and the Athenians, depending on whether he is emphasizing Southern resistance to Northern commercial power or the bravery of the Southern homefront in the face of widespread hunger and privation: "The Northern Union, represented by Athens, was a naval power. The Southern Confederacy, under the leadership of Sparta, was a land power";[23] but it was in the South, as in the Athens of Aristophanes, that "hunger was the dominant note of life."[24] In "The Limits of Culture," written in

1867, Gildersleeve concludes his attack on progressive educators with a passage linking their criticism of classical education to the recent Yankee invasion of the South:

> We of the South have little left except our system of higher education, and it is our duty to meet the assault that is making on it—an assault which is a part of the grand attempt to crush all individuality of development into a homogeneous centralization. Already do we see the snares spread; already is the "vast slave-net of mischief" preparing to draw all the educational institutions of the country into the meshes of a West Point system. In a few years the Minister of Public Instruction will send out his sergeants to drill the free citizens of this republic into passive tools of a great central power; and we can well understand why studies which stir so many earnest doubts of our present condition should be thrust into the background, so that none but dreamers may think of the wonders which Greek autonomy wrought or of the immeasurable woe which was the price of Roman unity and the cause of Roman ruin.[25]

Gildersleeve's view of Greece as positive exemplum, Rome as negative; Greece as the freedom-loving South, Rome as the domineering North was reinforced, perhaps even generated, by his fondness for German Romantic writers. The editor of Gildersleeve's letters pictures the young scholar as entering the Civil War in response to " the call of Goethe,"[26] and Gildersleeve himself describes how he discussed Faust with a fellow officer moments before the latter was felled by a Yankee bullet.[27] Gildersleeve's second-generation Romanticism is especially evident in his fondness for heroes who have dedicated themselves to hopeless causes. "Are we such strangers to faithfulness that we cannot understand how men can be true to a cause foredoomed?" he writes in a spirited appreciation of the recently executed emperor Maximilian of Mexico.[28] Gildersleeve likens Maximilian to Julian the Apostate, himself the subject of another lengthy eulogy,[29] calling one "the Romanticist on the throne of the Caesars," the other "the Romanticist on the throne of the Montezumas."[30] In his ability to hold fast to passionate idealism while "taking into account defeat and limitation"—again, Nemoianu's phrase[31]—and in his admiration of figures like Maximilian and Julian who share this ability, Gildersleeve repeats the pattern of "tamed romanticism" on American soil. What eluded Maximilian in Mexico and Julian in the Roman Empire Gildersleeve will seek to accomplish in the context of the American research university: the establishment of a strictly circumscribed form of paradise, a preserve against the turbulent forces of history.

Like Niebuhr, Gildersleeve constructs an Eden that can encompass historical Rome, its language and literature, but only as a counterexample: in defending Latin as a field of study in an address marking the tenth anniversary of the founding of Johns Hopkins, Gildersleeve resorts to a doubly Romantic argument, telling the story of a professor whose lecture on the vanishing of weak vowels linked this loss with the downfall of a nationality: "[G]reat linguistic, great moral, great historical laws marched in stately procession before the vision of the student, the airy vowels that had flitted into Nowhere seemed to be the lost soul of Roman life."[32] The Romantic assumption that the story of Rome is the story of loss coincides with the views of Herder and Hegel on the close connection between language and the spirit of a race.[33]

With allusions to lost greatness and to the innate spirit of a race, Gildersleeve's Romantic preference for Greece over Rome takes on a sinister cast. Roman unity comes at the price of immeasurable woe and leads to ruin; yet earlier in the same essay, "the old Greeks" are praised for holding on to their myths, thereby refusing "to break up the unity of their national life."[34] Unity alone cannot be the culprit in Rome's demise; nor in view of the Greek history of intra- and interstate strife can the Romans be regarded as having an ancient monopoly on woe. Why, then, should Rome persist as the target of criticism?

A further set of passages in the eulogy for Maximilian suggests some possible answers. Near the end of that work Gildersleeve refers to Napoleon III's assignment of the Austrian archduke to the Mexican throne as evidence of a scheme "to restore to the Latin race on this side of the water its power and prestige, and so to check the invasion of the Anglo-Saxons."[35] Gildersleeve calls attention to the irony implicit in Napoleon's use of "the most thoroughly German prince in Europe"[36] to carry out this scheme, then expatiates on the differences among Germans, Frenchmen, and other nationalities, in both his own view and that of Maximilian. "Frenchmen," we learn "are not good judges of race, and show an incredible philosophy in the matter of amalgamation. Those nations that keep their blood pure, that refuse to blend with an inferior stock, are those that are destined to the mastery; and 'Latin' America owes most of its misery to the degradation of race."[37]

There follows a lengthy quotation from Maximilian's own "Sketches of Travel" describing in exquisite detail a Peruvian mulatto named Antonio, a "strikingly handsome youth of seventeen years, as tall and slender as a poplar, with soft features and sparkling eyes. His complexion is not red, not black, not olive, not bronze, not light, not dark, a mixture of all conceivable colors. Corinthian brass may have looked that way—copper, gold, and bronze all mixed together."[38] Any appeal the youth may have held for Maximilian in his *Wanderlust* was apparently lost on Gildersleeve who regards "Antonio" only as an example of a racial "combination which a Frenchman like Michelet might admire, which the good sense of a man of Germanic stock can regard only as a curiosity not deserving of repetition."[39] But repetition, it seems, is exactly what "we" are headed for, according to Gildersleeve, who concludes the digression by noting that "we of the United States are fast developing in this direction, and if report tells the truth, the crosses in California of Indian, Chinese, Negro, Kelt, and Anglo-Saxon promise results which will throw utter contempt upon Maximilian's specimen of mixed breed."[40]

Empire, especially an empire run by unenlightened members of a Latin race, promotes the mingling of racial stocks, and such mingling leads to degradation and "misery." A related thought is applied to literature in a passage from the anniversary address that closely precedes the elegy for the lost vowels:

> I am not at all shaken by the self-satisfied edicts of those who rule so large a portion of the reading world, and I maintain with unwavering confidence that all healthy literature must be kept in communion, direct or indirect, with the highest exemplars of our Indo-European stock; and if anything could prove the necessity of a return to healthy human nature, with its com-passed form, its fair red and white, it would be the utter wearisomeness of so much recent fine writing, in which there is no blood, no sap, nothing but division and subdivision of nerve tissue. "A pagan suckled in a creed out-worn" is a joy and delight in comparison with the languid, invertebrate children of the great goddess Anaemia.[41]

It would take some effort to untangle the knot of biological, sexual, cultural, and literary anxieties latent in this brief passage, but the implication for Roman studies is clear: the unity that led to the loss of Roman soul was a unity, or mingling, of races, cultures, languages, and religions that stands in marked contrast to the preservation of distinctive national identity that Gildersleeve associates with the purportedly autonomous Greeks. The facts of Roman history were too obvious to permit it to serve the needs of those who sought ancient precedent for their own quest for national and cultural identity; at best Rome could serve as evidence of the risks involved in abandoning the pure Greek model.

According to Higham's analysis of American nativism, several varieties of "race thinking" circulated in nineteenth-century America; these genres run parallel to developments in Europe as traced by Bernal, although with different emphases and articulations in the distinctive American context. One sort of race thinking, predominantly literary and cultural in expression, made a "vague identification of culture with ancestry [that] served mainly to emphasize the antiquity, the uniqueness, and the permanence of a nationality. It suggested the inner vitality of one's own culture, rather than the menace of another race";[42] in the European context, this seems closest to the point of view of Schiller. A second type, which expressed itself in a form of scientific discourse, focused on physical differences between races, often, but not exclusively, from a perspective of white superiority over other groups. The melding of these two types of "race-thinking," supplemented by a Darwinian focus on the survival of the fittest, produced a third, more potent ideology that explained in natural, "scientific" terms the superiority of one race over another and was accompanied by deep anxiety over the mingling of races and the consequent diluting of the strength of the superior race. Gildersleeve's writing shows traces of all three types, ranging from admiration for the special virtues of Southern whites, to concern with the "fair white and red" that characterizes "healthy human nature," to the scientific metaphors contained in the discussion of healthy versus enervated literature and in the allusion to racial mastery. We might be tempted to dismiss Gildersleeve's vehemence toward "Latin" America as a response to French propaganda that sought to popularize precisely that notion as justification for intervention in the Western Hemisphere,[43] but it is hard to explain away the frequency or intensity of Gildersleeve's race-baiting so simply.[44] Indeed, in the eulogy of Maximilian, race is invoked precisely as a means of preventing the reader's natural sympathy for Maximilian from turning into support for further adventures in mongrelization. "The Romanticist on the throne of Montezuma" must be dissociated from "the Frenchman Michelet."

In view of the hostility toward Rome evinced in the writings of Gildersleeve and the close connection between that hostility and persistent aspects of American life, we may wonder why and how Latin came to be preserved as a field of study within the American research university at all. Its practical value for inculcating a sense of linguistic structure and of the history of the English and Romance languages seems to have been an important factor.[45] Gildersleeve's *Latin Grammar* is testimony to his own interest in Latin as pedagogy, as perhaps is his assignment of elementary Greek and Latin instruction to a Latinist colleague at Hopkins; he himself insisted on teaching only advanced or research students. The awareness in the culture at large of the connection between Roman legal, political, and social ideals and the realities of American life kept the teaching of Latin alive in secondary schools and in the lower levels of universities and colleges, as did the growing Catholic immigrant population and the educational system it developed. Finally, the role of the Romans in transmitting and preserving much of Greek culture and thought was undeniable, and so Latin had to be preserved, if only as an appendage to the project of Greek studies.

But in a certain sense the question of why Latin studies persisted is misconceived, for a genuine, independent study of Rome and Latin literature has scarcely existed in the Romantic research university. To the extent that Latin has been studied, it has been cast in terms acceptable to

philhellenic Romanticism; and even those who have made a profession of
Latin literature have found themselves called upon repeatedly to make
Latin Greek—or at least "Greek" as understood by Gildersleeve, his men-
tors, and his epigonoi. [46] Consider the efflorescence of Latin literary studies in the 1950s and '60s. The battle between critics and scholars that had
been waged earlier within Departments of English was played out anew
among classicists, and students of Latin were active participants. Bernard
Knox's essay on the imagery of the second book of the *Aeneid*,[47] although
written by a critic generally regarded as a Hellenist, and Steele Commager's work on Horace[48] seemed to offer a discourse concerning Roman
poetry that was bound to the text without limiting the imagination of the
interpreter. As with Gildersleeve's professionalization of American classical studies, so too this revolution in critical approach was prompted by
unarticulated ideological considerations that from the vantage point of
hindsight can only be viewed as problematical. On the one hand,
the work of America's literary Latinists continued and developed the efforts of postwar European scholars like Curtius and Pöschl, who sought
to universalize the implications of classical Roman texts as a way of establishing literature as a force that could ameliorate and even transcend
national and racial animosities.[49] Equally important, however, was the
example of the American New Critics of the 1930s who, for all their
purported anti-Romanticism,[50] nonetheless reinforced the view of literature as a realm independent of society and ideology into which only the
privileged few could enter. In the words of Roger Fowler, the writings
of these New Critics "are an apologia for a privileged and unproductive
elite, they deny literature any social responsibility, they mystify the
practice of writing."[51] Like Gildersleeve before them, who spoke of the
"vast slave-net of mischief," the New Critics in calling their journal *The
Fugitive* invoked the ugliest form of oppression to justify their own elitist
enterprise.

Fowler's critique of the New Critics' attempt to split literature from
society rings true for critics of English and American literature as well as
for their Latinist progeny. Commager's groundbreaking study of Horace
insists on the importance of tehcnique at the expense of meaning, alludes
to the "covenant" between critic and poet, and makes such tantalizingly
oracular pronouncements as "[Horace's] poems record only an imaginative apprehension of the world" or "an Ode's meaning . . . inheres in the
sounds, the figures, the tone, the emotional coloring."[52] Language of this
sort illustrates what one writer has called New Criticism's tendency to
resort to "declaration of literary infallibility" and to become a "technique
by which literature is actually protected from criticism."[53] Or again, in an
introduction to a collection of essays on Vergil, we encounter the New
Critical assertion that "*The Eclogues*, despite their contemporary politi-

cal and social allusions, are essentially an attempt to substitute a world of imagination for that of fact."[54] Vergil has become Goethe, and the critic is his Schiller, still hoping to recapture a vision of autonomy and aesthetic freedom, which is the legacy of Romantic Hellenism.[55]

The study of Roman culture and of Latin literature in its relationship to that culture has thus been characterized by a prolonged process of self-dismemberment. The first limb to go, it would appear, was chronological extension. Greece had a classical period, so Rome needed one as well, and it should come as no surprise that Augustine and Prudentius lost out to Vergil and Cicero. But Cicero was hopelessly enmeshed in the culture of his time, a representative of an outmoded (read: French) humanism that had been replaced by ideals of the aesthetic, and so he, along with Seneca, Quintilian, and others, could be relegated to the task of teaching writers of the modern languages a clear understanding of linguistic structure. The historians could remain, but only as historians; after all, someone had to bear witness to Rome's immeasurable woe.

What remained was compact and homogeneous enough to be no threat to the Greeks and to bear no resemblance to Papist Rome or "Latin" America, but it was still not sufficiently polished to attain to neo-Hellenic standards of excellence. And so the canon was reduced further: in the words of Gildersleeve, "Away with Marcus Manilius, Valerius Flaccus, Silius Italicus. . . . we earnestly hope that professors of Latin do not generally deem themselves bound to read, as poor Addison considered himself bound to quote the vapid productions. . . ."[56] Now at last we had our perfect torso of classical Latin poetry, unless, of course, some of these poets actually seemed to have and—worse—to express a vested interest in the power relations inscribed in Roman politics and society. What if they were implicated, embedded, compromised? Well, then out as well with the fourth book of Horace's *Odes* and of Propertius' elegies; farewell to the second half of the *Aeneid*; goodbye to Aristaeus in the fourth book of the *Georgics*—that poem ends, as everyone but Vergil seems to know, with the death of Orpheus and not the rebirth of the bees or the praise of Caesar.[57]

The persistent Romantic view of the university as a substitute Eden, coupled with distinctive, although hardly unique, American anxieties about cultural identity, have created and reinforced a devaluation of Rome within classical studies and, more important, an isolation of Roman culture from Latin literature within the narrower field of Latin literary studies. The current move toward secular canonization of Gildersleeve—eponymous chairs, adulation in the journals, publication of letters and biographical studies—threatens to reinforce these tendencies, but also bespeaks an anxiety about the continuing vitality of the larger projects, institutional as well as intellectual, that he initiated. On the one hand, a self-consciously American classical establishment seeks a founding hero, and with his professional record and international reputation, Gildersleeve is the likeliest candidate. At the same time, classical studies sees itself, in the title of a recent collection of essays, as a "discipline and a profession in crisis,"[58] under assault from the outside and also from dissenters within. Hero worship offers a sense of secruity, albeit a false one, and the clarity of Gildersleeve's intellectual program provides a useful means for restraining the more restive segments of the profession. An exemplum both empowers and constrains. For those interested in the future of classical studies, especially of Roman studies, and in their potential significance for the world as we and our students experience it, the exemplum of Gildersleeve is especially problematical. His privileging of Greece over Rome was part and parcel of a larger, significantly more complex project involving the emergence of national identity, the search for ancient prototypes of modern peoples, an essentialist view of the relationship between language and culture, the creation of an aesthetic realm within culture, and the self-aggrandizing heroization of supporters of doomed causes. Greece triumphed over Rome because it better served the needs of intellectuals, especially those who saw themselves as the spokesmen for emerging or embattled national identities. As in the writing of his German Romantic forebears, so in the work of Gildersleeve, the relative evaluation of Greece and Rome, and the relationship between literature and culture that plays into that evaluation, are largely the products of the aspirations and anxieties of the times.

In order to gain some perspective on the current configuration of classical studies, especially in the United States, it will be useful to consider briefly the ways in which Romantic ideals shaped the study of Greece and Rome in other national contexts. Such an investigation will help to clarify the relative significance of political and cultural factors in the formation of a classical agenda as well as suggest alternative paradigms for the relationship between literature and culture, Greece and Rome, the past and the present. Of course it would be possible to seek such paradigms in a variety of contexts, historical and geographical. But limitation to the Romantic period makes it possible to differentiate essential from accidental Romantic traits, while a focus on the cases of Poland, represented here by Adam Mickiewicz, and France, in the figure of Jules Michelet, provides the strongest contrast to the Germano-American situation.[59] To begin far from Gildersleeve, then, in geography, language, and religion we may consider briefly the career and influence of the Polish Romantic poet, activist, and professor Adam Mickiewicz (1798–1855). Mickiewicz, who was as much enamored of Goethe as was Gildersleeve, nonetheless managed to denounce the political absolutism of imperial Rome without rejecting its literary and cultural output. Indeed, his idealization of Greek autonomy and Roman unity can be regarded as the paradigm for a Romantic, and still vital, model of a free and united Poland.

Mickiewicz's early work, with its admiration of Walter Scott and Byron, contains disparaging comments on Roman political tyranny and Roman poetry.[60] Yet while in exile after the collapse of the Polish revolution of 1831, Mickiewicz served briefly and successfully as professor of Latin at Lausanne. The glowing reports of various academic officials in attendance on Mickiewicz's lectures deserve quotation at length, both for their own sake, and as an antidote to Gildersleeve's insinuations about Latin and the teaching of Latin:

> The knowledge of the intimate life of the Roman people with regard to the arts and letters, of the spirit of the Latin language and that of poets and orators whom this language served as their tool, an astonishing perspicacity in penetrating their individual characters in connection with the investigation of their writings, felicitous comparisons between the ancient literature of Rome and various modern literatures, the ability to express himself in a foreign tongue, finally the interest of freshness lent to a subject which seemed exhausted and the inspiration of a poet's soul enlivening these gifts of nature and these fruits of labor—these are in the eyes of Mr. Mickiewicz's audience, the reasons for the growing success of a course which captivates the young people, attracts each day more listeners, and most charms those who are best suited to judge it.[61]

> Though for many years he seems not to have made Roman literature his principal work, nothing in his exposition shows notions acquired or resuscitated overnight. The thought is always precise and complete; the judgements solid; the views broad and just. Listening to him one feels that his is a mind that has absorbed an immense amount and compared much, and that, as a result, sees all things from above. He is thoroughly familiar with the works of the most learned philologists, but he does not use them slavishly; he evaluates them according to their worth, and his erudition is always utilized with judicious comprehension and superior reason. Those who, in particular, hear him talk either of some little-known author, such as Lucretius, or of one well-known, such as Cicero, may observe that his opinions, equally sound in both cases, are his own. And when his subject leads him to compare authors of different nations, as he has done, for instance in the case of Catullus, it may be seen to what extent the eye of this experienced writer grasps ingenious connections without abandoning the truth and to the enhancement of beauty.[62]

The mixture of erudition and insight, the genial movement between ancient and modern, prose and poetry, literature and culture bespeak an altogether different conception of the significance of Latin literature and its vitality as a field of study from Gildersleeve's evocation of a dreary procession of disappearing vowels.

Mickieiwicz's treasuring of Latinity is characteristic of Polish intellectual and cultural life almost to the present moment. Why Polish Romanticism could accommodate Latin literature to an extent that German Romanticism and its American offshoot could not is not far to seek. Polish nationalism, like that of Czechs, Hungarians, and Romanians, defined itself in opposition to Russian- and German-speaking empires, not to one dominated by speakers of a Latin tongue. Roman Catholicism characterized the idealized Polish state, in opposition to the Protestantism of German Romantics, the Orthodoxy of Russia, and the Judaism of a large portion of the population within the proposed Polish territory.[63] Finally, the fervid nationalism among the Polish nobility of the eighteenth century confounded the easy equivalence among Romantic liberty, national identity, and anti-aristocratic sentiment that characterized other versions of Romanticism.[64] A passage in Mickiewicz's "Books of the Polish Pilgrims" (1830) praises the self-sacrificing virtue of Scaevola, Curtius, and Decius as definitive of "citizenship."[65] The theme of self-sacrifice reverberates throughout his descriptions of the Polish pilgrim, and is equally applicable to the 23,000 citizens massacred at Praga in 1794 and to Mickiewicz's own refugee contemporaries.

In his emphasis on the connection between citizenship and civilization via the medium of the Latin language and archaic Roman heroes, Mickiewicz anticipates, by a few years, a comparable connection made by the French historian Jules Michelet, whose colleague and friend he was soon to become at the Collège de France. The equation of Rome and civilization receives early emphasis in the preface to Michelet's *Histoire romaine* (first published in 1831), if only by indirection. Michelet describes his illustrious predecessor, Barthold Niebuhr, as a barbarian invader of the Roman world. "Rome was renewed by the invasion of northern peoples, and it has also taken a northerner, a barbarian, to renew the history of Rome."[66] "His first victory was at Verona, like that of Theodoric the Great" (p. xvi). "He has destroyed, but he has rebuilt as well" (p. xvii). Niebuhr's *History*, according to Michelet, is like the *forum boarium*, "so imposing with all its monuments, well or poorly restored. One can often sense a Gothic hand at work; but it is always marvelous to see with what strength the barbarian lifts the grand debris" (p. xvii).

Despite one scholar's identification of Michelet as a "disciple" of Niebuhr,[67] it is difficult to take his introductory description of Niebuhr as unadulterated praise. "It is the fate of Rome to conquer its masters," continues Michelet (p. xviii), in a reappropriation of the Horatian maxim. "Niebuhr became Roman. He knew antiquity in a way that antiquity never knew itself. . . . Don't you dare attack this colleague of the

Decemviri, or speak of him lightly. Be careful: the law is precise: *si quis malum carmen cantassit.* . . . " (p. xviii). But no sooner does Michelet warn against criticism of Niebuhr than he openly admits that he himself has made short shrift (*bon marché*) of Niebuhr's "audacious hypotheses." "I know that it is impossible to derive serious history from an epoch whose monuments have almost all perished" (p. xix). Michelet's own approach, which treats Roman history well into the historical period, is, with ironic understatment, recommended for its ability to cast the light of better known epochs on those that are obscure. Michelet's language seems to parody the nationalistic overtones of Niebuhr's work and to challenge his idealization of prehistoric Rome. Equally important, with its metaphors of light and darkness, harmony and proportion, in opposition to Niebuhr's concern with depth and surface and with critical analysis, Michelet introduces an alternative approach not just to the composition of historical narrative but also to the relationship between literature and culture. He proposes a division of Roman history into three epochs, which he designates Italian, Greek, and Oriental, largely on the basis of cultural factors. The divisions of political history are represented as analogous to these. Even the conventional distinction between Republic and Empire, which Michelet ultimately accepts, is deemed worthwhile because it corresponds to the contrast in religious history between the pre-Christian and the Christian era. In a final rebuff to Niebuhr, who denounced the capitulation of critical judgment to "the written word" and disparaged the eighteenth century's fascination with "vague, meaningless words,"[68] Michelet concludes his preface by reminding the reader of the Christian image of Jesus Christ as the "Word of God." "The empire becomes united and grows calm," he writes, "as if to accept with greater reflection the Word from Judaea or from Greece. . . . At the same time as the imperial leveling begins, due to proscription of the Roman aristocracy and the equality of civil law, the doctrine of Christian leveling asserts itself quietly. The invisible republic raises itself on the ruins of the other republic which knows nothing of it. Jesus Christ died under Tiberius" (p. xxiii).

Michlet's view of the constructive force of "the Word"—whether of Christianity, or Roman literature, or of his own historical narrative—is closely connected with his praise, in this case unironic, of Giambattista Vico earlier in the preface to the *Histoire romaine*.[69] Vico, who is sometimes regarded as a seminal figure in the development of Romanticism because of his interest in primitive peoples, in fact points in a different direction from that taken by Herder and his nationalistic disciples. Vico's essential insight, according to Michelet, is that "humanity is its own project unto itself. God acts on it, but through it. Humanity is divine, but there is no divine human being" (p. xi). As a consequence, history becomes not an account of the truth behind the facade of legends and symbols, but an investigation of the truth of those symbols. *Verum factum* is the Viconian phrase: What is true is what has been made, and only what has been made can be the legitimate object of investigation. Vico is thus the patron saint of all who study social, cultural, and literary constructs as such.

A further assertion on Vico's part, to which Michelet again alludes, is that the constructs of a given society tend to pass through historical phases, moving from particular to abstract, and from mythical to institutional. "And so humanity moves from symbol into history, law, religion. But from the materialized, individualized idea, it proceeds to the pure and generalized idea. It is in the immobile chrysalis of the symbol that the mystery of the transformation of the Spirit takes place. . . . And this process is especially recognizable in the law; the law dates its revolutions and engraves them in bronze" (p. xiii). This is why, according to Michelet, Vico develops a particular interest in archaic Rome: not because of any mystical racial spirit unique to these prehistoric peasants, but because the history of Roman institutions, especially as preserved in the Latin language, is paradigmatic of the historical processes undergone by humanity generally. "In changing the form of its government" (Michelet is now quoting his translation of Vico) "Rome constantly founds itself on the same principles, which are none other than the principles of human society. What gives the Romans the wisest of jurisprudences is also what makes of their empire the most vast and durable of all" (p. xiv).

Vico is not the most consistent or lucid of authors, and in his selection of a quotation stressing the supremacy of Rome, Michelet ignores the more relativistic dimensions of Vico's work. These stem from Vico's own reflection on the discovery of previously unknown "primitive" peoples who had followed courses of development quite different from that of the ancient Mediterranean communities. Michelet's attention to the universal, as opposed to the representative, significance of Rome in Vico's work is no doubt due to his own concern for the potential ideological significance of the new Rome in which he finds himself. Nonetheless, it is easy to see how the example of Vico—who, not incidentally, held the post of professor of Roman rhetoric at Naples—could push French historical and classical studies in a very different direction from that pursued in Germany under the banner of Winckelmann and Schiller. Where the German Romantic tradition idealizes Greece, values youth and liberty, and, most important for our purposes, asserts the validity of a segmentation between literature and culture, or the aesthetic and the political, the work of Vico moves in an opposite direction. It privileges Rome for its exemplarity, emphasizes the transformations of society and culture over the long duration of the historical process, and views language, institutions, and myths alike as social constructs, thereby invalidating distinctions among them either within an ancient society or on the part of the outside observer looking in. As Michelet rightly sees, this synthetic approach of Vico is precisely what makes his thought so challenging ("hardie," p. x) to those who prefer an analytical or "critical" approach. "In his vast system . . . exist already, in germ at least, all the works of modern science. . . . All the giants of 'la critique' are already comfortably ensconced in the little pandemonium of *The New Science*" (p. x).

According to Martin Bernal, Michelet's writing is characterized by "hatred of the Phoenicians,"[70] he is guilty of saluting Niebuhr "for having discovered the ethnic principle of history 'as early as 1811'" (in fact, Michelet says 1812), and his account of the revolt of the Carthaginian mercenaries in 240–238 B.C. served as the basis of Flaubert's quintessentially Orientalist sensation *Salammbo*. In fact, Gildersleeve's attack on Michelet for endorsing "incredible" ideas about race-mixing seems more on the mark. Michelet's approval of Niebhur, as has been suggested above, is tinged with irony. And the revolt of the Carthaginian mercenaries is specifically abscribed to an ethnically mixed group of soldiers and presented as an extreme instance of the high degree of violence that characterized "the bloody world of the successors of Alexander" (*Histoire romaine*, 2.92). As for a racial aspect to the war itself, Michelet points out that the Sicilian Greeks and the Romans themselves sent help to Carthage in putting down the revolt. To the extent that Michelet faults Carthage for relying so heavily on mercenaries, his judgment is political rather than racial.

To be sure, Michelet does approach history from a racialist standpoint. But he is alert to positive as well as negative characteristics of the groups he discusses, and in general his writing smacks of academic cynicism as much as of Romantic obsession with race. Surely the work that would have most disturbed Gildersleeve is Michelet's *Bible de l'humanité* (3e éd., Paris 1864). For all its stereotyping of various races, and its strongly philhellenic and Aryan bias, the emphasis of the work is on the contribution of all sectors of humanity to "une Bible commune." "Humanity places its soul ceaselessly in a common Bible. Each great people writes a verse" (p. 1). Much as the history of Rome was presented as benefiting from the incursion of barbarians like Niebuhr, so the Bible of Humanity must combine the genius of the people of light with the "sombre genius of the South." The book of nature, which, according to Vico, each nation writes for itself, is in Michelet's view actually being written by the totality of humanity—and it is the privilege of his own era, thanks to philological and colonial adventures, to have access to that totality (pp. ii ff.).

While Michelet never to my knowledge explicitly associates that totalizing impulse with Rome, others of his era emphasized the Latinity of the

French politico-cultural project. The term "Latin America," apparently coined by a Colombian publicist in 1856, was popularized by propagandists for French overseas adventurism.[71] The concept of "races latines" was irresistible to those who sought to unite Spanish, Portuguese, and French interests against incursions from Anglo-Saxon America. A pamphlet addressed to Napoleon III in 1858 urges his intervention in Latin America on the grounds that France is "the only nation that can claim for itself the right to exercise universal influence."[72] But this influence, we are told, will be "neither egoistic nor interested." Rather, France must resist the incursions of the North Americans who, "like all sons of the Anglo-Saxon races, excel in the means of exploiting the work and the fortune of others" (p. 25). Those who scoff at President Buchanan's schemes against Mexico and Cuba are like the Romans "who laughed at the pretensions of the barbarians who eventually overwhelmed them" (pp. 15–16). Little wonder Gildersleeve found it difficult to accept a Chair of Latin in the most Catholic city in the United States!

The examples of Mickiewicz and Michelet make it clear that even within the general intellectual and cultural framework of Romanticism other configurations of the relationship between Greece and Rome and between literature and culture were possible. For Mickiewicz the continuing vitality of Latin literary studies stemmed from a sense of the unity of the literary tradition and from fascination with the apparent blend of urban sophistication and rural simplicity found in an author like Ovid. Mickiewicz's own search, in his imaginative writing, for a creative middle course between the logico-rhetorical structure of the Renaissance and Enlightenment and the emotional-expressive pattern of Romanticism allowed for the continuing influence of classical Latin.[73] At the same time, larger cultural considerations not only did not militate against the study of Rome but indeed fostered it as a counterweight to Prussian and Austrian imperialism. For Michelet, who, like Mickiewicz, can be found to repeat the usual Hellenomanic platitudes, the example of Vico was paramount in both the privileging of Rome in his own historical practice (he wrote no *History of Greece*) and in the promulgation of the view of discourse as construct. Again, the attempt to maintain a balance between potentially competing tendencies—in Michelet's case liberalism and imperialism—created in Michelet's work as in Mickiewicz's space for Rome and Latin to flourish.

Given the variety of Latinisms and classicisms available at the founding of American classical studies and throughout its history (and of course the list could be expanded well beyond the brief survey offered here) we may well ask why the program of Gildersleeve, especially in its privileging of Greece over Rome and its employment of philology as weapon instead of tool, has had such sustained historical impact.[74]

Gildersleeve's actions fit Gildersleeve's situation, but that situation has
hardly remained constant for the profession as a whole. The problem of
the force of tradition and its imposition on succeeding generations is im-
mensely complicated in disciplinary history as in literary history; but a
few tentative clarifications and hypotheses are in order here. At a social
level, American racial thinking has in the past and continues even to day
to resemble the views of Gildersleeve more than those of "a Frenchman
like Michelet." American particularism, that is, the sense of its unique
and experimental status, is more easily reconciled with visions of a Bibli-
cal city on a hill or a Swiss-Hellenic miracle than with Roman universal-
ism. While the history of American political and legal institutions has far
more in common with the Roman model, American self-representation,
particularly on the part of intellectuals, inclines toward Hellenomanic
idealization of "Greek" youth, freedom, and autonomy. Indeed, the tense
relationship between the university, which enjoys a virtual monopoly of
discussion of the past, and culture at large, would seem to be the crux of
the matter. Hugh Lloyd-Jones has written of the eagerness of English
writers and artists "to protect their art from contamination by the sordid
reality of the post-industrial world. ... Scholarship," he continues,
"shared the fate of art and literature."[75] In the United States, as Graff and
Lentricchia have argued, literary scholarship and literary criticism have
been especially prominent in the academic movement to "prevent culture," that is to isolate literary and artistic discourse from the larger discourse of society.[76] It is perhaps not surprising that in a self-proclaimed
classless society anxieties over status should be more rather than less pronounced among American academics. James Halporn has discussed some
of the status aspects of classical studies in the United States and rightly
observed their closer resemblance to the German as opposed to the
French or British experience.[77] What I have tried to suggest is that the
resemblance to the German model derives from philosophical and ideological congruence as well. Finally, the obviously self-constructed nature
of American cultural identity seems to prompt claimants to hegemonic
status to be particularly assertive in their exclusivist claims—witness the
virulence and intolerance to which various parties in debates over "Great
Books" and "American cultures" have been known to succumb; this
again suggests an affinity with the exclusivist model of German Romanticism, as opposed to other types, and with the idealized view of Greek
autonomy and uniqueness as opposed to the countervision of Greek complexity and/or Roman unity.[78]

    "Ideology cannot be removed," writes Roger Fowler. "It can be
replaced—by alternative ideology. Criticism demonstrates that there
are ideologies; compares their structural characteristics, their geneses,
their consequences; cannot disperse them."[79] Something similar can be

said about disciplinary histories. They can help us to understand the historical constraints that shaped current practice and give us options as we reconfigure our own circumstances and ideologies. Historians of the future may attribute the present eagerness to dissolve disciplinary boundaries, to redesign the canon, and to reformulate scholarly projects to any of a number of contemporary political, economic, and social factors: the decline and resurgence of nationalism, the globalization of economic structures, the collapse of sooty industrialism with concomitant weakening of the barriers between "pure and free" intellectual life and "dirty" culture. They will see those who resist such changes and seek to maintain classical studies as one of several "historical parks . . . where members of the community relax and contemplate their ontological relics," [80] and will perhaps attribute the prevalence of this mode to a desire for stability in a fast-changing world. But let us hope that they will note as well a renewed engagement with Rome, its culture and its literature, its tyrants and its laws, on the part of those who agreed to confront the world as they found it.

Chapter 2

WHY WAS LATIN LITERATURE INVENTED?

THE CONVENTIONAL EXPLANATION for the invention of Latin literature, as expressed or implied in various handbooks and specialized studies, is that the Romans developed Latin literature at the end of the third century B.C.E. and the beginning of the second because during that period they came into contact with a variety of foreign cultures, that of the Greeks pre-eminent among them. Captivated by the literary models of the Hellenic world and aware of their own limitations in this regard, the Romans are said to have set about creating for themselves a literature that could compete with the masterworks of the Greek tradition. Whether attributed to a cultural inferiority complex or regarded as the expression of a new-found cultural self-confidence, the literary performances and productions of the period are routinely described by modern scholars as the consequence of Roman interaction with Greeks.[1]

This Hellenocentric approach to the commencement of Latin literature can be rejected for several reasons. First, it is contrary to historical reality; the Romans had been in contact with the cultures of the Greek-speaking world long before the end of the Second Punic War. While formal inter-state exchanges may have been few in number, trade and other forms of social intercourse are well attested by both the archaeological and the historical record at least as early as the fourth century B.C.E.[2] The traditional view of the development of Latin literature asks us to believe that it was only after centuries of contact and interaction that Romans took note of the cultural productions of their Greek neighbors. In addition, the continuing focus on Greek models or Roman-Greek rivalry perpetuates a Romantic view of the superiority of Greek culture over Roman, a view which has little to do with the historical attitude of the Romans toward the Greeks. For the Romans, Greek culture, like the Greek population and Greek material wealth, was a colonial resource to be exploited and expropriated; to the extent that Greek culture was admired, it was as much for its potential to augment Roman power as for any immanent qualities or characteristics. Cicero's remark in the *De officiis*, to the effect that if a local elite runs out of resources to satisfy its population it should take what it needs from weaker neighbors, can be applied to Rome's expropriation of cultural as well as material wealth. Finally, the emphasis on Roman-Greek relations in contemporary scholarly discussions reflects an outmoded insistence on the particularity of the classical experience and ignores ample evidence from other traditional societies concerning the development of literary discourse. Without doubt the Roman experience, like that of any culture, has its unique aspects, but such uniqueness can only be ascertained in a comparative context. Comparative evidence, as well as evidence internal to Roman culture, makes it clear that, whatever the ultimate impact of Greek literary forms on Roman culture, Rome had its own culture of verbal performance that would have continued to evolve even in the complete absence of Greek literature.[3]

It is my thesis in this chapter that Latin literature took the particular form it did in the late third and early second centuries B.C.E. in response to two contemporaneous yet countervailing developments in Roman society: the transformation of Rome from a city-state to a traditional aristocratic empire and the crisis of identity provoked in Rome's rulers by that very transformation. Prior to the Second Punic War Rome was an influential polis of central Italy. As such, it seems to have had a ritual and artistic culture not entirely dissimilar to that of other city-states of the ancient Mediterranean world. As a result of its crushing defeat of Hannibal and subsequent conquests in the East, however, Rome acquired a vast overseas empire that taxed the traditional aristocracy's ability to govern. The depredations of the Hannibalic invasion, together with the postwar importation of large numbers of slaves, devastated the peasant class and radically transformed patterns of farming and landowning on the Italian peninsula.[4] The integration of Italy and the pacification of the Mediterranean that followed upon the war provided the basis for economic expansion in both manufacturing and trade and led to the emergence of elites who owed their wealth to sources other than land and inheritance. As with the spread of Hellenism in the aftermath of Alexander's conquests, so in the Roman world the development and diffusion of an administrative dialect was crucial to the maintenance of unity among farflung territories. Moreover, record keeping, an enterprise essential to any centralized administration, came to include cultural records as well, a natural development in an aristocratic society, since it is through access to an authorizing past as well as through brute force that an aristocracy legitimizes itself. But unlike Alexander and his successors, who were able to extend preexistent notions of panhellenic cultural unity to territories occupied by non-Greek peoples, the Roman leadership was caught off guard by its success and, indeed, underwent what is best described as an identity crisis. Rome's Italian neighbors, who possessed their own cultural traditions and civic institutions, had been instrumental in Rome's success against Hannibal and later against the Macedonians, with the result that ownership of the imperial hegemony was open to competition from outside Rome. Were the leaders of the new empire best regarded as

Romans, as Italians, or as participants in a pan-Mediterranean Hellenic *koinē*? And what did the possibility of such choices imply for their own prerogatives with respect to the territory they ruled? Even within Roman society aristocratic hegemony was at risk, since the enrichment of individual aristocrats from war booty together with the increase in wealth from commerce and manufacturing had the potential to disrupt both aristocratic unity and aristocratic exclusivity. As a result, the literature created to protect and promulgate the interests of the Roman elite is from its commencement more narrowly focused in both subject and audience than is the literature of Hellenism. Even when written by non-Romans (as it usually was) Latin literature remained deeply implicated in the maintenance of a specifically Roman aristocratic hegemony.[5]

FROM MUSIC TO THE MUSES

Before exploring the invention of Latin literature in more detail we must first correct the false yet widespread impression that Latin literature actually "began" late in the third century B.C.E. As the recent work of Nevio Zorzetti makes clear, the ancient Romans believed, and there is little reason to doubt them, that they had a literary culture—or, more precisely, a musical culture from which literature could emerge—prior to the Second Punic War.[6] As in other archaic city-states, so in Rome citizens sang songs of praise and blame, recounted the achievements of their ancestors, persuaded each other through political oratory, hymned their deities at civic festivals, and taught their children proper behavior through anecdotes, examples, and precepts. They had a cultural system comparable to what the Greeks called *mousikē*, one linked, as in Greek cities, to the institution of the symposium celebrated by clusters of aristocrats, known in Latin as *sodalitates*.[7] The debunking of Niebuhr's view that the early Romans had a tradition of heroic lays, or protoepic poems, has left unexplained, until Zorzetti, the persistent references in a variety of Roman sources to literary and cultural practices that predate the work of Livius Andronicus, Naevius, Plautus, and other figures conventionally associated with the origins of Latin literature. We can reject Niebuhr's postulation of an early Roman epic tradition without thereby invalidating reconstruction of the early Roman civic and sympotic culture more generally. As Zorzetti puts it, "[t]he old idea of the typical Roman character, practical and unpoetic, is simply inadequate, besides being unhistorical."[8]

The transformation in cultural practice that occurred during and immediately following upon the Second Punic War is best regarded not as the invention of literature per se, but as a revolution in the sociology of literary production. Three developments define this revolution: reliance on writing, professionalization of performance, and importation of performers. Whereas archaic literary culture seems to have been characterized by performances that were not necessarily transmitted in writing, the new culture of the late third century and early second centuries B.C.E. was intimately connected with the preservation, importation, and circulation of texts. It is important to recognize that we are not speaking here of a transition from oral to literate society; archaic Rome was literate centuries before it developed what we have come to call literature.[9] Inscriptional evidence indicates that written language was used in Latium from the seventh or sixth century B.C.E. on, chiefly to mark ownership of property and to record sacral and legal regulations. Yet the earliest substantial remains of what is usually regarded as Latin literature, that is, fragments of the poetry of Livius Andronicus and the entire plays of Plautus, can be placed no earlier than the second half of the third century B.C.E. During that generation and the one immediately following it, we see evidence of the turn to written literature in the establishment of a *collegium*, or guild, for *scribae* and *histriones* (i.e., writers and performers together). The immediate stimulus was the commemoration of Livius Andronicus's contribution to the Roman state during the Second Punic War; it is perhaps significant that the contribution itself consisted of the re-performance of a hymn that had been sung at an earlier festival, and is therefore likely to have been preserved in writing.[10] Also relevant is the appearance in the late third century B.C.E. of individual authors associated with individual texts, in contrast to the generic *vates*, or priest-prophets, of earlier times.[11] The privileging of written texts implies and in turn is encouraged by a new model of authorship. Finally, it is in this era that we hear of the use of texts in schools, the division of texts into books, and the preparation of revised or annotated versions. While the songs of the *vates* are reported to have been written down—Livy refers to the confiscation of *vaticini libri*—such writing seems not to have been instrumental to the activity of the *vates* and may very well represent a last-ditch attempt to preserve the culture of the *vates* in the face of incursions by the new literary culture associated with the *poetae* and their Muses. In what may be a parallel strategy, native American "idolators" in sixteenth-century Mexico adopted the European writing system in order to preserve their cultural traditions in the face of aggressive colonization and Christianization.[12]

In addition to reliance on writing, the new literary culture of the late third and early second centuries B.C.E. is distinguished by its employment of literary professionals.[13] The preservation of a written literary tradition both requires and enables the professionalization of the literati. Again, the establishment of the collegium on the Aventine illustrates the point:

it was located in the temple of Minerva, protectress of the *artifices*, or skilled laborers, of Rome. An otherwise puzzling fragment of Cato the Elder also points to the disjunction between preprofessional and professional literary production, for Cato records approvingly the ancestors' disdain for poetry as skilled labor (poeticae artis honos non erat) even though he is elsewhere the source for the tradition that symposiasts themselves sang songs of praise at banquets, a practice of which he evidently approves.[14] By differentiating between *carmina convivialia* and the products of the *ars poetica*, Cato is not, as some would have it, distinguishing between poetic genres.[15] Rather, he is differentiating the longstanding preprofessional practice of producing *carmina*—song, in Nagy's extended sense of the term—from the newly developing reliance on outside professionals.[16] Indeed, the very expression *ars poetica* is a calque on the Greek lexical practice of denoting a *techne* by addition of a modifying adjective with suffix *-ik-*. In addition, by identifying the practitioner of the *ars poetica* as a *grassator,* or mugger, Cato alludes disparagingly to the making of poetry for profit. Cato's recounting of the ancestors' disapproval of professional poetry testifies to the new significance of professionalization in his era; otherwise there would be no reason to pronounce against it. This significance would have been augmented by the concomitant emphasis on written texts, since in a pre-print era writing is as likely to diminish access to a work of literature as to facilitate it, both because literacy is not spread evenly throughout society and, which is more important, because books are scarce commodities.[17]

Finally, in addition to being a culture of writing and a culture of professionalism, the new or Musaic culture was a culture of outsiders. With the exception of Naevius, who may have fought as a Roman soldier in the First Punic War,[18] and later Cato, who in effect invented Latin prose literature—in part by disembedding it from its poetical and musical context[19]—the chief figures of the so-called beginning of Latin literature were non-Romans. To explain this phenomenon is to move from the what to the why of the invention of Latin literature, since it seems perfectly possible that Roman citizens could have been trained to serve as literary professionals, like the Christian Indians of sixteenth-century Mexico;[20] like the rhapsodes of archaic Greece; or like Naevius himself. By importing outsiders, the aristocrats who fostered the development of Musaic culture effectively guaranteed that it would be their unique possession.

Writing late in the second century B.C.E. the poet Porcius Licinus remarked that it was during the Second Punic War that "the Muse winged her warlike way to the fierce tribe of Romulus" (Poenico bello secundo Musa pinnato gradu/ intulit se bellicosam in Romuli gentem feram [*FPL* fr. 1]). Skutsch is probably correct to see in Licinus's words a reference to the arrival in Rome of Ennius, the Muses' promoter, during the war against Hannibal.[21] If so, Licinus's remarks confirm our association of the invention of Latin literature with the survival strategies of the traditional Roman leadership in the wake of the Hannibalic invasion. At the same time, the unexpected identification of the newly arrived Muse as warlike, as opposed to her association with harmony from the earliest period of Greek culture,[22] may serve as an emblem of the strife, both external and internal, cultural and political, from which the Roman aristocracy and its client Muse emerged triumphant. The defeat of pre-Musaic culture (i.e., of the music of the *sodalitates* and the *carmina* of the *vates*), the creation and promulgation of a literary dialect, the invention of a constricting moral and cultural tradition, and the expropriation of Greek symbolic capital were neither inevitable nor uncontested developments. Rome did not abandon its pre-political and pre-imperial civic institutions without a struggle. Years later, during another crisis of aristocratic self-confidence, Cicero, writing in the *Brutus*, would try to naturalize the events of the late third and early second centuries B.C.E. by constructing an account of growth and gradual development (nihil est enim simul et inventum et perfectum [*Brut.* 71]) that involves special pleading with respect to chronology that still mystifies contemporary readers.[23] His erasure of the conflict and contestation that characterized the earlier period has long held sway among scholars eager to view him as a source of information about Roman culture rather than as the imaginative polemicist he was. As we shall see below, it is time to restore him, as well as his predecessors, to their rightful position as strategists in the conflicts that generated classical Latin literature.

THE LINGUISTIC POLITICS OF ARCHAIC ROME

Virtually every scrap of information that we have pertaining to Latin literature in the third century B.C.E. can be related to the preservation of social cohesion at Rome. Livius Andronicus's performance of a play at the *Ludi Romani* in 240 B.C.E. is associated with the celebration of Roman victory in the First Punic War (Cic. *Brut.* 72f.). The expanded opportunities for dramatic performance later in the century are linked in Livy's narrative with senatorial attempts to maintain unity and morale in the face of wartime catastrophes (e.g., 25.12, 26.23.3, 27.23.5–8). The performance of a hymn of Livius Andronicus in 207 B.C.E. is at a religious festival designed to channel and allay the fears provoked by the arrival of a second Carthaginian army in Italy (Livy 27.37.1–5). And the commemoration of Livius for the success of that hymn is effected through the establishment of a guild of scribes and actors under the protection of Minerva; literature thus comes to be associated with the politically significant operations of record-keeping and festival performance, under the watchful eye of the goddess of specialized crafts, with the permission of the Roman Senate (Festus 446L).

Social cohesion is an important motif in early Latin literary history in large part because the struggle with Hannibal taxed Roman unity, both within the Roman populace and between Rome and its allies. In Livy's narrative, as the Second Punic War drags on, we hear of an upsurge in foreign religious practices (25.1.6ff.); senatorial anxiety over the cooperativeness of the tax-farmers (25.3.8); the restiveness of allies, including the Latin colonies (26.15.4, 27.9.7); and arson in the city of Rome (26.26–7). The problems of the years 213–212 B.C.E. and the state's response to these problems are particularly instructive. According to Livy (26.1.5ff.), the long duration of the war, combined with the crowding of many refugees from the countryside into the city of Rome, produced an upsurge in religious superstition. Particularly to blame were men he describes as *sacrificuli* and *vates*—that is, people who proposed alternative rites and alternative discourse to the officially sanctioned (i.e., statist) religious practice. The response of the magistrates was to confiscate the offending writings, including *libri vaticini*, and to forbid public observance of new or foreign rituals.

Among the *libri vaticini* that came into the hands of the praetor urbanus were some verses by one "Marcius," whose single name, it should be noted, links him to the pre-literate world of legendary heroes—or, as Livy would like us to believe, to other figures of low or foreign extraction. According to the account offered by the authorities, these verses had not only predicted the disaster at Cannae, but also promised victory to the Romans if they established new games in honor of Apollo. This the city praetor duly undertook in 212 and in each succeeding year, until in 208 the Ludi Apollinares were vowed in perpetuity as part of the regular cycle of festivals (27.23.5). Livy does not give much detail about the content of these early Festivals of Apollo, although he regards them as consisting of some sort of spectacle (populus coronatus spectavit [25.12.15]). Within a few years they had certainly become the occasion of dramatic performances.[24] Regardless of any uncertainty about the original nature of the games, their invention, in a context of civil unrest, and on the advice of confiscated vatic texts provides a concrete instance of the cooptation and replacement of pre-Musaic by Musaic culture and of the purposeful involvement of the senatorial, or statist, aristocracy in that endeavor. Moreover, the sequence of events, which is more fully recounted than the incident of the Livian hymn or indeed of any of the earliest events in Latin literary history, clarifies the motives that directly or indirectly shaped those episodes as well: the need of a threatened aristocracy to preserve morale and social unity under their leadership.

Far from weakening in the wake of victory over Hannibal, the Roman leadership's sense of its own vulnerability apparently intensified. A newly integrated Italy was just that: Italy, not Rome. As a consequence, the Roman Senate devised a number of strategies for securing its dominance throughout the peninsula without diluting its membership or antagonizing its allies. The suppression of the Bacchanals in 186 B.C.E. can be understood in this light, as can the extension of usury laws to the allies (193 B.C.E.) and the various machinations concerning citizenship, allied status, and military recruitment. In the case of the Bacchanals, the Senate sought to regulate a potentially seditious religious practice but arranged for enforcement to be handled by local officials in communities outside Rome.[25] In the financial legislation of 193 the Senate sought to gain control of the economic integration of the peninsula by applying its own standards to bankers from allied communities.[26] With respect to military recruitment, the Senate engaged in various machinations (described by Toynbee as a game of "beggar-my-neighbour") designed to secure maximum military manpower from depleted allies without extending citizen rights to them, a move that would have weakened the senatorial aristocracy's hold on political power.[27]

The Senate's attitude, a mixture of anxiety and aggression, is reflected in the linguistic politics of the era as well—a subject generally neglected in histories of the period, yet of great importance to our account of the invention of Latin literature. During the conduct of the war against Hannibal, language appears not to have been an issue, at least not on the Roman side. Livy is aware of linguistic differences throughout his narrative, but his emphasis is on the incompatibility of Punic with the languages of Italy rather than on any linguistic difficulties within the Roman alliance. Hanno needs a translator at Nola (where Oscan was spoken), the Romans do not (Livy 23.43.9). Greek and Roman residents of Tarentum trade control of the city, but their differences are described as political and military rather than cultural or linguistic (e.g., Livy 25.11). Despite numerous references to the linguistic gulf between Hannibal and the peoples whose territory he invades (e.g., 21.42.1, 22.13.6, 23.5.11, 23.34.6, 27.28.9, 27.43.6, 30.30.1), only once does Livy describe use of a translator in a Roman context, and that is when Fabius Pictor, himself the author of a Roman history for a Greek-speaking audience, recites a Latin translation of a Delphic oracle (23.11.4). In contrast to the mutual comprehensibility of the Roman allies, Hannibal's army is described as heterogeneous in ethnicity, custom, dress, religion, weaponry—as well as language (28.12.4; cf. 30.33.8, 30.34.2). While we must be cautious of overreliance on a history composed some two hundred years after the events in question, it seems reasonable to suppose that if language problems had been severe on the Roman side, Livy's narrative would have

preserved some evidence of that fact, especially in light of his express
concern with sociolinguistics in other contexts.

In the aftermath of the war with Hannibal, however, the linguistic politics of Italy become more volatile, or at least more readily observable.
The spread of Roman and Latin colonies inevitably led to the expansion
of the use of Latin.[28] Rome's prestige as head of the anti-Hannibalic
confederation and the size of the Latin-speaking population of Italy enhanced the status of the Latin language itself. Campanile's analysis of
inscriptions from Delos and of linguistic evidence from Spain reveals the
extent to which speakers of Oscan adopted Latin for public purposes
while preserving Oscan, at least in the case of Delos, for private affairs.[29]
Livy reports that in 180 B.C.E. the Cumaeans petitioned the Roman Senate for permission to use Latin in commerce and administration (Cumanis
eo anno petentibus permissum ut publice Latine loquerentur et praeconi-
bus Latina vendendi ius esset [Livy 40.43.1]). That the petition was
granted suggests the Romans' awareness of the value of a uniform medium of communication. Yet that such a petition was necessary or advisable, especially in the case of the Cumaeans, who had long enjoyed
Roman citizenship (civitas sine suffragio) and were signally loyal to Rome
during the Hannibalic invasion, shows the uneasiness felt by the Romans
with respect to the possible leveling of linguistic distinctions, an uneasiness justified a century later during the Social Wars when the Italian confederation used Latin as a means of communication among those in revolt
against Rome.

As for the city of Rome, there is also evidence of competition among
languages and corresponding cultural forms. In a fragment attributed
to a speech against the tribune Marcus Caelius (ORF 8.115), the Elder
Cato denounces the target of his invective for such unconventional behavior as bursting into song, performing Greek verses, and telling jokes.
Cato's use of Hellenism as a club for beating up on political opponents is
well known, but in this instance he seems to object to the specified actions
themselves and not their connection, real or imagined, with degenerate
Greece. In fact, in a fragment from the same speech (8.113), Cato rails
against "a wandering minstrel and a Fescennine," declaring, "I wouldn't
enroll him in a colony."[30] Cato's opponent is to be politically marginal-
ized because he attempts to appeal to the burgeoning, diversified population of the city. And the mark of his marginalization is that he is not fit
to participate in the colonial project of extending Roman hegemony.
Both the problem—the complexity of postwar Italian society—and one
solution—increased Roman colonization—become apparent from Cato's
invective.

Other scraps of evidence also point in the direction of persistent linguistic and cultural competition. A fragment of Titinius, contemporary of

Terence and first attested author of the *fabula togata*, or comedy in Roman dress, refers to those who "talk [or perhaps perform plays: *fabulantur*] in Oscan and Volscian because they don't know Latin."[31] Later evidence documents the performance of plays at Rome in both Greek and Oscan during the first century B.C.E. While it is possible that these are antiquarian or academic revivals, it seems more likely that the representatives of the various cultures of Italy and the Mediterranean that either flooded or were forced into Rome as early as the Second Punic War simply brought their forms of entertainment along with them.[32] During the late second century the poet Lucilius refers to the opposite phenomenon when (or if) he attacks an unnamed impresario for taking his Roman show on the Italian road.[33]

But the best and by far the most abundant evidence for the sociolinguistic complexity of second century Latin is to be found in the surviving literary texts themselves. In the plays of Plautus, for example, we encounter not just the adoption, in a loose sense, of the Greek literary form of New Comedy, but, more important, the easy and persistent use of Greek vocabulary, Greek oaths, and Greek linguistic forms. As Meillet long ago observed, Plautus takes his Greek not from a literary elite, but from the streets and the marketplace.[34] Words such as *balineum* and *camera*, *macina* and *tecina*, *mina*, *talentum*, and *dracuma* make it clear, according to Meillet, that "Greek civilization infiltrated among merchants and sailors and the lower classes of the city of Rome before having a profound effect on the dominant classes."[35] While it may be possible to dispute Meillet's conclusion concerning the relative Hellenization of the upper and lower classes at Rome, his evidence for the "Greekness" of Plautus's Latin does call attention to the permeability of linguistic and social boundaries between Latin- and Greek-speaking communities.

If Plautus's language helps to document the sociolinguistic situation, it also suggests the variety of individual responses to that situation, particularly with respect to competition between Latin and Greek. The hellenization of Latin literature, which is sometimes regarded merely as the submission of an inferior culture to a superior or the gradual evolution from primitive to sophisticated, is in fact the product of a clash between literary and linguistic paradigms. As Devoto puts it, Greek operated like a "pincer" on Latin, proceeding "from both the highest and the lowest social levels."[36] In the case of comedy, the varieties of grecizing are evident in the contrast between the interpenetration of linguistic and social levels found in Plautus and the *purus sermo* canonized by the younger comic playwright Terence.[37] With respect to epic, the fragments of Livius Andronicus's translation of the *Odyssey* reveal a tendency, as one scholar put it, to latinize Greek, while Ennius in his *Annales* hellenizes Latin.[38] That is to say, Livius finds Latin equivalents of Greek terms, whereas Ennius intro-

duces Greek terms, Greek inflections, and Greek versification into his epic
account of the origin and development of the Roman state. The net effect
of Ennius's stylistic inventiveness is to distance literary language from
that of everyday speech. Even the Greek that he introduces is, unlike Plautus's Greek, the Greek of elite literature or sophisticated philosophizing
as opposed to the Greek of the marketplace.

The Latin language never fully dominated the Italian peninsula either
during the period of the Roman Republic or later. Indeed, linguists attribute the contemporary linguistic diversity of Italy in part to the varied
non-Latin substrates that affected the development of later dialects.[39] But
linguistic unity was never the aim of the Romans, although linguistic
unity of the elites may have been. From the standpoint of the elites, the
linguistic situation that obtained by the end of the second generation of
Latin literature, that is, by the "death" (if such it was) of Terence in 159
B.C.E., was ideal. Latin was secure as the prestige language of Italy, and
good Latin had been nicely distinguished from bad in the public medium
of comedy. If the masses rejected the comedy of Terence and opted for
dancing bears and rope tricks, so much the better; at least they had been
exposed to the language of the elite and might recognize it when it was
used to give them orders. As Ernst Gellner put it regarding the development of formal, standardized languages at later periods of history, "The
most important and persistent message is generated by the medium itself.
. . . That core message is that the language and style of the transmissions
is important, that only he who can understand them, or can acquire such
comprehension, is included in a moral and economic community and that
he who does not and cannot, is excluded."[40] As for the members of the
elite themselves, the invention of literary Latin and the production of a
sizable number of texts in it gave them just the vehicle needed for communication among themselves. Moreover, the very artificiality of the new
language guaranteed its inaccessibility and its timelessness—so much so
that even today Terence is regarded as the quintessence of *Latinitas*.

Eric Hobsbawm has written that in order for a people to become a
nation three requirements must be met: "historic association with a current state or one with a fairly lengthy past": "a proven capacity for conquest"; and "existence of a long-established cultural elite, possessing a
written national literary and administrative vernacular."[42] At the end of
the Second Punic War the Romans met the first and second criteria; two
generations later they had fulfilled the third as well. Nor is it anachronistic to relate a study of modern nationalism to the control of a traditional
aristocratic empire, for that is precisely how the Romans came to regard
their own role within their empire: one nation among many, destined to
rule and to civilize. From the linguistic/political struggles of the late third
and early second centuries B.C.E. emerged the "imagined community" of

Roman nationhood, one replacing the face-to-face communities of pre-Hannibalic *sodalitates*. The newly established literary tradition, with its characteristic preferences for writing over performance and professionalization over amateur production and its reliance on vulnerable outsiders, was an overdetermined response to the social and cultural challenges facing the Roman elites of the era.

EXISTIMATIO AND THE FORMATION OF THE ROMAN ARISTOCRACY

All aristocracies must devise strategies of recruitment and acculturation. Recruitment can be along strictly biological lines (i.e., the children of aristocrats become aristocrats) or on the basis of other criteria and through other means, such as adoption and adlection, which were common strategies at Rome. Whatever the background of the new aristocrats, they must be inculcated into the protocols of aristocratic behavior, and their qualifications as aristocrats must be defended against rival or alternative claimants to authority.[42] At Rome literature participates in the "formation" of the aristocracy in both senses of that word, that is, by defining, preserving, and transmitting the standards of behavior to which the individual aristocrat must aspire and by valorizing aristocratic ideals and aristocratic authority within the broader cultural context. By definition, an aristocrat is someone who lays claim to special privileges on the basis of a connection with an authorizing past. Literature is an important means of both preserving (or, as is more often the case, inventing) that past and of asserting its authority. While we can well imagine a scenario in which the process of acculturation is carried out without the circulation of written texts—early Greece and perhaps late Aztec cultures provide examples—the Roman drive simultaneously to solidify and to expand aristocratic hegemony makes the use of written literature as a tool of acculturation all but inevitable. Writing, especially writing by outside professionals beholden to the aristocrats individually and/or collectively, comes to supplement and ultimately almost to replace the rituals of acculturation that characterize a smaller, less expansionistic Rome. It does so precisely because of its double characteristics of permanence (relatively speaking) and mobility or portability. In the early stages of its development, we can see Latin literature lay claim to its destiny as acculturator of imperial elites in its promulgation of language and associative structures designed to evoke rituals of acculturation, ranging from the sympotic performance of praise and blame to the funeral laudation, with its construction and inculcation of authoritative exempla of right thinking and acting. The terms by which literature defines its own social role provide an important avenue to the process whereby it establishes its authority. The verb *existimo*, its nominal counterpart *existimatio*, and the related noun *exemplum* are especially important. As we shall see, this lexical nexus helps to define literature's role as inventor of an authorizing tradition and as promoter of that tradition over and against rival sources of social authority.

Crucial to our analysis is recognition of the widespread and continuing tension within traditional societies between a static—even essentialist— view of authority as embedded in clearly defined social roles and hierarchies and a more dynamic, changeable view of authority as attributable to unique achievement or acquisition.[43] While this tension can manifest itself along any of a number of parameters, it is perhaps easiest to observe (and in the context of Roman history most important to observe) in the competition between landed senatorial aristocracy and market-oriented commercial interests. Not coincidentally the very word through which Latin literature promotes its own social significance, *existimare*, denotes, among other things, the interconvertibility of different sources of social authority.[44] The literal meaning of the verb is to evaluate, or assess; according to Festus (23 Lindsay), the simplex *aestimare* refers to the establishing of a relationship between *aes* or money and other forms of property (sheep or cattle in the example he gives). Festus also uses the verb in relationship to the noun *exemplum* (72 Lindsay). An *exemplum* is something "taken out of" (*eximo*) a group in order to serve as a standard by which other instances of the type can be evaluated (*existimare*). Thus it would seem that *existimatio* implies both evaluation according to a standard and the possibility of conversion from one system of value to another. As a result, the term captures precisely the double function we have attributed to literature in early Roman society: first, establishment of traditional standards and second, assimilation or repudiation of systems of value different from the aristocratic reliance on tradition.

As it happens, the verb *existimare* figures prominently in the opening paragraphs of Cato's *De agricultura*, a passage expressly concerned with competing systems of value that occurs in the context of a work seeking to transmit appropriate standards of conduct from one generation to the next. Thus the *De agricultura* as a whole and the introductory paragraphs in particular recapitulate and exemplify, both within the text and in the relationship between text and context, the uses of *existimatio* that interest us here.

The opening of the treatise is thus worth quoting in full:

Est interdum praestare mercaturis rem quaerere ni tam periculosum siet; et item fenerari, si tam honestum siet. Maiores nostri sic habuerunt, et ita in legibus posiverunt, furem dupli condemnari, feneratorem quadrupli. Quanto peiorem civem *existimarint* feneratorem quam furem, hinc licet *existimari*. Et virum bonum quom laudabant, ita laudabant, bonum agricolam bonumque colonum. Amplissime laudari *existimabatur* qui ita laudabatur. Mercatorem autem strenuom studiosumque rei quarendae *existimo*; verum, ut supra dixi, periculosum et calamitosum. At ex agricolis et viri fortissimi et milites strenussimi gignuntur, maximeque pius quaestus stabilissimusque consequitur, minimeque invidiosus: minimeque male cogitantes sunt, qui in eo studio occupati sunt.

It's sometimes advantageous to seek riches through commerce—except that it's so dangerous. And it's the same with moneylending—if only it were respectable. Our ancestors thus determined, and thus placed it in their laws, that a thief was subject to double indemnity, a moneylender to quadruple. How much worse a citizen they considered (*existimarint*) a moneylender than a thief, from this it can be assessed (*existimari*). And as for a good man, when they praised him, they praised him thus: a good farmer and a good landsman. Most fully was he thought (*existimabatur*) to be praised, who thus was praised. I adjudge (*existimo*) a businessman to be energetic and eager for gain, but as I stated above, plagued by danger and disaster. But it's from farmers that the bravest men and most energetic soldiers are born, and the most honorable income and most stable follows from farming, the one least subject to envy. And least ill devising are those who are occupied in this pursuit. (Cato *De agricultura Praef.* 1–4)

The question posed at the outset of the passage concerns the most appropriate means of pursuing wealth (*rem quaerere*). Commerce is rejected because of its dangers, moneylending because it is not respectable. The language of praise and blame suggests that we are in the environment of cultural constraint, and constructed self-interested attempts to regulate discourse and behavior. It is not surprising, then, that Cato proceeds to elaborate on the disreputability of moneylending by contrasting it with the appropriate means of acquiring wealth, namely agriculture (or, more precisely, agribusiness), the topic of his treatise. The ancestors (*maiores*) are introduced as authorizing the privileged status of agriculture, and their general preferences are expressed in terms of widening circles of *existimatio* or evaluation. The ancestors set the price/punishment on usury as twice the price/punishment for theft and from this the contemporary reader is invited to evaluate the ancestors' evaluation. The ancestors praised good men, and, at the same time, they evaluated the praise by which good men were praised. Cato imagines the collectivity of the ancestors, individuals among the ancestors, himself, and his readers as engaged in a complicated and ongoing process of praise and blame, pricesetting and evaluation, the persistent nature of which is underscored by the incantatory and reduplicative nature of the language of the preface. And the end result of this process of cross-generational transmission of evaluation is that Cato himself is empowered to make his own assessment or evaluation: *existimo*, "I appraise," as he says in the first use of a first person verb after a string of impersonal and passive constructions.

Up to the time of Cato, the verb *existimo* seems to have retained its etymological association with *aes*, meaning money. Indeed, Plautus frequently uses the compound *existimo* and the simplex *aestimo* with the genitive of price construction, for example, "I put a price on this of . . ."[45] Cato toys with the etymological significance of *existimo* when he refers to the calculation of proper restitution for property alienated through theft or usury. Yet within the same passage, he seems to shift from this concrete, etymological use of *existimatio* to the looser, more metaphorical sense ("judge" or "determine") familiar from later Latin. Indeed, the switch from *existimo* to *laudo* in the middle of the paragraph seems to signal Cato's own uncertainty or hesitancy about using *existimo* in this newfangled way.

What we have been observing in the language of the *De agricultura* may be described as the surface tensions produced by a deeper cultural anxiety over value, in particular the value of an aristocratic or gentrified lifestyle in its relationship to new sources of power within Roman society. Winkler's observation that in Greek society the insistence on the naturalness of a practice is a good indicator of its conventionality finds a counterpart in the Roman world where the assertion of *mos maiorum* frequently masks some novelty of interest or acquisition. The *De agricultura*, as is well known, is not just a hodgepodge of traditional recipes and prayers, but an attempt to develop a set of rational principles for the newly altered conditions of Roman agriculture in an era that saw the decline of the traditional peasant farmer and the spread of large and far-flung estates known as *latifundia*.[46] By attributing admiration of farmers to the *maiores* and loading the *De agricultura* with age-old prayers and formulas, Cato seeks to ascribe what Gellius calls in another context the *color vetustatis*, or appearance of antiquity, to what is in fact a revolutionary enterprise. At the same time, by insisting on the connection between land and tradition, Cato seeks to give to the landowning class an inalienable resource in its power struggle against other fractions of society and potential new sources of cultural energy. Landowning, as opposed to banking, commerce, and pillage, has the authority of tradition, and tradition, in turn, is uniquely the possession of the class that owns land. Soldiers may grow rich by sacking cities, upstart equestrians may seek political influence to match their economic clout, and Greek literati may revel in their exhibitions of the supple power of sophistic rhetoric, but one thing to which none of them can lay claim is the Roman past. The irony that it is Cato, a new man, at least in the political sense, and a diversified participant in the dynamic economy of second-century Rome, who articulates this nexus of *existimatio*, tradition, and land merely underscores the ideological nature of the preface to *De agricultura* and its linguistic innovations. Cato the man was evidently not disturbed by the prospect of accumulating wealth through means other than agriculture. But the insistence on the traditional privileging of landowning allows Cato and his class to have their cake and eat it too—enjoying the material benefits of a new economy, increasingly oriented toward commerce and manufacturing, as well as the social and political privileges associated with traditional aristocratic hegemony.

By attributing *existimatio* to the ancestors, Cato seeks their validation for what is in essence his own and his contemporaries' attempt to resolve anxiety over the ambiguity of value. While *existimare* at an earlier stage of linguistic and cultural development means "to set a price on," in the concrete sense of assigning a monetary value, it now comes to signify assessment by the vaguer and more easily manipulable standards of goodness (*bonus*), reputability (*honestus*), and largesse (*amplissime*). Cato assigns to the inevitably controversial and ambiguous determination of a man's worth the simplicity of an economic calculation. Yet in so doing he seeks also to establish a disparity between aristocratic *existimatio* and the tawdry processes of exchange and evaluation characteristic of other groups in society. Indeed, although Cato does not specify the context in which the ancestors delivered their praise and blame, the emphasis on their plural, anonymous performance and on the transmission of their judgment over time may well have evoked for the contemporary reader the kind of sympotic setting Cato praised elsewhere in his discussion of *carmina convivialia*.[47] In other words, both the content of the evaluation and the context can be taken to reinforce the link between Cato's advice and traditional aristocratic wisdom, in contrast to the social commitments implied in a privileging of wealth. We witness a repetition and confirmation of Cato's strategy of differentiation between aristocratic evaluation and mere lucre in the words of Gaius Gracchus, who told the Roman people in 123 B.C.E.: "I seek from you not money, but a good evaluation" (peto a vobis non pecuniam, sed bonam existimationem [*ORF* 48.44]). That Gracchus, whom we might ordinarily associate with a different political program from that of the Elder Cato, can be invoked as a parallel suggests that we are dealing not with factional in-fighting among aristocrats but with an attempt by the elites as a whole to construct Roman culture in their own interests. The aphoristic contrast between *pecunia* and *existimatio*, we may note in passing, persists into Cicero's day, as evidenced by his speech in defense of Roscius, where we are told pecunia levissima, existimatio sanctissima (money is most fickle, *existimatio* most sacred) (*Rosc. Am.* 15).

In the preface to *De agricultura* we observe the textualization of the process of *existimatio*: that is, *existimatio* takes place within the work of literature itself—although it is authorized in part by a process of *existima-*

tio described as having occurred outside the text. In a set of related texts from the same era, we find more direct reference to a process of *existimatio* that takes place independent of the work of literature. Ennius, Polybius, and the authors of the Scipionic epitaphs all describe the assessment of aristocratic performance in accordance with agreed-upon standards as a process that takes place outside of the text, that is, as a standard ritual of Roman culture. While we cannot rule out the possibility that their representations correspond to historic reality, it is worth keeping in mind that it is in the interests of the literati to foster a process that requires someone within society to preserve and articulate the exempla against which the aristocrat is to be measured. Thus an important additional aspect of *existimatio* that emerges from examination of these passages is the need *existimatio* creates for literature.

In book 31 of his history of Rome, the Greek intellectual Polybius recounts the commencement of his long friendship with the younger Scipio, who was certainly one of the most renowned aristocrats of the Roman republic, thanks in no small part to the successful public relations campaign conducted by his client—Polybius. According to Polybius, Scipio, while still a young man, asked Polybius why he was in the habit of addressing Scipio's older brother while ignoring him: "Evidently you also have the same opinions of me that I hear the rest of my countrymen have. For, as I am told, I am believed by everybody to be a quiet and indolent man, with none of the energetic character of a Roman, because I don't choose to speak in the law courts. And they say that the family I spring from does not require such a protector as I am, but just the opposite; and this is what I feel most."[48] Polybius describes himself as astonished at Scipio's outspokenness and eager to offer him assistance: "I myself would be delighted to do all in my power to help you to speak and act in a way worthy of your ancestors. For as for those studies which I see now occupy and interest you, you will be in no want of those ready to help both of you; so great is the crowd of such men that I see flocking here from Greece at present. But as regards what you say now troubles you I don't think you could find anyone more efficient than myself to forward your effort and help you." Polybius alludes to the widespread availability of rhetorical education at Rome, but offers himself as an adviser on character formation, and in particular on the matter of assisting Scipio to "speak and act in a way worthy of his ancestors."

The passage should be read in tandem with the Ennian episode sometimes referred to as "The Good Friend."[49] In a scene that probably comes from Ennius's account of the death of the consul Cn. Servilius Geminus during the battle of Cannae, the poet provides, in the view of Aulus Gellius, who preserves the important fragment, a model of the proper relationship between men of unequal birth and fortune (*Noctes Atticae* 12.4).

Servilius delivers a final official speech or message, then calls to his side a longtime companion, one whom he had felt free to address openly about all of his plans, anxieties, and accomplishments after a day hard spent in government and business. The friend's responsibility, we learn, has been to keep the consul from any bad pursuit (malum facinus), to listen, but also to speak when the time is right (secunda loquens in tempore) since he has knowledge of "many ancient matters, which a long expanse of time has buried," and knows "customs both old and new, the laws of the ancients both human and divine." The inferior friend is "capable of speaking and of keeping quiet": qui dicta loquiue tacereue posset (*Ann.* 285). A tradition originating with the grammarian Aelius Stilo (first century B.C.E.) treats the passage as allegorical of Ennius's own relationship with his patron Fulvius Nobilior. Even without such speculation, it is clear that the *amicus minor* as described fulfills a function comparable to that of literature. By providing a historical and cultural context for the real and proposed behavior of the great man, he indirectly constrains him to behave in a way that is the opposite of *malum*, that is, *bonum*, or as an aristocrat should.[50]

The exchange between Scipio and Polybius suggests that the constraint upon aristocratic behavior provided by the well-informed *amicus minor* in fact derives from tradition and from the unspecified "everybody" who by their talk enforce the tradition. Even in the passage from Ennius's *Annales*, it seems to be taken for granted that the great man needs a friend of lesser rank because in his relationship with other great men he is always on display and in a state of implied yet intense competition before an audience. Two elements of this construct—the power of tradition and the expectation that it will be enforced by a contemporary audience—seem to have been particularly important to the Scipios and their proteges, for they figure prominently in the inscriptions on the family tomb.[51] Tradition is invoked both by comparisons between the recently deceased and the ancestors and by the arrangement of epitaphs in a familial context, while the role of the judging audience is specifically mentioned in several places. The oldest of the *elogia* begins by declaring that the "greatest part of the Romans agree that this one man was the best of the aristocrats" (honc oino ploirume cosentiont R[omani]/ duonoro optumo fuise viro [*CIL* I^2.8–9 [*CLE* 6]). The list of high offices, military achievements, and pious activities is not left to stand on its own, but is validated by the prior assertion of widespread recognition and evaluation of those achievements.

The great-grandson of the man thus eulogized could not match the accomplishments of his predecessors, since he died at the age of twenty. But his *elogium* refers explicitly to the reader's imagined expectation that he should have accomplished more:

> Is hic situs quei nunquam victus est virtutei
> Annos gnatus XX is l[oc]eis m[an]datus:
> Ne quairatis honore quei minus sit mand[at]u[s]

> Here lies one never defeated in manliness (*virtus*)
> Twenty years old he was entrusted to this place.
> Ask not after honor, wherefore the less it was entrusted.
>
> (*CIL* I².11 [*CLE* 9])

In the case of Scipio Africanus's son, who also died at an early age, the expectation of great achievement is expressed as a past contrary-to-fact condition, addressed to the dead youth himself:

> Quibus sei in longa licu[i]set tibe utier vita,
> Facile facteis superases gloriam maiorum

> Had it been permitted to you to enjoy a long life
> Easily would you have surpassed with your deeds the glory
>   of your ancestors.
>
> (*CIL* I².10 [*CLE* 8])

Finally, the most recent of those honored by the surviving *elogia* is represented as speaking in his own defense, in this case with an eye to the explicit judgment of the ancestors:

> Virtutes generis mieis moribus accumulavi,
>   Progeniem genui, facta patris petiei
> Maiorum optenui laudem, ut sibei me esse creatum
>   Laetentur: stirpem nobilitavit honor.

> I heaped up the virtues of my clan through my behavior.
>   I begot offspring. I pursued the deeds of my father.
> I obtained the praise of the ancestors so that they
>   rejoice that I was born to them. Honor has ennobled the stock.
>
> (*CIL* I².15 [*CLE* 958])

While the concentration and interconnectedness of the epitaphs invite the reader to imagine the continuity of the Scipionic tradition, the allusions to a judging audience, either living or deceased, suggest that the force of tradition must be reinvented and reasserted in each succeeding generation, and, furthermore, that the reader is instrumental in the validation of that tradition.

Polybius would have us imagine that adherence to tradition is a natural psychological state for the Roman aristocrat and that expectation of such adherence is the normal attitude for the well-informed Roman observer of aristocratic conduct. In his famous account of the Roman funeral he describes the ritual whereby members of the deceased's household don the *imagines*, or death masks, of the ancestors, parade through the streets to the accompaniment of the flute, then seat themselves in some public location in anticipation of the *laudatio* or eulogy. Facing the assembled ancestors, the eulogist is reminded of the prior achievements of the household and of the code of conduct to which all are expected to adhere. The eulogy, if surviving fragments and allusions are an accurate reflection of the general tenor, consists of an attempt to reconcile the life of the recently deceased to the standards and expectations established by the prior history of the clan—a defense of the dead man, as it were, before a jury of his ancestors.[52]

Polybius recognizes the intended impact of the event on the young aristocrat delivering the oration. He is put in mind of the clan's traditions, and reminded that he too one day will face a final reckoning by the living and the dead. Yet what is evident to those of us who view the event from afar is the degree to which it manipulates the audience as well. The ritual asks them to believe not only what is said about the recently deceased and about the ancestors, but to believe that this is what matters; that is, that the self-congratulatory history of the clan should be the basis against which the actions of the recently deceased and, more importantly, of those still living, are to be measured. Contemporary scholars are right to doubt the veracity of the specific claims made in the family eulogies and annals of early Rome; but when they limit themselves to debate over the truth or falsity of detail, they fall into the trap set by the funeral ritual and its promoter Polybius, both of which take for granted the legitimizing force of aristocratic tradition. Just as the historiographical tradition of post-Hannibalic Rome has recently been reinterpreted in light of the ideology of its composers, so too should the ethical tradition of the same period come under similar scrutiny.[53] It was in the interests of the members of the aristocracy to claim that they were acting in accordance with a distinctively Roman *mos maiorum* and to implicate the lesser members of society in the enforcement of that *mos*. There is no reason to think that the *mos maiorum* had a real, historical force independent of that ascribed to it by its contemporary promoters.

To say that tradition matters is to support the aristocracy at Rome, since tradition is a source of authority over which aristocrats have primary control. Merchants have money, peasants their outlandish cults, and Greek professors their lessons in rhetoric and philosophy; but the past, as Appadurai reminds us, is a scarce resource, and the literati help to make certain that the aristocrats maintain their hoard.[54] Yet what is particularly striking about Ennius's legend of the Good Friend, and perhaps even more so about Polybius's astonishing claim that he—a newly arrived foreigner—can help Scipio to "speak and act in ways worthy of his ancestors" is the implication not only that preservation of tradition as a means of acculturation is one function of literature but that it is a function for which literature, or the literate man, is uniquely qualified. It is this assertion that unites writers as diverse as Cicero, Horace, Livy, Vergil, Seneca, and Tacitus, and that motivates the continuing interest of Latin literature both in the Roman past and in the rituals of acculturation whereby the representatives of Rome's future are initiated into the *mos maiorum*. Roman historiography, for example, starts out and remains moralizing and hortatory because the traditions on which it draws are created and re-created as a means of assuring group identity and enforcing the authority of one sector of society over another. And hortatory literature—the dialogues of Cicero, the satires and epistles of Horace, the treatises of Seneca the Younger—continually reconstructs the primal scene of evaluation: friend helping friend to live and act in a way worthy of the ancestors. Indeed, by a distinctively Roman improvisation, tradition becomes both the content of acculturation, that is, the system of constraints and options in which the subject is embedded, and the means by which one establishes one's standing in Roman culture. The *mos maiorum* is something you know, but also something you do. And one of the things you do in observing the *mos maiorum* is to participate in the ritualized exhortations, evaluations, and self-criticism that have as their purpose the enforcement of your own adherence to the *mos maiorum*. Thus Latin literature of the early classical period both participates in the invention of tradition and makes itself a part of the tradition that is being invented. In this way it secures for itself a permanent role as an agent of aristocratic acculturation.

In a narrower historical framework, the instances of *existimatio* and related terms in early classical Latin also help us to understand why Latin literature, despite its similarities in its preclassical phase to Greek, did not remain rooted in the sympotic environment as long as Greek literature did. As the encounter between Polybius and the younger Scipio indicates, and the funeral inscriptions imply, the audience for the aristocratic performance at Rome is not limited to other aristocrats. Whereas Archilochus or Alcaeus may praise or blame an individual for his adherence or lack thereof to group standards of conduct largely as a way of reinforcing the solidarity of the relevant group, the praise or blame of a Roman aristocrat has ramifications chiefly for his status within the larger community and with respect to potential rivals for the approval of that community, rivals who may hail from other sectors of the aristocracy or from elsewhere in society altogether. In this respect Pindar seems the archaic Greek figure most closely parallel to the early Roman *existimatores*, with the epinician serving something of the same function of reintegrating the victor into the community of the living as the Roman funeral laudation does with respect to the recently deceased and the community of the dead.[55]

Cato's depiction in the *De agricultura* of expanding circles of *existimatio* maps onto a temporal axis the sociological conditions under which the subject of evaluation conducts his life, while the good friend in Ennius's *Annales* functions in part as an acting coach for his higher-status companion, who, not coincidentally, is prominent not just as part of an elite sector of society but as an official of the imperial state. In short, Roman culture moves from pre-political to political and from political to imperial in relatively short order, in contrast to Greek and with significantly less documentary residue. The result is that on at least some occasions the very texts that provide evidence of Roman culture's similarities to other archaic cultures are also the bearers of its transformation into what we might regard as a "theatricalized" or "spectacular" culture, that is, one in which the aristocratic subject of literary attention is always already on display well beyond the confines of his *sodalitas*.[56]

We may conclude this investigation of *existimatio* and literature in early Rome by considering two passages from Terence that exemplify both the enactment of *existimatio* characteristic of Cato's *De agricultura* and the implication of a broader audience in the process of *existimatio* and the aristocratic culture it supports, which we encountered in Polybius, Ennius, and the Scipionic epitaphs.[57] In Terence, as in Cato, the term *existimatio* is specifically employed to refer to assessment of aristocratic performance and rejection of alternative sources of authority; hence the passages in question are important also by way of linking the term *existimatio*, which is of course absent from Polybius's Greek and from the Scipionic epitaphs, with the process they describe. In the prologue to the *Heautontimoroumenos* (*Self-Tormentor*) the speaker defends the playwright against the charge of having spoiled or contaminated many Greek plays in composing but a few in Latin. The speaker uses language that has rightly been likened to that of contemporary oratory.[58] But in so doing he invokes a more generalized model of evaluation of which forensic oratory is but one instance. "I would tell you the author of the relevant Greek play, were it not that I evaluate (*existimarem*) the majority of you as likely to know anyway" (*Heaut.* 7–9). The speaker offers a positive evaluation of the audience in the hope of receiving a positive evaluation in response. Indeed, he specifically anticipates that evaluation or *existimatio* a few lines later (arbitrium vostrum, vostra *existumatio* valebit [25–26]), thereby implying that the playwright and the audience constitute a mutual admiration society, or artistic economy, exchanging positive evaluation for positive evaluation. This exchange system is, on the other hand, designed to exclude another, unnamed poet, clearly a competitor and detractor, who is described as running the risk of making a false evaluation (ne ille pro se dictum *existumet*, [30]) in assuming that Terence's request for open-minded evaluation should apply to his own innovations as well.

The salient feature of the Terentian concept of evaluation employed in the prologue to the *Heautontimouromenos* is that it is constructed in alliance with the culture of the aristocracy and in opposition to means of evaluation associated with other segments of society. The term *contaminare*, for example, refers to the spoilage of goods, rendering them unusable.[59] In this context it applies to the charge that Terence, by using more than one Greek play in fashioning the plot of a single Latin play, is rendering those Greek originals unusable by other Latin poets. Terence's breezy dismissal of what may have been a serious concern about the finite number of Greek plots available for adaptation (after all, Terence himself is reputed to have lost his life seeking new texts by Menander), is phrased in terms of the "example of the good" (*exemplum* bonorum [*Heaut.* 20]). This is how the good behave, and this is how Terence will continue to behave. Commentators assume that the noun *boni* here refers to "good playwrights" on the basis of a parallel passage in the prologue to the *Andria*, where Naevius, Plautus, and Ennius are specified by name (*Andria* 15ff.); but the word *boni*, used in the citation from *Heautontimoroumenos* without further specification, can be taken to refer to anyone who allies himself with the upper ranks of society. Indeed, the argument from exemplum only makes sense if one already privileges the behavior of figures from the past, or at least cultural role models. (Thus, in a certain sense, it does not matter whether Terence is thinking of specific playwrights or high-class types in general; the social implication of the rhetorical gesture is the same in either case). Moreover, Terence deals with the other charge leveled against him, namely that he took to theatrical pursuits quite suddenly, relying on the talent of his friends rather than his own nature, by ignoring it. If these friends are the same, or at least of the same rank, as the *homines nobiles* mentioned in the prologue to the *Adelphoe* (15), then Terence's reference to the charge can be taken as acceptance of a compliment, or display of a social connection, rather than rehearsal of an accusation. Indeed, the rhetoric of the passage concerning contamination and reliance on friends establishes a parallel between the example of the good and the evaluation of the audience; each stands in opposition to the accusations of the malevolent. Thus Terence seeks to ally the audience with an aristocratic circle of *existimatores* and to differentiate this expanded aristocracy's process of evaluation from that of the unnamed poets. If numerous readers have been mystified by Terence's unclear or paradoxical defense of his poetic practice in this and other prologues, that is because mystification was Terence's aim. Much as Cato seeks to naturalize the radical innovations in Roman agriculture by associating them with tradition, Terence seeks to popularize what is in fact an innovative and elitist literary form by attributing to himself and his audience the habits of evaluation characteristic of aristocrats. We may note as

confirmation that the poet who will be denied the generosity of evaluation Terence claims for himself is specifically charged with a startling violation of social decorum; he depicted the *populus* (i.e., members of the
citizen body) as "giving way" (*decesse* [*Heaut.* 32]) before a slave running
in the street.[60]

One aspect of Terence's assimilation of his artistry to the cultural practices of the elites demands further attention: his placement in close prox-
imity of the terms *exemplum* and *existimo*. The words fit into the same
semantic field; if one is to conduct an evaluation, a standard is a necessity.
An exemplum is both a striking instance of its kind, hence something to
be held up for praise or blame, imitation or avoidance, and a standard,
the coin that sets the canonical amount of precious metal for its particular
issuance. Given the connection between *exemplum* and *existimo*, we
should not be surprised to learn that the historical development identified
earlier for *existimo* is repeated in the case of *exemplum*. For Plautus the
term *exemplum* is available to describe any standard of measurement or
setting of a precedent—most memorably an exemplary punishment—but
seems not to be used specifically to describe exemplary good behavior,
least of all elite cultural models. In Terence, by contrast, we witness the
assimilation of the term *exemplum* to the aristocratic program of acculturation and ongoing evaluation of character and behavior. This redeployment of the term is itself exemplified by its confluence with uses of
existimo. We have already considered the parallelism Terence establishes
in the prologue to the *Heautontimoroumenos* between the *exemplum bonorum* and the *existimatio* of the audience. Terence makes the connection
more specific at the end of the prologue, when, after declaring his dependence on the *existimatio* of the audience for validation of his theatrical
innovations, he has the prologue speaker conclude by asking the audience
to establish him as an exemplum:

> *exemplum* statuite in me, ut adulescentuli
> vobis placere studeant potiu' quam sibi . . .
>
> Set a precedent in my case, so that young men
> will be eager to please you rather than themselves . . .
>
> (Terence *Heaut.* 51–52)

Terence wants to be set up as an exemplum of the proper respect for
existimatio, which, as we have learned earlier in the prologue, involves
evaluation in accordance with exempla. The language of pricing has been
completely transposed to the realm of determining cultural models and
enforcing cultural constraints, and the union of traditional exempla and
on-going evaluation that is implied in Ennius' episode of the good friend
is here transferred from the private to the public sphere.

Does Terence's concern for proper *existimatio* come at the expense of economic calculation? That is, is the expansion of the semantic field of *existimatio* and *exemplum* in fact a gesture that privileges the new emphasis on ethical as opposed to economic models? I argued as much for Cato's use of *existimatio* and believe the same point can be made for Terence, provided we accept the evidence of two suggestive passages, both of which, curiously enough, have been athetized (i.e., identified as inauthentic) by some modern editors. Immediately preceding the prologue-speaker's invitation to the audience to make of him an exemplum for the young, all manuscripts preserve the line "If never greedily did I set a price on my art" (si numquam avare pretium statui arte mea [48]) and all but the Bembinus continue with two more lines:[61]

> et eum esse quaestum in animum induxi maximum
> quam maxume servire vostris commodis . . .
>
> And if I decided in my mind that there was no greater return
> Than to serve your interests to the utmost . . .

(Terence Heaut. 49–50)

All three lines have been excised by modern editors because they are repeated in a similar context near the conclusion of the prologue to the *Hecyra*, where there is no uncertainty in the textual tradition and where they are felt to fit better because they allude to a past poetic practice less appropriately evoked in the early *Heautontimoroumenos*. If retained in *Heautontimoroumenos*, the verses offer splendid confirmation of the specific reevaluation of terminology that has been ascribed here to Terence and Cato, since they have Terence, through the person of the prologue-figure, arguing that because the playwright does not seek financial gain through his productions he therefore deserves to be set up as an exemplum for the future. In the *Hecyra* context, the lines lack the specific linguistic force that would be present in *Heautontimoroumenos* but convey the same train of thought: disdain for lucre entitles the playwright to exemplary status.

Later in the *Hecyra*, in a verse that is more secure than the problematical trio at the end of the *Heautontimoroumenos* prologue, the nexus of *existimo* and *exemplum* reappears in a speech by a character who specifically proposes to replace mercantile evaluation with ethical. A young man forced into an unwanted marriage refrains from sexual relations with his wife and continues to seek the services of a courtesan of whom he is enamored. To his surprise, the latter ups her price, while his wife treats him with the respect due a husband. This, so the slave narrator informs us, is what prompted the groom to leave the prostitute: "He came to know himself, and the prostitute, and the one at home sufficiently / evaluating (*existimans*) the character of each by the *exemplum* of the other" (et ipse se / et illam et hanc quae domi erat cognovit satis / ad *exemplum* ambarum mores earum *existimans*, [161–163]). The originality of Terence's phrasing here, where the words *ambarum* and *earum* have to do double duty as genitive of price with *exemplum* and genitive of possession with *mores*, has caused some to doubt the authenticity of the verse.[62] It can be argued in opposition that it is precisely the interpenetration of the genitives that conveys the complexity of the evaluation involved (not to mention the novelty of the sexual relationships) and, further, that the economic subtext present in the terms *exemplum* and *existimans* here serves to carry a significant theatrical and ideological irony: Pamphilus is represented as reverting to what is figured as a pre- or noneconomic code of conduct (husbands should sleep with their wives) by the financial demands that a prostitute makes upon him.

Terence's use of *exemplum* and *existimo* to describe the relationships within the play as well as the relationship between playwright and audience allows us to observe a more complicated set of ironies at work in the scene in question.[63] No sooner have we—and the characters onstage—been informed of Pamphilus's economically motivated rejection of pleasure and acceptance of tradition than we discover that the problem the play confronts stems not only from Pamphilus's failure to consummate his marriage, but more specifically from his consignment of his wife to the care of her mother-in-law while he leaves town to collect a legacy under orders from his father. Moreover, the whole story of the young couple's entangled legal/financial/sexual/familial affairs is narrated empathetically by a slave who, by definition, has no stake in the self-contradictory system his behavior defends. Pamphilus's setting of a price on his wife and his concubine by evaluating their behavior through a process of side-by-side comparison is emblematic of Roman culture's ambivalence at this time with regard to the transmitted mores and the allure of new modes of acquiring wealth and status. More than that, it is emblematic of the use of *existimatio* and *exempla*, themselves terms from the increasingly significant realms of finance and monetary exchange, as linguistic devices for privileging and enforcing noneconomic codes of conduct. Like landowning in *De agricultura*, so in Terentian comedy "traditional" forms of behavior (marital or otherwise) are validated by their purported transcendence of mere economic calculation. And like the clever slave or aging prologue-speaker who articulates the terms whereby the members of the elites transmit their culture to one another and solidify it at the expense of other sources of power, so Terence and other writers of the period fashion the discourse by which they themselves are constrained.

The Colonization of Greece

To return to the general argument of this chapter, if the invention of Latin literature is intimately connected with the growth of the Roman empire and the preservation of aristocratic Roman identity, then one may with good reason ask why the Latin literary tradition that emerges from the formative period of literary history is so powerfully Greek in its appearance. If the simplistic model of primitive culture yielding to superior is to be rejected, what model can we put in its place? The linguistic situation in archaic Rome reminds us that borrowing from the Greeks had both a practical and a symbolic dimension, practical in the sense that new devices, procedures, institutions, and ideas brought with them new vocabulary and modes of description; symbolic in the sense that the complex intertextual relationships between the elite literature of the age and its Greek counterparts served as a means of widening the gap between sectors of Romano-Italic society. The contrast between the Greekness of Plautus and the Greekness of Ennius should make it clear that Greekness alone is not the issue; rather, we must consider the ways in which phenomena identified as Greek are incorporated into Roman culture.[64]

In 155 B.C.E. Cato the Elder had the philosopher Carneades and others of his profession expelled from the city of Rome after they had held a successful series of public lectures. Yet this same Cato, far from contemning Greek learning, saw to it that a learned Greek tutor was retained in his own household and on numerous occasions demonstrated his own familiarity with the classics of Greek literature.[65] The paradoxical nature of Cato's attitude and actions suggests that the critical issue with respect to Greek culture was not the possibility of its influence, but the control and management of that influence by the appropriate sectors of Roman society. Thus the expulsion of the philosophers, at least in Plutarch's version of the story, is due to the immense popularity that they enjoyed among the people and especially the youth of Rome. In the Senate Cato denounced the Greek visitors as capable of persuading "the people to what they pleased." They should "go home again to their own schools, and declaim to the Greek children, and leave the Roman youth to be obedient, as hitherto, to their own laws and governors." A similar move in 92 B.C.E. was aimed at closing the schools of the Latin rhetoricians with their new type of education. This measure, if successfully enforced, would have restricted rhetorical training to those who had access to Greece or to Greek teachers. As Narducci has argued, the episode reveals the importance the elites vested in maintaining control of what he describes as "l'arma potentissima della parola."[66] In later years Cicero's own friends encouraged him to study abroad, as he in turn encouraged his son. The elite Greek culture of rhetoric and philosophy was too valuable to be squandered on those who could not pay the appropriate price for it.

Yet, at the same time, each move to limit access to Greek culture met with resistance. Cato is described as tongue-lashing a reluctant Senate in the matter of Carneades; Crassus, one of the censors who issues the decree of 92 B.C.E. is presented as defending it against criticism in Cicero's *De oratore*; and the purpose of Cicero's *Rhetorica* and *Philosophica*, composed late in his life, is, in his own words, "to provide a great assistance to his countrymen" (magnum adiumentum [*De officiis* 1]) by making Greek rhetoric and philosophy available to them without their having to study the relevant treatises in Greek. Thus running throughout the history of the Roman aristocracy's relationship with Greek culture is an opposition between sequestering and displaying the thoughts and works of the Greeks.

The vacillation in attitude toward the symbolic capital represented by Greek learning corresponds to the aristocracy's anxiety and indecisiveness over the display of other forms of wealth as well.[67] In the century and a half from the time of the Second Punic War to the consulate of Cicero, the aristocracy made repeated attempts to control the public display of wealth through the passage of a series of sumptuary laws.[68] The Oppian Law of 215 B.C.E. was designed to regulate the display of wealth on the part of Roman women by limiting the amount and nature of their jewelry and clothing. A tribunician law, the *lex Orchia* of 181, set a limit on the number of guests that could be invited to a meal, while a senatorial decree of 179 regulated expenditures on public games. In 161 the *lex Fannia*, carried by one of the consuls for the year, set limits on expenditures on meals, and in 143 the *lex Didia* extended the *lex Fannia* to all of Italy. The *lex Aemilia* of 115 placed further regulations on banquets, as did the *lex Licinia* of 95, which was carried by the same Crassus who three years later was involved in the effort to close the Latin schools of rhetoric. The ancient sources persistently describe these laws as attempts to resist the decline in public morals, and modern scholars have not always been sufficiently critical of that self-serving description on the part of aristocrats and their apologists. In fact, the laws can equally well be interpreted as strategies for strengthening the propertied elites by protecting the less well-off among the senatorial aristocracy from having to match the expenditures of the wealthiest (the tendency toward "autoconservation" described by Clemente) but also by making the difference between the elites and the rest of society less visible and therefore less invidious.

Under the classical Athenian democracy, the distinction between visible and invisible poperty was a crucial one, inasmuch as liturgies could only be imposed upon those whose wealth was apparent.[69] In Rome, the

institution of the census was designed to guarantee that property would
be accounted for and state obligations and privileges correctly assigned.[70]
Thus there was less practical motivation for an individual aristocrat to
conceal his wealth and indeed much reason to display it, thereby advertis-
ing his own glory and that of his household, attracting clients and allies,
and gaining a competitive edge over his peers. But for the aristocracy as
a group, the competitive display of wealth could lead to debilitating internal strife and/or to the widening of the gap between elites and the mass of
the population. Cicero makes a great deal out of the alienation wrought
by conspicuous consumption when he attempts in the second speech
against Catiline to rally the small property holders of urban Rome against
the "spendthrift" aristocrat and his impecunious supporters.[71] The followers of Catiline are said to include those who have squandered their
parents' fortunes on luxurious living as well as those prone to sexual and
personal liberties incompatible with the virile manliness required of vig-
ilant Romans. It does not seem farfetched to propose that similar considerations prompted Cato and others, in the face of the massive increase of
wealth in Rome following the Second Punic War and the conflicts of the
early second century B.C.E. and in particular in response to the augmentation of personal fortunes, to propose restrictions on public display of
such wealth. The sumptuary laws do not seek to limit the possession of
property per se; rather they limit the use of property in ways that might
be seen as articulating the status difference between aristocrats and com-
moners. This is why the rhetoric of "traditional Roman morality" is so
easily invoked in connection with sumptuary legislation: the point of the
legislation is to make it seem as if there is indeed just such a thing as
traditional Roman morality and that it does in fact unite all segments of
society. But the net effect of passing sumptuary legislation or repealing it,
enforcing it, or ignoring it, is the same: the enhancement of aristocratic
power. It is simply a question of whether the hidden or open exercise of
power is more effective at securing its continuity.

   Literature, as earlier sections of this chapter have argued, carries with
it various sorts of power: the power to enforce status differentiation, to
constrain human belief and conduct, and to finesse disputes over value.
Greek literature is for the Romans especially effective as a means of social
dominance precisely because it is alien and access to it can be regulated.
It is a power that can be contained or exercised at will, a symbolic form
of capital that can be conserved or displayed as the circumstances de-
mand. In this context it should be remembered that physical access to the
texts of Greek literature was restricted to a small sector of society, and
that not every text would have been available to every interested member
of the aristocracy.[72] As with the sumptuary laws, so with the goods of
Hellenic culture, it is not a question of a moral struggle between nativists

and cosmopolites. Rather the debate is over the best use of a newfound form of wealth. The point can be seen most clearly with regard to rhetoric, that is, formal training in the construction and performance of public speeches. The systematic training that Hellenistic rhetoric offered in brainstorming (Gk. *heuresis*, Lat. *inventio*) in consideration of alternative stances (Gk. *taxis*, Lat. *dispositio*), in developing self-confidence and self-consciousness about performance strategies (Lat. *elocutio* or *pronuntiatio* or *actio*) conferred practical benefit on the Roman engaged in the give-and-take of senatorial debate and judicial politics and accordingly was seized upon as a valuable resource by ambitious Romans, much as new technology is promptly exploited by contemporary artists, musicians, and propagandists. But whether to provide a self-conscious display of the resources of Hellenistic rhetoric is another matter, as the contrast between Catonian rhetoric and Ciceronian reveals and the conflict between Cicero and his Atticist detractors brought to the fore. Cicero virtually advertises his indebtedness to Asiatic instructors through his pronounced reliance on figures of amplification and almost musical cadences, while first Cato and then the Attici favor a prosaic art that conceals its artistry.

While there are traces of the sequester/display dichotomy within the literature of the second century B.C.E.—one thinks of Lucilius's attack on the philhellene Albucius, an attack that in its own structure and terminology betrays a grasp of some rather nice distinctions in Stoic ethics[73]—the contrast between the two strategies is most evident to us in the relationship between earlier and later Republican literature. Although the Hellenic inspiration for Terence's comedies is apparent throughout the plays, in nomenclature, setting, and social context, the strategy of the prologues—and indeed of those few passages in which we can compare Greek "original" and Latin "translation"—is to downplay the specific Greekness of the plays. The prologues, for example, seek to place Terence's work in an established Latin literary tradition as represented by Plautus, Caecilius, Naevius, and others, while the translations suppress the details of geography and cult that will come to form such a crucial aspect of the Alexandrian affectations of Catullus and his successors.[74] Cato's historical work, the *Origines*, while taking its form and title from Greek *ktisis*-literature, has as its chief project the differentiation of the Italic from the Hellenic versions of the development of Rome and the allied Italian cities.[75] In contrast, Cicero's philosophical and rhetorical treatises, written a century after the deaths of Cato and Terence, present themselves as translations of Greek works or indulgences in Greek specialized investigations when in fact they constitute highly independent and original improvisations on Roman cultural themes.[76] The differences between and among Cato, Terence, Catullus, and Cicero with regard to Greek culture represent alternative strategies of exposure and concealment and not fundamentally different conceptions of the nature and function of Latin literature or of the relative merits of Greek and Roman cultural achievements.

It is appropriate to close a chapter on the invention of Latin literature with a brief consideration of the writings of Cicero, since they are to a large extent responsible for the view of early Latin literature and the early Roman tradition that this chapter has been resisting. In the *Brutus* Cicero constructs a teleological account of the development of Roman oratory and other Roman literary forms that valorizes a contrast between primitive, rough-and-ready early Romans and the sophisticated, philhellenic figures of the later Republic. In his creation of a set of national *exempla virtutis*, through his speeches and other writings, Cicero not only regularizes the content of the *mos maiorum*; more importantly, he gives the very notion that there is a *mos maiorum* against which conduct and policy must be measured a new vitality. And it is Cicero who, by canonizing such writers as Ennius, Terence, and Cato, in opposition to Livius Andronicus, Naevius, and Plautus, flattens the contours and smoothes over the divisions within the early Roman tradition.

Yet it is the same Cicero who is widely regarded as the most important transmitter of Greek culture to succeeding generations, the man who virtually singlehandedly made overt philhellenism socially acceptable to the Roman aristocracy. How can we reconcile Cicero's role in the invention of a national literature with his apparent reliance on the alien literature of the Greeks? Cicero himself provides the answer in a variety of passages, nowhere more clearly than in the introduction to *Tusculan Disputations*. This treatise is in some ways the most Greek of Cicero's many writings, since it quite openly adopts what Cicero regards as the Greek manner (*Graecorum more* [*Tusc.* 1.7]) of philosophical debate—posing a thesis, followed by dispute pro and contra.[77] Yet Cicero makes it clear that what he is doing is not in fact Hellenizing his own practice, but rather Romanizing Greece. The metaphors he uses at the outset of the treatise are those of illumination and guardianship:

hoc mihi Latinis litteris inlustrandum putavi, non quia philosophia Graecis litteris et doctoribus percipi non posset, sed meum semper iudicium fuit omnia nostros aut invenisse per se sapientius quam Graecos aut accepta ab illis fecisse meliora, quae quidem digna statuissent in quibus elaborarent. Nam mores et instituta vitae resque domesticas ac familiaris nos profecto et melius tuemur et lautius, rem vero publicam nostri maiores certe melioribus temperaverunt et institutis et legibus.

I calculated that it was necessary for me to illuminate this by means of Latin letters not because philosophy could not be perceived through Greek texts or Greek teachers, but because it has always been my judgment that our people have either invented everything more skillfully than the Greeks or improved upon the things we have taken from them—at least the ones that we have deemed worthy of elaboration. For just as the habits and institutions of life in matters domestic and familial we most assuredly look after (*tuemur*) better and more luxuriously (*lautius*), so did our ancestors at least (*certe*) manage the common wealth with better institutions and laws.

(*Tusc.* 1.1–2)

The illumination with which Cicero is concerned is not just the casting of light on something that is in darkness, but also the showing forth to others of something that they had not previously seen. Thus he emphasizes in the preface to *De finibus* and again in *De officiis* the presentation of Greek culture to his fellow citizens and the great benefit that they will derive from his endeavor; and he boasts in the final years of his life (in the preface to *De divinatione*) of his ability to make the totality of Greek philosophy available to readers of Latin: "We were prepared," he writes, "had not a graver matter blocked the way, to turn to the remaining issues, so that no topic of philosophy would be allowed to remain that had not been illuminated by Latin letters" (ut . . . nullum philosophiae locum esse pateremur, qui in Latinis litteris inlustratus pateret [*Div.* 2.14]). Cicero thus opts, in a spectacular way, for the display—the illumination and the bringing to light—of the property that Rome has expropriated from Greece.

Cicero's exhibitionism with regard to Greek culture would seem to run counter to the other metaphor he employs for the relationship between Rome and Greece: that of *tutela*, the protection of the property of a weaker figure by the conservative investment strategies of the stronger.[78] A guardian's task is to protect the tutee's property, not to merge it with his own. On this matter we need to examine more closely Cicero's account of the reasons for his expropriation of Greek capital. Greece, he makes clear in the preface to *Tusculans* and elsewhere, has done a commendable job of creating cultural forms, but is hopelessly inept at transmitting them. This alleged failing explains why Greek culture can be depicted as in the dark or in need of resuscitation. Yet Roman culture, it turns out, is confronting its own crisis of transmission, one that threatens to make it as inept and moribund as Greece. In the passage quoted above there is a fluctuation between first and third person forms of the verb, and present and perfect tenses, that betrays an ambivalence about the role that Cicero and his contemporaries are to play in the management of Rome's own symbolic capital. "Our people have always made shrewder discoveries than the Greeks or improved upon that which they received": the use of *nostri* for "our people" is sufficiently openended to allow for the possibility that the implied "we" unites Cicero, his reader, and previous representatives of the Roman elite. In the next sentence, this transgenerational unity is replaced by a dichotomy between the "we" of the present and "our ancestors." We know how to manage private wealth, and our ancestors at least (*certe*) knew how to manage public wealth (as well). While the passage is not as overtly critical of present affairs as are some in Cicero's other treatises (e.g., *De officiis*), the implication is clear: Rome is in danger of destroying its *res publica*, or common wealth, through too much emphasis on private enrichment. Precisely what distinguishes the Romans, past and present, from the Greeks—the ability to augment and transmit one's inheritance, that is, to reproduce the patterns of aristocratic hegemony—is now at risk. The proposed solution to this crisis of transmission is at first glance paradoxical, but in fact completely logical within the system outlined here. Rome is to become more rather than less Greek. By absorbing Greek culture into Latin letters Cicero both enriches the Roman common wealth and provides a new means of transmission of that wealth from one generation to another. It is thus no accident that Cicero's illumination of Greek philosophy occurs in the context of uncertainty over the continuing efficacy of "institutions and laws" (*institutis et legibus* [2]).

The representation of rhetoric and philosophy, indeed of *litterae Latinae* generally, as offering a symbolic as opposed to a practical means of reuniting a fragmented aristocracy and preserving the continuity of its control over the Roman world is a recurrent feature of Cicero's rhetorical and philosophical prefaces.[79] In *De oratore* his entire political career, the making of speeches and holding of offices, is regarded as an intrusion on his original project of developing a glorious form of Roman rhetoric. It is only in writing the treatise *De oratore* that he has returned to the "attention-getting pursuits" (*praeclara studia*) appropriate to the true aristocrat. Later, in the account of the historical development of rhetorical studies at Rome he acknowledges the practical utility of Greek rhetorical training (*utilitas*) yet suggests in a lengthy exhortation that it is rhetoric's *magnitudo*, that is, its grandeur, that makes it the proper pursuit for those "whose renown and status are dear to us"(19). In *De natura deorum* Cicero writes that when it appeared that the republic was doomed to succumb to one-man rule, he decided that he was obliged "for the sake of the common wealth" to "explicate philosophy for our countrymen, determining that it would be of great value to the honor and praise of the state for matters so serious and so renowned to be contained in Latin letters" (*ND* 1.7) The symbolic capital of literature augments the common property of the Roman elites and thereby works to resist autocracy as well as to suppress claims to empowerment of other sectors of society. As Bourdieu remarks in connection with the general relationship between power and prestige, when "real" forms of dominance fail to maintain social control, "symbolic" forms arise to take their place.[80]

In the era of Cato and Terence, the Greeks, along with the Oscans, Faliscans, and other peoples of Italy, could be regarded as rivals for the cultural identity of the peoples of the peninsula. Ennius's claim to have three hearts—Latin, Greek, and Oscan—was as much an observation as a boast, albeit one disturbing in its implications for continuing Roman hegemony. In Cicero's day the challenges posed by Hellenization and by the cultural diversity of the Italian peninsula were real ones, but secondary in comparison to the threat posed by the instability and disunity of the Roman aristocracy. Cicero's works partake of the earlier strategies of Latin literature—construction and promulgation of national identity, acculturation of the aristocracy, negotiation of disputes over value—while exemplifying another one as well: the open and obvious expropriation of the cultural capital of colonized Greece. Cicero represents his use of Greek cultural resources as a rescue of Greece from itself, but also as an augmentation of the *res*, or property, to be shared by his fractious contemporaries and their aimless descendants.

The remarkable thing about Cicero's approach to Rome's crisis of cultural transmission is that it worked, albeit in ways that he himself may not have anticipated. In opposition to Syme, Habicht, and other scholars who assume that because Cicero's narrowly legal and structural solutions to the crisis of the late republic were not adopted by Julius Caesar and his successors he therefore had no discernible impact on later Roman politics, we can see that it was Cicero, and the approach to culture he represents, that made later Roman politics possible. By expanding the common wealth of the Romans and making that wealth available to later and larger groups of readers through his extensive literary output, Cicero succeeded in widening the circle of self-conscious, interconnected elites to whom Hobsbawm refers and in making it possible for them to believe, regardless of their status or place of origin, that they too had a stake in the preservation of a distinctively Roman *mos maiorum*. Czeslaw Milosz has observed that where ideology fails, military force cannot in the long run hold a society together. Cicero, and the literary tradition he canonized, provided the ideological framework that made the *pax Romana* possible.

Cicero's recognition of Greece's failure to overcome its crisis of transmission coincides with his and his contemporaries' acknowledgment of Rome's own potentially fatal afflictions. The habit of juxtaposing Greek, Roman, and other chronologies, familiar from the work of Cicero's contemporaries Nepos, Varro, and Atticus, and reinforced by Cicero's own work, the *Brutus*, would not only have provided Romans with an excuse for the supposed poverty of their youthful culture vis-à-vis the older, more mature Greek civilization;[81] more to the point, it would have alerted them to the cyclical nature of all human affairs, and, in the cataclysmic years of the '40s B.C.E. would have, reinforced their own sense of impending doom. Against what he represents as the demise of rhetoric, the collapse of fidelity between friends, the abandonment of a sense of civic duty, and the failure of morals and laws, Cicero rallies not armies or legislators, but the force of the Latin literary tradition, enriched with its acquisitions from moribund Greece. The embeddedness of this literature, from its conception, in the power struggles of the Roman elite—that is, the very politicization that Romantic readers seek to deny or evade—is what made Latin literature available as a means of resolving Rome's own crisis of transmission.

Chapter 3

CICERO AND THE BANDITS

WHEN ALEXANDER THE GREAT asked a captured pirate what prompted him to harass the sea, the quick-thinking desperado replied, "The same thing that prompts you to harass the world. I do it with a little boat and am called a bandit; you do it with a big fleet, and are called emperor."[1] The emperor Tiberius received a similar reply when he asked the slave who was impersonating Agrippa Postumus how he had managed to become Agrippa: "The same way you became Caesar."[2] And when the praetorian prefect Papinianus interrogated the bandit leader Bulla Felix early in the third century C.E., the question and answer followed the same pattern: "Why did you become a bandit?" "Well, why did you become a prefect?"[3]

The popularity and adaptability of this anecdote remind us of two important aspects of ancient political life. First, the legitimacy of the state and its elites was always open to contestation, even if only through jokes or apocryphal stories; and second, bandits, whether real or imagined, figured prominently in such contests for legitimacy.[4] While the degree of political, economic, and social disruption caused by banditry varied by era and location, the resemblance of banditry or *latrocinium* to the dominant class of the ancient state was not lost on the state's enemies or its defenders. Like the Senate at Rome or other "legitimate" authorities, the bandit troop was an organized, hierarchical, and ritualized mechanism for controlling and redistributing the material resources of ancient society.[5] If the stories of Alexander and the pirate or Bulla and the prefect permit the resentments of the state's enemies to enter the historical record, equally do they reveal the elite propagandists' eagerness to remind their audience of what is in store for them should aristocratic hegemony fail. Fear of bandits, like fear of gangs or terrorists today, is as potent a force as are the bandits, or gangsters, or terrorists themselves.

The analogy to contemporary criminality can be pursued further as a means of clarifying the rhetorical and ideological significance of banditry in the ancient world. As Brent Shaw has argued in his study of banditry in the Roman Empire, *latrocinium* is neither a form of class revolt, as Hobsbawm and others would have it, nor an infiltrative activity supported by outside powers, as terrorism sometimes is today. Rather, bandits are criminals who operate in the spaces that are claimed by the political authorities but are not well integrated into the social, economic, and cultural life of mainstream society.[6] Geographically, ancient bandits are a feature of rural rather than urban society, and, because an absence of social control is prerequisite to their success, the temporal space they occupy is the night, as opposed to the day. In American society, the analogous phenomenon is the urban drug gang, which operates in geographical and cultural spaces that are claimed by the authorities (i.e., inner cities) but are not fully integrated into the social, economic, and political structures that unite the rest of the community. It is precisely this marginal yet reflective character of banditry as an organized "counterstate" within society that makes it such a challenge to the mainstream authorities' self-image. Ancient bandits, like modern gangsters, frighten (or can be made to frighten) precisely because they offer an alternative to the structures of mainstream society, and in particular to the dominance of the ruling elite. Why should the inhabitants of a bandit-dominated territory respect the commands of central authorities if it is in fact the bandits who have the power to enforce patterns of economic and social behavior?

The significance of banditry as a challenge to the legitimacy of the status quo can serve as the starting point for an analysis of Cicero's defense of the Roman establishment throughout his career, but especially in the four orations against Catiline delivered late in 63 B.C.E.[7] The speeches in question have recently been described as Cicero's response to a crisis of legitimacy posed by the disaffection of the aristocratic Catiline and his followers. They thus constitute a politically conservative defense of the Roman establishment, yet one which, as we shall see, draws imaginatively on a full range of linguistic, ritual, and historical resources to advance and enforce a novel distinction between citizens loyal and disloyal to the Roman state. In the context of this book, an analysis of the language of banditry employed by Cicero brings to light the full performative force of Ciceronian oratory, a force against which virtually all Latin literature measures and finds itself wanting. Cicero in the Catilinarians is the *existimator* of his own performance, the arbiter of political, social, and ethical divisions, and the hero of a founding myth of his own creation. In his expulsion of Catiline and his bandit troop through nothing but language, he concentrates in one set of textual events the aspirations and achievements ascribed throughout this study, albeit in refracted form, to Latin literature more generally.

The charge of banditry figures prominently in Cicero's attacks on Catiline (e.g., impio latrocinio, scelerate susceptum latrocinium, tanto latrocinio, and latrones Italiae, to cite the first speech alone) and we can see immediately why this should be so.[8] To the extent that Cicero seeks to differentiate his opponent from the other members of his audience, accusing him of the most radical and most highly charged form of opposition to the status quo is an effective rhetorical technique. The orator aims to deny his opponent standing within the community and to exclude him from the place of reasoned debate by aligning him with the very forces that the community cannot incorporate if it wishes to remain the same community. Insults like "slave" or "gladiator" seek to lower the opponent's standing within the community, but do not exclude him from it. Charges of disreputable financial, political, or sexual practices may create a division between opponent and audience, and give the speaker a psychological advantage in debate, but they fall short of delegitimizing the opponent's response: the possibility remains that he will be equally vitriolic in his denunciation of his attacker. But calling one's opponent a bandit, provided the accusation can be made to appear plausible, excludes the opponent from the very community whose rules and procedures make political debate possible. Indeed, Cicero applies this logic to his own advantage in the *Paradoxa Stoicorum* when he argues that he was not in fact exiled from the Roman state, since the state had been replaced by the banditry of Clodius and his followers.[9] Again, we have an analogy in our own era in which the accusation of drug running has been successfully used to deny a foreign official access to the normal channels of international political dialogue.

Banditry, precisely because of its quasi-political character, serves in Roman oratory as a point of intersection for the various codes that constitute the official discourse. That is, just as the state that Cicero is defending is a construct infused with ideological, economic, military, and religious significance, so too banditry, as the mirror image or evil twin of the Roman aristocratic state, can be opposed to the state along any of these axes of analysis. And just as the state looks slightly different depending on whether we emphasize its ideological, economic, military, or religious aspect, so too banditry and resistance to banditry can be made to align themselves with different institutions, symbols, and patterns of behavior, depending on the aspect of banditry being emphasized. Thus, the charge of banditry is interesting not just for its own sake, but also as a means of access to a variety of strategies—verbal, symbolic, and physical—that Cicero and others employ to differentiate between the state and its opponents, or, in the case of the Catilinarian orations, between the speaker and his rival.

As suggested above, the mere reference to *latrocinium* in the orations against Catiline sets him apart from most of Cicero's other oratorical opponents.[10] The banditlike nature of Catiline's behavior and the need for a counterconspiracy on the part of Cicero's audience are emphasized in various details, apart from the simple identification of Catiline's activities as *latrocinium*. Catiline's conspirators meet at night, as bandits are ordinarily reputed to do; and so the meeting of the Senate on November 8 is called for night as well, despite the proviso that decrees of the Senate

passed between dusk and dawn have no binding force.[11] The reference to
perverted religious rituals, carried to an extreme in the story retailed by
Dio to the effect that the Catilinarian conspirators swore loyalty to one
another by killing a free-born boy and devouring his entrails, alludes to
the possibility that bandits, like participants in all conspiracies, seal their
pact through ritual slaughter (an issue to which we shall return below).[12]
Cicero's repeated request that there be a wall between Catiline and himself—a rather unimaginative way of dealing with the potential destroyer
of the fatherland, it might seem—reinforces the view of Catiline as someone who, like a bandit, will find his natural abode in the territory beyond
and between the walled cities of Italy.[13] The domestic turmoil associated
with the Catilinarian conspiracy (rich women accused of paying conspirators to murder their husbands[14], sons plotting against their fathers[15]),
whether historically accurate or not, corresponds to the prospect of complete replacement of one social order by another that Cicero invokes
through his accusations of banditry. Even Cicero's references to the appearance of the senators (nihil horum ora voltusque moverunt?, "Haven't
the expressions on the faces of these men set you in motion, Catiline?"[1]), to the physical manifestations of Catiline's moral turpitude
(Quae nota domesticae turpitudinis non inusta vitae tuae est?, "What
mark of domestic shamelessness has not been branded on your life?"
[13]), and to the need for visual evidence of the senators' support for his
own course of action (sit denique inscriptum in fronte unius cuiusque
quid de re publica sentiat, "Let every man's political views be written on
his brow for all to see" [32]) may be taken as alluding to the difficulty of
distinguishing bandits from good citizens in the normal bustle of Rome or
any other Italian town. Two and a half centuries after Cicero, a group of
bandits is said to have nearly succeeded in overthrowing the emperor
Commodus by joining in with the disguised revelers at the festival of the
Hilaria.[16] Cicero seems to have a comparable prospect in mind when he
informs his audience of Lentulus's desire to delay the slaughter of the *boni*
and the burning of the city until the Saturnalia, that is, until a time when
the usual protocols of social interaction have been suspended.[17] With this
single detail Cicero raises fear of social revolution in the form of slave
revolt, religious sacrilege in the form of abuse of a festival, and the dangers of disguise in a society that uses outward appearance as a means of
social differentiation and political control; all of these anxieties are made
plausible by the association of Catiline with bandits.

Bandits pose a threat to the established political order either directly or
indirectly by offering an alternative model of political structure and by
doing so in territory claimed by the "legitimate" rulers. Bandits are also,
at least potentially, just as dangerous to the state in its economic manifestation as *res publica*, or common wealth.[18] In its earliest occurrences the

Latin word *latro* refers to those who drain the public treasury, such as mercenary soldiers or bodyguards of the king; later it is applied to what we might call rural gangsterism, such as assaults by runaway slaves, landless veterans, shepherds, and others on travellers moving between cities, and the infiltration of cities and villages by similar characters.[19] In one sense, then, Cicero's description of Catiline, Clodius, and Antony, all of whom had professional satellites or bodyguards, as *latrones* may be the revival of a traditional meaning of the word with its mixed political and economic connotations. But Cicero's use of *latro* also constitutes a metaphorical extension of the term in that he likens the assault of the conspirators on the *res publica* or common wealth to bandits' theft of the property of individual citizens or households.[20] In either case, banditry is the organized use of force to dispossess another of his property, and the chief defense against banditry is the city wall. As Cicero himself asserts in *De officiis* 2.73, cities were first built in order to protect the property of their residents from theft by outsiders: nam etsi duce congregabantur homines, tamen spe custodiae rerum suarum urbium praesidia quaerebant. The same notion is to be found in Cicero's declaration elsewhere in *De officiis* that as a result of the dictatorship of Julius Caesar, "the building walls of the city remain . . . but we have lost the common wealth from deep within" (parietes modo urbis stant et manent . . . rem vero publicam penitus amisimus [2.29]). The sentence unites the image of theft from the storehouse of an individual household with theft of the common property from the city that protects it. The economic role of bandits as plunderers of property thus explains the rhetorical association with city walls.

The opposition between city as protector of the *res publica* and bandits operating in the countryside yet eager to plunder the possessions of those inside the city structures much of the second speech against Catiline, which was addressed to the people of Rome, in contrast to the senatorial audience of the first oration. Zvi Yavetz has argued that one of the chief reasons for the failure of Catiline's conspiracy was his loss of support among the urban plebs.[21] Initially attracted to Catiline's call for cancellation of debt, the *tabernarii* and other small property owners (who would have been part of Cicero's audience on November 9) lost confidence in Catiline once it became clear that his coconspirators were willing to rely on freed or runaway slaves.[22] The temporary economic gain to be realized by the cancellation of debts would have been heavily outweighed in the small property owners' calculations by the potential for social chaos, including proscriptions, slave revolt, arson, and ultimately the loss of all property rights. Yavetz emphasizes the straightforward economic calculation that would have motivated the plebs, but we should not underestimate the power of Cicero's rhetoric in presenting the alternatives available in such a way that only one choice could be made.

To the modern reader perhaps the most striking feature of the second speech against Catiline is Cicero's seemingly self-righteous and moralistic critique of the character of Catiline and his followers.[23] Catiline's sexual crimes are described vividly, and his well-known stamina is attributed by Cicero to the rigors of a lifestyle of seduction and debauchery. The list of Catiline's followers culminates in a memorable denunciation of the hand-picked elite (de eius dilectu [22]) men who manage to enjoy both the active and the passive role in sexual intercourse (amare et amari [23]), who sport expensive haircuts (pexo capillo nitidos [22]) and lavish effeminate wardrobes (manicatis et talaribus tunicis, velis amictos, non togis [22]), enjoy lewd dancing and singing (saltare et cantare [23]), and follow up their late night parties (antelucanis cenis [22]) with the waving of daggers and sprinkling of poisons (sicas vibrare et spargere venena [23]). Yet such attacks, suggestive as they have sometimes seemed to students of Ciceronian character and of late Republican social life, fit into a more elaborate pattern of Cicero's critique of the misuse of property. The other supporters of Catiline listed by Cicero include aristocrats who refuse to sell property in order to pay off debts,[24] veterans whose land grants have prompted them to live beyond their means,[25] politicians exhausted by the financial burdens of campaigning and too stupid to see that seizing office by force will only encourage others to do the same to them,[26] lazy and incompetent property owners who went bankrupt long ago,[27] and parricides, assassins, and other such lowlifes who have nothing left to lose.[28] In short, Cicero manages to associate Catiline at once with have-nots eager to take from those who have, and with those who have so much that they can afford luxuriant lifestyles inaccessible to the average member of the urban plebs. His rhetoric speaks to both the class envy and the status anxiety of the small urban property owner.

And the emphasis, throughout the speech, is indeed on *urbes*: both the great and wondrous city of Rome and the other cities and towns of the Italian peninsula. "Now at last, Quirites, Lucius Catiline, burning with boldness, panting outrage, plotting unspeakable evil against his country, threatening sword and flame against you and against this city (vobis atque huic urbi), out of this city (ex urbe) we have cast. . . . No longer will destruction against these walls be prepared inside these walls (moenibus ipsis intra moenia). . . . No longer need we be fearful—not in the Campus Martius, not in the forum, not in the curia, not inside the walls of our own houses. . . . We have driven him out of his secret hiding place into open banditry (ex occultis insidiis in apertum latrocinium)." All of these quotations are taken from the opening paragraph of the second oration. Catiline's departure from the city subsequent to Cicero's first performance provides Cicero with the perfect opportunity to continue the depiction of him as a rural bandit, only this time with the emphasis on his and his followers' greed for financial gain. Hence from the outset Cicero invites his audience to reflect on the buildings and places that constitute the *urbs*.

Later in the same speech, after listing and categorizing the followers of Catiline, Cicero expands his account of the imminent showdown between city dwellers and Catilinarian bandits to include the other cities of Italy. "Already indeed the cities (urbes) of the *coloniae* and *municipia* will respond to the hilly woodlands of Catiline (Catilinae tumulis silvestribus [24])." "Nor do I consider it necessary to compare the other forces, the armaments, the garrisons that belong to you with the impoverishment and the neediness of that bandit" (neque ego ceteras copias, ornamenta, praesidia vestra cum illius latronis inopia atque egestate conferre debeo [24]). "I will protect the city, you should protect your own rooftops, the residents of the colonies and municipalities will protect their cities and their border from the nighttime excursions of Catiline."[29] Once again, Catiline's behavior is described as characteristic of a bandit, with his nighttime assaults and forest hideaways; and the battle he incites with Cicero's audience becomes one over the resources of Rome and of the other cities of Italy. At the end of the speech Cicero lists the gods themselves as among the vigilantes of Italy, describing them as defending their own temples and the rooftops of the city (qui iam non procul, ut quondam solebant, ab externo hoste atque longinquo, sed hic praesentes suo numine atque auxilio sua templa atque urbis tecta defendunt [29]). It remains for the members of the audience, the people of Rome, to continue to beseech them to protect "this most beautiful, most prosperous, most powerful city" against "the unspeakable criminality of utterly profligate citizens" (quos vos, Quirites, precari, venerari, implorare debetis, ut, quam urbem pulcherrimam florentissimamque esse voluerunt, hanc omnibus hostium copiis terra marique superatis a perditissimorum civium nefario scelere defendant [29]). The adjective *perditissimorum*, here applied to the conspirators, in its dual meaning of "profligate" and "depraved" recapitulates Cicero's argument throughout the speech: because of their profligate misuse of property, Catiline and his conspirators have turned to banditlike depravity. They have fled the city in shame and now in open banditry (apertum latrocinium [1]) plot their assault against it. The tenor of Cicero's appeal to the people in the second speech is reproduced in the triumphant opening of the third, where Cicero lists all that has been rescued through his endeavors: the *res publica*, or common wealth, the lives of all citizens, goods, fortunes, wives, children, and most of all "this domicile of noble power, this most fortunate and most beautiful city" (rem publicam, Quirites, vitamque omnium vestrum, bona, fortunas, coniuges, liberosque vestros atque hoc domicilium clarissimi imperii, fortunatissimam pulcherrimamque urbem [3.1]).

In his appeal to the gods to defend the property of the Romans, Cicero incidentally introduces the related issues of the military and religious aspects of Catiline's banditry and of his own resistance to it. As an organized group of armed men, bandits can easily be likened to a military force. The Latin word Cicero employs to describe the conspiracy, *coniuratio* (e.g., 1.6, 1.30bis, 2.4), allows him to exploit the ambiguity of bandits as common criminals or fierce military unit.[30] Of *coniuratio* applied to groups resisting either the political or the economic power of the state we have numerous instances. For example, Cicero himself applied the word to a slave revolt and to a shepherds' conspiracy against Sicilian landowners in his Verrine orations (*Verr.* 2.5, 2.17). Cognates of the word figure prominently in the text of the *Senatus consultum de Bacchanalibus*, where they are used to describe the activities of the worshippers of Bacchus.[31] Livy in his account of the years immediately following the suppression of the Bacchanals in 186 B.C.E. twice applies the term *coniuratio* to a conspiracy of shepherds in Apulia, who, we are told, were infesting the roads and public grazing grounds with banditry (vias latrociniis pascuaque publica infesta habuerant [39.29.8; cf. 39.41.6–7]). That Cicero should wish to associate Catiline and his followers with such miscreants will come as no surprise to anyone.

But there is another, nonderogatory use of the term *coniuratio*, and its relevance to the orations against Catiline has not yet been fully explored. Two notes of Servius (*Ad Aen.* 7.614 and *Ad Aen.* 8.1) explain the different forms of military recruitment in ancient Rome and the types of oathtaking associated with them. Under ordinary circumstances (so-called *legitima militia*) each recruit swears to obey the commands of the consul during his period of enlistment. The oath he takes is called a *sacramentum*. Under extraordinary conditions, when the city is endangered, a *tumultus* is declared, and soldiers are sworn in en masse in a procedure known as *coniuratio*, or "swearing together." Livy, whose accounts of military recruitment by and large corroborate the Servian description, suggests that *coniuratio* could take place within the regular recruitment and induction process as well when small units of soldiers elect voluntarily (ex voluntate) to swear together (coniurare) not to break ranks except to recover a weapon, assault an enemy, or rescue a citizen (see in particular Livy 22.38.1–4). Indeed, Livy describes as unprecedented (and, one infers from the outcome, ominous) the forcible use of *coniuratio* to swear in all the recruits prior to the catastrophic battle of Cannae (id ex voluntario inter ipsos foedere ad tribunos ac legitimam iuris iurandi adactionem translationem [22.38.4]).

Another episode in Livy also reveals the dangers of misuse of *coniuratio* while illustrating an important feature of the process, namely the performance of blood sacrifice. In book 10, chapter 38, Livy recounts the gruesome process whereby the Samnites initiated their recruits not long before suffering a catastrophic defeat at the hands of the Romans.[32] According to Livy, a large linen enclosure was erected, sacrifice was performed within, and recruits were led into the enclosure one by one. There they were forced to swear a dire oath cursing family and offspring in case of desertion or failure to kill deserters. Those who balked at the oath were slain on the spot and their bodies left among the sacrificial victims as warning to others not to refuse the oath. The procedure mixes the time-consuming individual oath taking of *legitima militia* with the heightened seriousness of the *coniuratio*. Far from relying on a voluntary commitment among soldier peers, it exercises compulsion of the most extreme sort.

The Samnite ritual perverts *coniuratio* in another way as well. As Livy remarks, each soldier was led to the altars "more as victim than as participant" in the sacrifice (admovebatur altaribus magis ut victima quam ut sacri particeps . . . [Livy 10.38.9]). Given the regularity with which ancient peoples marked solemn occasions with the performance of animal sacrifice, we should regard the victimization of the recruits rather than the slaughter of the animals as the perverted aspect of the ceremony. Indeed, Bleicken has relied on Livy's account of the Samnite oath to connect a series of third- through first-century Italian coins with *coniuratio*.[33] The coins depict a group of soldiers (*gregarii*, or common soldiers, with various sorts of military garb) surrounding a sacrificial animal, in most cases a suckling pig. Because the human figures are clad in military, as opposed to civilian, garb, it is unlikely that the coins depict the striking of treaties. Instead, Bleicken argues, the coins depict scenes of oath taking, specifically the *coniuratio* as opposed to the individual *sacramentum* of *legitima militia*. In light of their provenance and date the coins can thus be interpreted as commemorating various occasions on which Italian cities, Rome foremost among them, undertook *coniurationes* in the face of military emergencies. The earliest of the series of coins dates from the time of the Hannibalic invasion; but others almost certainly commemorate *coniurationes* of Italian cities during the Social Wars at the end of the second and beginning of the first centuries B.C.E.—that is, within the memory of many in Cicero's audience. Thus, in addition to evoking a certain kind of military recruitment, the term *coniuratio* also calls to mind the religious aspect of the oath taking, that is, the animal sacrifice that marks the compact between soldiers.

The term *coniuratio* is, as another note in Servius reports, *tōn mesōn*, that is, ethically neutral, with the potential of being applied to good or bad swearings together.[34] Romans participate in *coniurationes*; so do their Italian rivals. Shepherds, runaway slaves, and bandits like Catiline swear together in their upland lairs, but so do the residents of walled cities. The Janus-like character of the term *coniuratio* makes it an extremely useful element in Cicero's performance of the Catilinarian orations. Catiline's conspiracy can be made to evoke not only fears of bandits, mythical or real, but also historical memories of military struggles against and between fellow Italians. Moreover, the organized agitation that Cicero conducts against Catiline's conspiracy raises the possibility of a counterconspiracy, a *coniuratio* of upstanding Roman citizens, with Cicero at its center. It is this second aspect of Cicero's use of *coniuratio*, that is, the raising of the possibility of a counterconspiracy, that must now be considered in some detail.

Willems, in his study of the Roman senate during the Republic, mentions in passing that a *tumultus* was decreed at Rome some time after the 27th of October in 63 B.C.E.[35] He bases this observation on Sallust's description of the placing of night watches throughout the city (*Catil.* 30.7), a description that follows the narrative of the Senate meeting of October 27 and precedes the narrative of the meeting of November 8. But this act alone hardly qualifies as declaration of a *tumultus*.[36] As Cicero informs us in the *Philippics* (5.31; cf. 6.2, 8.2–3, 8.6, 14.1) declaration of a *tumultus* (i.e., a state of emergency), implies as well the suspension of ordinary business (iustitium edicere) and the donning of military garb in place of the toga of civilian life (saga sumere). What Sallust describes is a state of not quite *tumultus*, or panic in abeyance, that exactly corresponds to Cicero's repeated assertions that he did not declare a *tumultus* in the struggle against Catiline, although (the implication seems to be) he might very well have done so. According to Sallust (*Catil.* 31.1–3), gloom (tristitia) replaced the customary joy and playfulness of the city (laetitia atque lascivia), residents became fearful and untrusting, and the city was in a state of neither war nor peace (neque bellum gerere neque pacem habere). In his first speech against Catiline, Cicero declares that when Catiline, at the electoral assemblies in July, had wanted to kill Cicero along with some of the candidates for office, he, Cicero, crushed the attempt with the help of his friends and without raising a public tumult (*nullo tumulto* publice concitato [*Catil.* 1.11]). The following sentence begins with the word *nunc* (now) and one might expect Cicero to say something to the effect that he has since learned better and has called for a *tumultus*. Instead, the sentence in question, while proceeding to describe the even more outrageous behavior in which Catiline has engaged since July, indicates that Cicero is once again stepping back from the brink and will not take some action that he could legitimately take: faciam id quod ad severitatem lenius, ad communem salutem utilius (1.12). The next day, in addressing the popular assembly, Cicero again raises the possibility of a *tumultus*, only to reject it: "You, Quirites," he exhorts his audience, "defend the shelters of the city with night watches and guardians: I for my part have taken sufficient precautions that the city be protected without terror on your part and without any tumult" (sine vestro metu ac *sine ullo tumultu* [*Catil.* 2.26]). A few sentences later Cicero again reassures the populace that the conspiracy will be crushed without any tumult: atque haec omnia sic agentur ut maximae res minimo motu, pericula summa *nullo tumultu*, bellum intestinum ac domesticum post hominum memoriam crudelissimum et maximum me uno togato duce et imperatore sedetur (2.28). In the third oration Cicero declares that Lentulus has gone north to stir up war among the residents of the Transalpine territory and a tumult among the Gauls (*tumultus Gallicus* [3.4]); when the Allobrogians decide to inform on the conspirators, well-meaning leaders of the Roman state beg Cicero to open the incriminating letters before taking them to the Senate, lest a tumult be rashly imposed on the state (ne . . . temere a me *tantus tumultus* iniectus civitati videretur [3.7]). In the last pair of passages *tumultus* becomes the expression of fear and panic on the part of a desperate foreign people and concurrently an inappropriate strategy in the well-ordered Roman state.

If nothing else, Cicero's use of *tumultus* throughout the orations suggests that he did not in fact declare a military state of emergency although he wished to remind his audience that the senatorial decrees of late October gave him the power to do so. The threat posed by Catiline is serious enough to justify a full-scale panic, emergency recruitment, suspension of ordinary business, and the donning of military garb, but it is better handled in another way.[37] This way is precisely the expression of political and social unity among all classes of Roman society that Cicero seeks to foster in all the Catilinarian orations and describes as realized in the fourth and final speech: "All people of all classes are at hand, of all types and of all ages. The forum is full, the temples around the forum are full, full are all the approaches to this temple and to its environs. For this is the only issue that has been identified since the foundation of the city on which all have one and the same point of view—with the exception of those who, although they see that they must perish, prefer to perish with all rather than alone" (Cicero *Catil.* 4.14).[38] Thereupon follows Cicero's enumeration of the ranks and orders of Rome, and their eagerness to join the cause against Catiline: the knights, who compete with one another instead of against other orders to show their love of the republic; the treasury tribunes and the scribes; the freeborn youth, even the youngest among them, here in force; freedmen and slaves, all orders join together in mind and will and voice for the preservation of the republic (omnes ordines ad conservandam rem publicam mente voce voluntate consentiunt [4.18]). Unlike the Samnites, who in a moment of despair must force all males in the society to submit to an oath of military loyalty, or the Romans themselves, who in their past have called tumults and ordered all men to take up arms, Cicero describes himself as having managed to rid Rome of the conspirators and simultaneously to create a "tumult" based not on fear and desperation but on love of country, not to mention its civilian form of government headed by himself. In purely political terms, especially insofar as he seeks to secure the support of the urban plebs, Cicero has demonstrated to the residents of Rome that the orderly senatorial government, oppressive as it may be, is preferable to the fear and disorder of a tumult—whether that tumult is created by Catiline and his fellow *coniuratores* or imposed by a military dictator such as Pompey, who is at this very moment returning from the East.[39] At the level of symbolic action, Cicero has managed to construct and enforce an image of a unified Roman community that works simultaneously to exclude Catiline and his bandits and, at least momentarily, to restore the desperate loyalty associated with the harrowing events of the Second Punic War without the corresponding call to arms and loss of life.

According to Servius's note (*Ad Aen.* 8.1), *tumultus* and *coniuratio* are related events. It is under conditions of *tumultus* that soldiers swear together, or *coniurant*. In the case of Cicero's handling of the Catilinarian conspiracy, the quasi-*tumultus* created at Rome is matched by the quasi-*coniuratio* among the Romans. Cicero (3.15) tells us that at its meeting on December 3 the Senate voted a *supplicatio* and days of special sacrifices to commemorate the end of the threat to Rome. Dio (37.6.3) refers to a *ieromenia* decreed after the execution of the captives—perhaps a separate action, perhaps a misplaced reference to the same event. In any case, the days of religious celebration neatly fit the symbolism of the deferred, or incomplete *tumultus*, for they substitute a celebratory sacrifice with concomitant banqueting for the oath-taking ritual identified with the *coniuratio*.

Since there was no way of knowing at the outset of the conspiracy and its suppression that things would turn out as they did, the juxtaposition of the joyful sacrifice and the peaceful *tumultus* of early December must be regarded as a serendipitous improvisation rather than as the fulfillment of a carefully contructed plan on Cicero's part. Yet the symbolic force of the climactic *supplicatio* was surely intensified by the fact that Cicero had incorporated the discourse of sacrifice into his polemic against Catiline from the outset. Rumors about the conspirators' own sacrilegious rituals no doubt originate in part in Cicero's campaign of slander. Sallust recounts accusations that the conspirators drank wine mixed with human blood as a sign of their loyalty to one another, although he expresses uncertainy about their accuracy (*Catil.* 22.1–3). Dio indicates that Catiline slaughtered a freeborn boy and distributed the roasted entrails to the leading men of the conspiracy, a detail that intrigues since it corresponds exactly to Roman sacrificial procedure in which the leading men of the community, known as the *participes*, immediately eat of the entrails while the roasted flesh is carved for later distribution to the wider community as well.[40] The stories of the Catilinarians' sacrilege became wilder as they were circulated over the years, with Minucius Felix in the third century C.E. reporting that Jupiter himself taught Catiline how to establish a conspiracy with a compact of blood (*Oct.* 30.5).

Whether or not we choose to believe such accusations, or to believe that the Romans believed them, we can understand how they originated. *Coniurationes*, which are, to cite Servius's dictum again, *tōn mesōn*, or ethically neutral, involve sacrifice. This is how the oath is ratified and the unity of the group reinforced. To call Catiline and his followers a *coniuratio* is to imply among other things that they performed a ritual sacrifice. Cicero may call attention to this aspect of *coniuratio* when he describes Catiline as *princeps coniurationis*, since the word *princeps* originally designated the person who receives the first and best piece of the sacrificial victim.[41] It is an easy move in the logic of invective and innuendo to turn the sacrifice that marks a *coniuratio* into something ghastly and sacrilegious. Cicero is too cautious to repeat the more outrageous accusations, but he certainly facilitates their circulation when he refers to the dagger that Catiline has devoted in an unknown ritual, when he denounces Catiline's impious hand (impia dextera [*Catil.* 1.24]) and his participation in impious banditry (impium latrocinium [1.23]), and when he speaks knowingly of a silver eagle, placed on an altar and sheltered in a scandalous shrine in Catiline's house (1.24).

Yet for all that the religious accusations against Catiline work to differentiate him and his followers from loyal Romans, by their very nature they remind the listener of the essential similarity between the two groups. Catiline creates not a new religious system but an alternative version of practices familiar to the Romans. With the allusion to a counter-*coniuratio* and the creation of a quasi-*tumultus*, we are back where we began with banditry: Catiline and his conspirators are a dangerous and distorted image of the government they seek to overthrow. They threaten the state by their mimicry of it. The conspiracy is neither an outside force that can be contained nor a legitimate expression of political dissent with which compromise might be achieved. It represents instead a fundamental challenge to the legitimacy of the state. To Cicero's implied question, why did you become a bandit, Catiline may well reply, why did you become a consul?

When Pompey the Great became consul in 70 B.C.E., seven years before Cicero, it was evident to some that the man would need assistance in managing the affairs of civilian life. This, we may surmise, is one of the reasons why Varro of Reate composed a handbook of senatorial procedure for him. Bits of this text (actually, of Varro's recollection of the text, since the original did not survive) are preserved for us by Aulus Gellius, and among the details recounted is Varro's prescription that any magistrate who is about to hold a meeting of the senate perform a sacrifice and take the auspices.[42] This piece of information dovetails with the additional requirement that the Senate can only meet in a place that has been inaugurated (i.e., made fit for religious ritual), and it is supported by the story Suetonius tells of Julius Caesar's last day alive: although Caesar sacrificed many victims and could not obtain acceptable auspices, he nonetheless entered the meeting place of the senate (dein pluribus hostiis caesis, cum litare non posset, introiit curiam spreta religione [Suet. Iul. 81]). Taking the auspices in this situation is not a question of determining whether the day is a good one for conducting business or not, as is the case with the notorious checking of the sky prior to assemblies. Rather, it is a matter of making certain that one has killed an appropriate sacrificial victim, and of repeating the ritual until one gets it right. Julius Caesar in this instance stands convicted of impatience rather than neglect.

Cicero, as consul in 63, had full authority to call meetings of the Senate. He did so on the night of November 8 and chose the temple of Jupiter Stator as the location.[43] The sources say nothing of his performing a sacrifice prior to the commencement of the meeting, but there is no reason to suspect that he ignored religious procedure on so solemn and carefully orchestrated an occasion. The animal would have been slain, the auspices taken, and the roasted entrails distributed among the participants. The first piece of the victim would have gone to the *princeps senatus*, and the distribution of entrails as well as roasted meat would have determined the limits of the sacrificial circle. Cicero began to inform the Senate of the latest information he had acquired against Catiline when in walked the culprit. Too late for the opening ceremonies, confronted by the hostile senators who left their seats to avoid being near him, deprived of his share of the sacrifice, Catiline was an outcast even before Cicero began his harangue. The text that survives for us merely confirms and elaborates on the identity that Cicero had already set for Catiline as outsider, bandit, and representative of a counterstate. Bandits meet at night: so does the Senate. Bandits conspire together after performing sacrifice: so does the Senate. Bandits have an energetic leader, one who works day and night to advance the interests of the group and receives the highest honor and greatest loyalty as a result: so does the Senate, in the person of its consul Cicero.

Building on a traditional ideology that pits bandits against the state, Cicero constructs an account of Catiline's behavior that leaves him no option but to abandon the city and join the bandits in Etruria who, as Cicero points out, are eagerly waiting for him. Catiline is not a dissident politician whose views can be incorporated into a general consensus, or the representative of a class with legitimate demands on the attention of the Senate. He is a bandit: a representative of a counterstate, a threat to the property rights of free citizens, an organizer of a military assault, and, perhaps most important, a participant in a perverted and parasitic religious system. "And still," in Cicero's words of outrage, "he enters the Senate, he becomes a participant (*particeps*) in public debate" (*Catil.* 1.2). In Cicero's view, Catiline's fatal error consists of entering the Senate, that is, of trying to be in the state yet not of it.

Structuralist interpreters of ancient religious practice have argued that key to the determination of an appropriate sacrificial victim is its possession of characteristics both like and unlike those of the group performing sacrifice.[44] In Greek and Roman cult, it is the similarity of domestic animals to human beings, combined with their obvious dissimilarity, that makes them, and not wild beasts, the standard sacrificial victims. In Greek tragedy, it is combination of sameness and difference that marks the hero, such as Oedipus, for expulsion from the community. Catiline, through his conspiracy, becomes the figure of the other; in his entry into the Senate he blurs the categories of same and other and marks himself as a victim. This is why, in the final section of the first oration, Catiline is no longer an enemy of the state or a promoter of revolution, but a sacrificial victim whose expulsion and murder will confirm the unity and dominance of the senatorial order:

> With these omens, Catiline . . . proceed to your impious and nefarious war. And you, Jupiter, who were established here by Romulus under the same auspices by which the city was established . . . this man and his comrades you will drive away from yours and all the other temples, from the rooftops and walls of the city, from the lives and fortunes of all the citizens. And these men, enemies of good men and the fatherland, bandits of Italy (*latrones Italiae*), joined together by a compact of crime and unspeakable type of union, with unending punishments, living and dead, you will immolate (*mactabis*). (Cicero *Catil.* 1.33)[45]

The last word of the passage, and of the speech, *mactabis*, is the hardest to translate yet of the greatest significance. It refers of course to the performance of blood sacrifice, the slaughter of the victim, roasting of his entrails, and distribution of his flesh among the participants; "Kill sacrificially" is the concise expression employed by the *Oxford Latin Dictionary*. The struggle between the *coniuratio* of *boni* and the *coniuratio* of the bandits, between one sacrificial system and another, can only be resolved by transference of the conflict to a higher order, a transcendent priest. And so Jupiter is called upon to perform the very action with which Cicero, as consul, would have opened the meeting that night, and to pursue Catiline, the bandit-senator, the carrier of the mark of sameness and difference, as the victim whose departure and/or slaughter will secure the prosperity and well-being of the community.[46]

Banditry is a useful marker within the synchronic ideology of the Roman state, in the context of which it can be invoked at any moment as the mirror image, and hence the quintessential threat to legitimacy, of the ruling elites. But banditry has another place in the Romans' account of themselves, namely, as an important feature in the story of Rome's origin. Romulus, after all, was a bandit, a renegade who overthrew a king, created a *coniuratio*, and invited other desperadoes to join him through the institution of the asylum.[47] And Romulus, as was widely accepted by Cicero's time, had a double, a twin who had to be eliminated before the newly founded state could achieve its identity.[48] Cicero alludes to Romulus throughout the orations against Catiline. The temple of Jupiter Stator in which Cicero delivers the first oration was, according to legend, inaugurated by Romulus to commemorate Jupiter's role in preventing the original Romans from fleeing in panic before the onslaught of the Sabines.[49] Cicero alludes to this story in the climax of the first speech, linking Romulus's inauguration of the temple with the foundation of the city and with Cicero's own performance of sacrifice in his capacity as consul in the passage quoted above. At the beginning of the third speech Cicero again establishes an explicit connection between himself and Romulus when he declares that there is even greater cause for rejoicing when we are rescued from death than there is when we are born: "Since we have elevated among the gods the one who founded this city . . . the one who has preserved it in its settled and magnified condition will deserve to be honored by you and by posterity."[50] The *supplicatio* that Cicero has been voted, he reminds us, is the first awarded a civilian since the foundation of the city (primum post hanc urbem conditam [*Catil.* 3.15]). We knew dire days were in store for Rome because a few years ago the heavens sent down a massive storm, statues of the gods and images of men of old were cast down, and (in the only memorial Cicero mentions by name here), the golden statue of Romulus, small and sucking at the teats of the she wolf was struck by lightning (tactus etiam ille qui hanc urbem condidit, Romulus, quem inauratum in Capitolio parvum atque lactantem uberibus lupinis inhiantem fuisse meministis [3.19]). The soothsayers ordered the erection of a new statue of Jupiter facing eastward and only on the day on which the conspirators were paraded through the forum was it finally set in place (3.21).

The Augustan poets were deeply troubled by the story of the dissent between Romulus and Remus and the resulting fratricide. The story was a painful reminder of the massive slaughter of Roman by Roman during the civil wars that marked the end of the republic. It has even been suggested that the story of fratricide is one of the reasons that Vergil opted to write an *Aeneid* instead of a *Romulid*.[51] Even earlier, it has recently been suggested, "identification of a Roman leader with Romulus was an ambiguous distinction at best."[52] In Cicero's orations against Catiline the ambiguities of the Romulus story operate with full force. Consider again the golden statue touched by lightning as an omen of impending disaster for Rome. Cicero states explicitly that it is a statue of Romulus, small and nursing with the she wolf. But how common were depictions of the wolf with only one twin? Whether we follow Wiseman in believing that Remus was added to the foundation myth in the fourth century B.C.E. or other scholars who regard him as always already there, by the late Republic Romulus implies Remus and vice versa. Indeed, one modern scholar makes an interesting and perhaps unintentional supplement to just the passage of Cicero under consideration here when she lists the objects destroyed by lightning as "statues of gods and heroes, the bronze table of the Laws, and the statue group of Romulus, Remus, and the wolf."[53] Like Romans of Cicero's day, so too modern interpreters take it for granted that doubling is central to the story of Rome's foundation, just as it is to many other Roman legends (e.g., the Romans and the Sabines, the Romans and the Aborigines, the Horatii and the Curiatii). The problem of the excluded other and of rivalry between peers is fundamental to Roman identity. Cicero's omission of Remus in all his allusions to Romulus is therefore a silence that speaks louder than any words.[54] If Cicero is Romulus, then it is obvious to all that Catiline is his Remus—indeed, Remus, like Catiline, is described elsewhere as a sacrificial victim, one whose death secures the longevity of the city and its walls.[55] The mirror imagery that marks the relationship of Catiline's bandits and the Roman state is repeated in the relationship of Cicero and Catiline, in both its contemporary description and in its legendary analogue. Repeatedly throughout the speeches Cicero alludes to the personal danger he willingly accepts in his struggle with Catiline. It is not just that Catiline is out to assassinate Cicero, but that the Roman people themselves may prefer the image of the martyred Catiline to that of the savior-consul.[56] To be sure, we may see such passages as part of Cicero's campaign of self-defense during the years after the conspiracy when indeed his own life was on the line because of his role in the suppression of the *coniuratio*. But such passages work equally well in the context of 63 B.C.E. as part of Cicero's rhetoric of exclusion. Like Romulus against Remus, like any of a number of legendary heroes who engage in one-to-one combat to determine the fate of the city and the people of Rome, Cicero acknowledges the possibility of his own annihilation in his confrontation with the enemy double.

If Cicero accepts certain implications of the Romulus story, and indeed uses them to his advantage in his assault on Catiline and defense of his role therein, equally does he seek to transcend other ramifications of the legend. The story of Romulus and Remus, like the story of the Romans and the Sabines, like the struggle between Cicero and Catiline, like the legends of bandits against the state, are expressions of Roman anxiety over identity and legitimacy. Starting from a small palisade near the Tiber, the Romans ended up, through absorption, annexation, and conquest, the rulers of a massive empire. Internally, their double population of patricians and plebeians was united thanks to careful political arrangements, but was often in danger of fracturing along one socioeconomic fault line or another. It is not suprising, then, that the nature of "Romanness" and the boundaries of community are central and recurring problems in Roman culture.[57] The Romans employed legal, military, religious, and economic strategies to enforce a model of community at home and throughout Italy and the Mediterranean. Surely it is time to acknowledge literature's involvement in the same process. Cicero's speeches against Catiline as they have been described here offer a particularly spectacular example of the intersecting codes of religious, political, military, and economic discourse, and of their ability to function together to create a myth that differentiates between those within the community and those outside it.

Literature can also serve the needs and interests of the individual author in his relationship to the larger society. This is the final aspect of Cicero's imagery of bandits and senators, *coniuratio* and *tumultus*, victims and priests, the consul and the missing twin, to be considered here. After a consul or other magistrate declared a *tumultus*, citizens could be ordered to don the garb of soldiers.[58] Military dress, the wearing of the *saga*, became the outward sign of the political and psychological transformation of the state and its inhabitants. In the years preceding Cicero's consulship, the appearance of soldiers in Rome was a hallmark of disaster. It scarcely mattered what one's politics were; Marians, Sullans, Cinnans, and independents had suffered grievously in the repeated collapse of civil order that accompanied military control of the city. Cicero appeals to the personal memories of his audience, but also to the long-term cultural memories inscribed in the legends and monuments from earlier periods of Roman history, when he speaks of his ability to save Rome from Catiline without any fear in the city, without any tumult. "All these affairs," he predicts at the end of the second oration, "will be carried out in such a manner that the greatest achievements will come to pass with the slightest fear, the most intense dangers dismissed with no declaration of panic, the cruelest and most severe internal and domestic war in the history of mankind put down with me alone, general and commander-in-chief, but dressed in a toga" (me uno *togato* duce et imperatore sederetur [2.28]). In the triumphant third speech, immediately after drawing the analogy between himself and Romulus, Cicero declares "I have extinguished the fires that have been carried against the city, and, what is more, I have blunted the swords that were drawn against the republic and thrust aside the daggers at your throats"(3.2). Again, when Cicero announces the *supplicatio* that has been awarded him, he declares that it is the first granted to a civilian (*togatus* [3.15]) and that he has received it for saving the city from fire, the citizens from slaughter, and Italy from war (3.15). "You have been saved from the cruelest and most wretched turn of events, and you have been saved without slaughter, without bloodshed, without an army, without combat. Dressed in your togas with me alone, a toga-clad general and commander-in-chief, you have conquered" (*togati* me uno *togato* duce et imperatore vicistis [3.23]).

Ennius, in the passage of his *Annales* describing the struggle between Romulus and Remus over the founding of Rome, has Romulus declare to his brother, who has just leapt over the new city wall, "No one who lives will behave thus with impunity—not even you. You will pay the penalty to me with your warm blood" (Nec pol homo quisquam faciet impune animatus/ Hoc nec tu: nam mi calido dabis sanguine poenas [*Annales* 94–95 Skutsch]). Like Ennius's Remus, Catiline, too, paid the penalty with his blood, but in Cicero's representation of the conspiracy, it was his departure from the city, and the rallying of all the orders against him, that constituted the real victory, a bloodless one, led by a general in a toga. It was not Cicero who killed Catiline, but Catiline who marked himself as Jupiter's sacrificial victim. According to Cicero, no one before him had blunted the drawn sword or thrust aside the threatening dagger without drawing a sword or a dagger himself. The victory over Catiline thus becomes in Cicero's account not just the crushing of a troop of bandits, but a victory over the bloody legacy of Rome. Cicero employs the old myth of Roman legitimacy, based on the superiority of one troop of bandits over another, one twin over his brother, to construct a new myth, one rooted in the potential of civilian government to parry weapons with the toga and to defeat military might through the power of language.

Chapter 4

CULTURE WARS IN THE FIRST CENTURY B.C.E.

THE ITALIANNESS of the Augustan settlement has been a topos of historical scholarship at least since the publication of Syme's *The Roman Revolution*.[1] Indeed, with respect to the bloody conflicts of the first century
B.C.E. and their resolution in the *pax Augusta*, one group of scholars has
gone so far as to claim that "Italy emerged as the true winner of the civil
wars."[2] But Italy, then as now, is a complex country and a complex idea,
and we should be as wary of equating slogans such as *tota Italia* or *cuncta
Italia* (both recorded in Augustus's *Res gestae*) with a unified cultural
identity as we would be of arguing that the United States is a cultural
unity because its coinage declares *e pluribus unum*. The patchwork nature of Italy was recognized rather than repressed late in the Augustan
regime when the princeps organized the peninsula into eleven administrative units based roughly on traditional ethnic divisions and developed a
discriptio Italiae that tallied not just cities and rivers but *gentes* as well.[3]

It is disappointing to have to remark that, despite the abundance of
modern discussion of the relationship between Augustan literature and
Augustanism, relatively little has been written about the relationship
between Augustan literature (or any period of Latin literature, for that
matter) and the problem of the integration of Rome and Italy.[4] Classical
studies persists in its Romantic preference for the personal over the ideological, for narrative history over cultural studies, and for events and pol-
icies over the representations that shape and are shaped by them. These
preferences manifest themselves in mistakes as simple, yet as persistent, as
the use of *urbs* and *oppidum*, *Latinus* and *Italus*, even *Roma* and *Italia*,
as if they were interchangeable terms rather than highly charged referents
in a complex and dynamic discourse of cultural and national identity.

In the case of Horace, who is the focus, although not the sole topic, of
the present discussion, the Italian problem comes to light most clearly in
the late writings, specifically the fourth book of the *Odes* and the *Letter
to Augustus*. This observation will surprise no one, in view of the historical background of the works—Augustus's return to Italy and Rome in 13
B.C.E. after a three-year absence in Gaul and Spain—and Horace's status
at the time as in effect poet laureate.[5] What is perhaps surprising is the
bold, paradoxical, and at times negativistic way in which Horace argues
for a brave new construction of poetry and the world in the poems of this
period. In them we hear a "pre-echo" of contemporary debates over the

literary canon and its relationship to cultural identity, and gain a "preview," to switch metaphors, of the contemporary struggle between verbal and visual means of regulating behavior and enforcing identity. In effect, Horace solved the Italian problem by denying it, and broke the old connection between poet and community by privileging a new relationship between writer and reader. In so doing, he produced a vision of an imperialistic Latin literature that was not seriously challenged for many centuries to come and authorized an isolation of writer and reader that has political and cultural consequences even today. An exploration of Horace's handling of the Italian problem against the backdrop of its representation in a wide range of earlier authors (Catullus, Cornelius Nepos, Atticus, Cicero, Vergil, and Varro) will thus serve two purposes within the larger framework of this book: first, it will supplement the list of the social functions of Latin literature by considering its role in the negotiation of conflicted cultural and ethnic identity; and second, it will continue our exploration of the oscillation between performance and text, stability and movement, that characterizes Latin literature from its inception. Whereas Cicero, both through the performance of a myth of Roman legitimacy and through his philosophical expropriation of the cultural capital of conquered Greece (as discussed in chapters 3 and 2, respectively), seeks to localize authority in an expandable but always Romanocentric aristocracy, Horace is here seen to enact a more polyvalent model of cultural authority. In this model texts, their elite producers and consumers, and even the emperor himself, remain in circulation, thereby strengthening their interconnections while mystifying their relationship to other sectors of society.

ITALY AND ROME IN THE POETRY OF HORACE

We can trace Horace's sensitivity to and participation in the shifting balance of power between Rome and the rest of Italy throughout his long poetic career. In some of his poems, Italy constitutes an entity distinct from and by implication subservient to the city of Rome. Thus in *Satire* 1.6, the poet describes a candidate for a magistracy as one who proposed to take as his *cura* or concern the city of Rome, the *imperium*, Italy, and the temples of the gods (sic qui promittit cives, *urbem* sibi curae / imperium fore et *Italiam*, delubra deorum [*S.* 1.6.34–35]). Concern for Italy is but one of a jumble of political promises, among which, however, attention to the city takes pride of place. In *Satire* 1.7, Italy is quaintly described as the metaphorical vinegar that douses the Greek Persius in his contest with the Praenestine Rupilius (At Graecus, postquam est *Italo* perfusus aceto [*S.* 1.7.32]). The contest between the Greek and the Praenestine is to be decided by Brutus, who is expressly invoked as descendant of the regicide and founder of the Roman Republic (per magnos, Brute, deos te / oro, qui reges consueris tollere [*S.* 1.7.33–34]). In *Satire* 2.6, along with rumors of Dacian invasion, something else that does not concern Horace, secure on his Sabine farm, is the question of the settlement of the Actian veterans either in Sicily or on land pointedly described as Italian:

> Quid, militibus promissa Triquetra
> praedia Caesar, an est *Itala* tellure daturus. . . .
> (Horace *S.* 2.6.55–56)

The speaker's eschewal of interest in political affairs conveniently disregards the legitimate anxieties of his Italian countrymen concerning disposition of land in their communities.

In the first collection of *Odes* this cavalier and Romanocentric approach to Italy is tempered by an awareness of the role of Italy in Rome's military successes. Caesar in *Odes* 1.37 hastens from Italy (ab *Italia* volantem [*Odes* 1.37.16]) to reckon with the *fatale monstrum*, Cleopatra, who plotted against the Roman citadel (*Capitolio* [*Odes* 1.37.6]). In *Odes* 2.7, Horace's comrade-in-arms under Brutus has at last returned to Italy (*Italo* caelo [4]) as an amnestied Roman citizen (quis te redonavit *Quiritem*? [3]). The Parthian of *Odes* 2.13 is said to fear chains and an Italian stronghold (*Italum* robur [*Odes.* 2.13.18]). The phrase *Italum robur* can be taken as referring both to the historical custom of imprisoning dangerous enemies throughout Italy and to the Roman army's dependence on Italian manpower. The historical connection between Rome and Italy is invoked in the Regulus Ode as well, with Carthage there described as uplifted by the downfall of Italy (o pudor / o magna Carthago, probrosis / altior *Italiae* ruinis [*Odes* 3.5.38–40]), an accurate reflection of the devastation sustained by the communities of Italy during the Hannibalic invasion. In contrast to an earlier representation of Italy as rustic hinterland, then, *Odes* 1–3 lay emphasis on the Italian contribution to Rome's greatness.

Yet even this vision can take on a more sinister cast, as passages from the early *Epistles* illustrate. When Iccius in *Epistle* 1.12 is to be informed how things stand with the Roman state (ne tamen ignores, quo sit *Romana* loco res [*Ep.* 1.12.25]), Horace tells him that Spain has given way to Agrippa, Armenia to Claudius Nero, Phraates of Parthia has knelt before Augustus, and—the climax of the list of imperial successes—"golden abundance has poured forth her fruits on Italy" (aurea fruges / *Italiae* pleno defundit Copia cornu [28–29]). Italy is here the beneficiary of Rome's successes, but later in the same collection it becomes clear that she will continue to pay a heavy price for this largesse. Thus in *Epistle* 1.18,

Augustus is said to leave to Italian military might whatever he has not already settled of the world's affairs (et si quid abest, *Italis* adiudicat armis [1.18.57]), this in the course of advice to Lollius to participate willingly in the manly and aristocratic Roman pursuits of hunting and athletic competitions on the Campus Martius (proelia . . . *campestria* [54]). While the golden youth of Rome enjoy the benefits of imperialism, the dirty work, as always, is left to the Italian soldiery.

These shifting and at times conflicting representations of the relationship between Rome and Italy in Horace's poetry mirror Augustus's own troubled and bloody history of involvement with the Italian problem. In the Perusine War of the late '40s, the then Octavian directed the destruction of a movement that represented itself as a revival of the early first-century concept of *tota Italia*: that is, all of Italy and to hell with Rome.[6] Yet a few years later, in 36, after the destruction of the fleet of Sextus Pompey off Naulochus, Octavian made certain to return to Rome via the cities of southern Italy, where he was welcomed as a deity, albeit as much for clearing the countryside of bandits as for defeating the remnants of the Pompeian forces.[7] In the Actian War of 31 B.C.E., sustained by the celebrated oath of loyalty from all of Italy (iuravit in me verba *tota Italia* sponte sua et me bellum quo vici ad Actium ducem depoposcit [*Res gestae* 25.2]),[8] Octavian employed the classic strategy of uniting the home front in opposition to a demonized external enemy. Part and parcel of this rejection of Egypt and the East was the development of Rome as *altera Alexandria*.[9] While such a move may have been designed to allay fears of a transfer of power from West to East, it necessarily privileged the city and soon-to-be world capital of Rome at the expense of its Italian environs. When Horace, in *Odes* 3.30, predicts that his lyric monument will outlast the pyramids (symbol of Egyptian strength and longevity) and endure instead as long as "the *pontifex* [head of Roman religion] mounts the Capitoline," the center and symbol of Roman power, he alludes, among other things, to the triumph of Rome over Alexandria. Yet in the movement of the ode, Rome's victory in the battle of the cities precedes and makes possible the poet's enduring fame along the river Aufidus and in the rural domain of Daunus.

Horace's representations of Italy, Rome, and their shared relationship stabilize in the works of his later years. *Odes* 4.14 and 4.15 and *Epistle* 2.1 paradoxically take advantage of Augustus's extended absence in Gaul, Germany, and Spain to construct an image of Italy and Rome as balanced partners and of the princeps as divine dissolver of ethnic differences. Thus in *Odes* 4.14, the subjugation of the Alpine tribes is represented as the completion of the process of pacification that has brought Augustus and/or his army into contact with peoples encircling Rome and

Italy on the north, west, south, and east. Sitting in the center, both geographically and formally within the catalogue at the end of 4.14 are Italy and Rome, of which Augustus is now the sacred guardian:

> o tutela praesens
> *Italiae* dominaeque *Romae*
>
> (Horace *Odes* 4.14.43–44)

The positioning of the adjective *dominae* between the names *Italia* and *Roma* reflects the shared dominion that the poem celebrates.

In 4.15 the focus is not so much on the protection of the imperial heartland as on the movement of power from the center to the periphery, with the Latin name and Italian vitality and renown (note again the balanced pairing) spreading from west to east:

> per quas *Latinum* nomen et *Italae*
> crevere vires famaque et imperi
> porrecta maiestas ad ortus
> solis ab Hesperio cubili
>
> (Horace *Odes* 4.15.13–16)

Yet even here the pacification of the frontier is interpreted as making possible the revitalization of the center, inasmuch as the Ode proceeds to refer to the cessation of civil strife (*non furor civilis* [17–18]) and, in the culminating image of Horace's lyric career, to the performance of poetry in the context of familial and social conviviality (nosque et profestis lucibus et sacris / inter iocosi munera Liberi / cum prole matronisque nostris . . . canemus [*Odes* 4.15.25–32]).[10]

As if in fulfillment of Horace's predictions concerning the impact of his return, Augustus, at the outset of *Epistle* 2.1, is specifically described as tending to the affairs of Italy:

> Cum tot sustineas et tanta negotia solus
> res *Italas* armis tuteris, moribus ornes
> legibus emendes. . . .
>
> (Horace *Ep.* 2.1–3)

Whereas in the late *Odes* Augustus's absence gives Horace the freedom to imagine the effect of his return, and to speak proleptically of the future greatness of Romano-Italic culture, in the *Letter to Augustus* Horace assumes the responsibility of advising the emperor on the tasks at hand, and thus, not surprisingly, the opening verses are full of topical references to the recent achievements of the princeps. In line 1, for example, the word *solus*, according to Syme, refers to the death on March 12 of Agrippa, who had taken responsibility for Rome and Italy in Augustus's absence.[11] In lines 14–16 there is clear reference, as Lily Ross Taylor noted, to the reorganization of the worship at the *compita*, or crossroads, a process whereby the image of the genius Augusti was substituted for that of the rustic Liber pater, who is mentioned in line 5. This religious reorganization, we may note, was concurrent with Augustus's election in 13 or 12 B.C.E. as *pontifex maximus*,[12] an event that, according to the *Res gestae*, was the occasion of the largest influx of citizens from throughout all of Italy that the city of Rome had hitherto witnessed: cuncta ex *Italia* ad comitia mea confluente multitudine quanta *Romae* nunquam fertur ante id tempus fuisse (Augustus *Res gestae* 10.2). Augustus returned the favor, as it were, by spreading the worship of his genius throughout the peninsula, while Horace contributes to this expansionist religious project by likening Augustus's achievements to those of a series of demigods whose spheres of influence represent expanding circles, starting at Rome and moving outward (i.e., Romulus, Liber pater, Castor and Pollux, and Hercules, all listed in lines 5 and following). Even the list of the achievements of these cult figures is as much a compilation of the accomplishments of Augustus: in recent years it is he who has tended to lands and to people, set aside harsh wars, founded cities, and assigned fields—or, as happened upon his return to Rome in 13 B.C.E., publicly and spectacularly refused to assign fields, offering the veterans of the Alpine campaigns cash instead of land, much to the relief of the whole Italian populace.[13]

After this array of references to the tendance of Italy and the clear expression of Horace's desire not to waste the emperor's time (in publica commoda peccem [*Ep.* 2.1.3]), the body of the letter to Augustus comes as something of a surprise. It turns out that the population's recognition of Augustus's greatness, indeed, of his ability to transcend the very categories "them" and "us," only proves by contrast its folly with respect to the evaluation of literature (cetera nequaquam simili ratione modoque / aestimat [*Ep.* 2.1.20–21]). As the letter proceeds, Horace repudiates the popular preference for ancient as opposed to contemporary literature, and for spectacular performance over well-crafted text. He argues for the privileged position of the poet as a moral teacher and as recorder of the great man's achievements, and concludes by asserting that he would rather see his poems turned into wrapping paper than be honored in a cheap or shoddy manner. No wonder many critics regard the opening lines of the poem, with their political and topical references, as a mere *captatio benevolentiae* to the addressee prior to consideration of the "real" topic, the contemporary state of literature. In contrast to this position, it is my contention that the very form of literary chronology that structures the body of the letter raises issues of precisely the sort adumbrated in the preface, and that the letter as a whole attempts to articulate a concept of literature appropriate for a new Romano-Italic cultural or national unity.

Canons and Chronologies

To understand Horace's intervention in the canon debates of his era, we must first consider those debates as they evolved in preceding generations. From extant works of Catullus, Cicero, and Vergil, as well as from the fragmentary treatises of Cornelius Nepos, Atticus, and M. Terentius Varro, it is possible to identify salient features, formal as well as ideological, that permit us to read the letter to Augustus as a polemical cultural chronology and to ascertain its strategic intent. As contemporary debates over "the canon" have made clear, there is a close connection between a people's construction of its past and its sense of identity in the present. Thus it should not surprise us to discover that the passion for literary chronology and cultural antiquities that characterizes the texts of the late Republic and early Principate corresponds to and expresses the broader cultural conflicts of the period.

The intersecting discourses of literary canonicity, cultural chronology, and ethnic identity make themselves apparent as early as the opening poem of the Catullan *libellus*. There Catullus identifies his dedicatee, Cornelius Nepos, as "the only one of the Italians who dared to unravel all of time in three volumes, learned ones, by Jupiter, and laborious" (cum ausus es unus *Italorum* / omne aevum tribus explicare cartis [Catullus 1.5–6]). The contrast between the slender Catullan *libellus* and the *Chronica* of Nepos has led some scholars to interpret the praise of Nepos as ironic; more persuasive is the view that Nepos's *Chronica*, emulative of Apollodorus's verse-history of the same title, represented a Latin transformation of a learned Hellenistic work that would have appealed to the literary sensibilities of Catullus.[14]

Shared literary interests do not rule out—and indeed may even support—shared political commitments as well. What little we know of Nepos's *Chronica* suggests, as Timothy Wiseman has observed, that Catullus's praise of Nepos as *unus Italorum* at the outset of his own collection of poems was "no accident."[15] As the analysis of various scholars indicates, Nepos's study incorporated material from both mythological and historical time; that is, it went back beyond the historical founding of Italian locales.[16] Moreover, the work was Italian, as opposed to exclusively Roman, in outlook, relating the history of the Italian peninsula, rather than just the city of Rome, to the history of the Greek-speaking world, and perhaps revealing a particular interest in northern Europe and the territory of the Celts.[17] Catullus's poem adds the information that the work purported to cover all of time (omne aevum) and that it did so in three books. In addition, the final line of Catullus's epigram—plus uno maneat perenne saeclo, "may my collection last longer than a *saeculum*"—would seem to point to the organizing principle, or at least a possible organizing principle, whereby Nepos could squeeze all of time into three volumes: that is, the *saeculum*, or period of time roughly equivalent to a century.[18] If this is the case, then Catullus's final request, that his own *libellus* survive longer than one *saeculum*, is also a request that it merit incorporation into the scheme of Italianizing cultural history promulgated by his friend and patron Cornelius Nepos.

Supporting evidence for this interpretation of Nepos's project and, by extension, Catullus's commitment to it, can be found in the ancient responses to the *Chronica*. Not long after Nepos undertook to describe all of history in three volumes, his acquaintance Atticus, the close friend of Cicero, also composed a chronology, the success of which seems to be largely responsible for the displacement of Nepos's chronology from the historical record.[19] Atticus's chronology seems to have been designed to resist the implications of Nepos's work by constructing a self-consciously Romanocentric version of comparable material. Cicero, in his *Brutus*, praises Atticus's chronology because it permits him "to see everything in a single glance, with the sequence having been unraveled." The language of his praise points to similarities and differences between Atticus's and Nepos's enterprises: "unus Italorum / omne aevum tribus explicare cartis," spoken by Catullus of Nepos (1.5–6), in contrast to "uno in conspectu omnia viderem explicatis . . . ordinibus" spoken by Cicero of Atticus (*Brut.* 15). The phrase *omne aevum* matches Cicero's *omnia, tribus cartis* corresponds to *uno in conspectu*, and the verb *explicare* occurs in both expressions.[20]

If nothing else, comparison between the praise of Nepos and the praise of Atticus suggests that the latter's work must have been more condensed and exhibited better layout than Nepos's did. The title of Atticus's project (*Liber annalis*) tells us how he achieved this improvement, namely, by listing events year by year. But it also suggests a connection with the traditional senatorial and pontifical *annales* that focused on events concerning the city of Rome. Indeed, elsewhere Cicero refers to Atticus's chronology by praising him for "binding together the memory of seven hundred years [that is, the history of the city] in a single book" (*Orator* 120). Münzer suggests that Atticus "improved upon and brought unity" to Nepos's work; if so, the "improvement" came in the context of a radically different construct of history.[21] Nepos, a newcomer from across the Po, a man honored in poetry by a fellow transpadane, takes his place as historian of and about the Italians, while Atticus, with the evident approval of Cicero and perhaps Brutus, limits history to the achievements of Rome and their Greek comparanda.[22]

Imitation is the sincerest form of flattery. In Cicero's case, imitation of Atticus comes in the form of the *Brutus* itself, a text whose generic and ideological framework fits the pattern set by his friend and predecessor:

comparison of matters Greek and Roman, interest in literary as well as
political history, focus on distinguished men. To the extent that Italy enters into Cicero's chronology of Roman oratory, it is in its conventional
role as a source of manpower—in this case for the conflicts in the forum
rather than abroad. Thus at section 169ff., several non-Roman orators
are noted as having acquired distinguished reputations among the Latins
and their allies. These orators, however, are promptly slighted by Cicero
for their lack of *urbanitas*, or "citiness" (quod non est eorum urbanitate
quadam quasi colorata oratio [170]); and it is only their speeches at
Rome that earn them the dismal commemoration they achieve.[23] Early in
the *Brutus* Cicero notes that Greek oratory is by and large a product of
Athenian culture (49–50), yet proceeds to use the adjectives *Atheniensis*
and *Graecus* almost interchangeably. No such carelessness (or generosity) with respect to the distinction between Rome and Italy infects his
account of "our own kind": indeed, his discussion of the non-Roman
Italian orators concludes by relegating them to the realm of otherness: sed
domum redeamus, id est ad nostros revertamur (but let's return home,
back to our own kind [*Brut.* 172]).[24]

Another well-known passage of Latin literature continues the dialogue
begun by Catullus and Nepos and extended by Atticus and Cicero. The
second speech of Anchises to Aeneas in the Underworld, that is, his long
exhortation on Roman history and Roman glory beginning at *Aeneid*
6.756,[25] exhibits the now-familiar features of chronological literature:
comparison of Greek and Roman (excudent alii . . . [6.847]);[26] the mingling of cultural history with political and military events; and the tension
between identification with Italy and identification with Rome. While
later books of the *Aeneid* seem to work towards a model of cultural
unity,[27] this pivotal passage in effect displaces the historical Italians from
the history of Rome.

At the outset of his speech Anchises promises to tell of his and Aeneas's
descendants of Italian race (qui maneant *Itala* de gente nepotes [6.757]).
Silvius is described as the first shade to return to the earth "mixed with
Italian blood" (primus ad auras / aetherias *Italo* commixtus sanguine
surget [6.761–762]). Yet with the arrival of Romulus on the scene at line
778, this Italianness gives way, even as the catalogue of Italian people and
places (Pometios Castrumque Inui Bolamque Coramque [775]) gives way
before the celebrated name of Rome (incluta *Roma* [781]), the praise of
the Roman people (*Romanosque* tuos [789]), the establishment of the
institutions of the city (qui legibus *urbem* / fundabit [810–811]), and the
parade of Roman heroes that culminates in the direct address to the unnamed Roman: tu . . . *Romane*, memento (851).[28]

Even Marcellus the elder, who warded off the Carthaginians and the
Gauls in the course of a great *tumultus* (magna turbante tumultu [857]),

is said in so doing to have protected the Roman estate (hic *rem Romanam* . . . sistet eques [856–57]). In the account of the fateful events of the third century B.C.E. and Marcellus's role in them it is only in the word *tumultus*, which refers to the arming of all of Italy against an inruption of the Alpine Gauls,[29] that we find any allusion to the Italian contribution to the salvation of Rome and the peninsula. The contrast between Vergil's account and Polybius's narration of the same events makes clear the distinctive perspective of each. As Polybius puts it:

> The Romans ordered their allies to furnish lists of men available for mobilization. . . . They prepared a stockpile of food and other necessities of war of a size previously unknown. Everyone from all sides came to their assistance. For the inhabitants of Italy, stunned by the Gallic onset, considered not that they were fighting as Roman allies nor that the war was undertaken on behalf of the Roman hegemony; rather each one believed that the danger touched himself and his own city and his land, and so they readily submitted to Roman instructions. (Polybius 2.23.8–14)[30]

In Vergil's version, by the time we reach this point in Anchises' speech, there are no longer any Italians left to submit.

In Horace's *Letter to Augustus*, the conventions of the implied genre of "cultural chronology" are invoked throughout, but chiefly for the purpose of deconstructing the opposition between Rome and Italy that had sustained, and had been sustained by, that genre in recent memory. Horace reviews history—in his case, literary history—from the earliest records through the present; he makes explicit comparisons of Greece and Rome; and like Catullus, who asks to enter Nepos's chronology, or Anchises, who uses the Roman past to exhort his audience to future action, Horace argues for a future vision of literature based on analysis of past accomplishments and failures. Horace may even allude to one of the examples of cultural chronology discussed thus far, namely the *Brutus*, in his description of captured Greece's conquest of its captor (compare Cicero's remark, Quo enim uno vincebamur a victa Graecia [*Brut.* 254]) and in his application of imagery from the human life cycle to the evolution of culture (compare *puella—infans—mature* in *Ep.* 2.1.99–100 to the contrast between *senes* and *adulescentes* at *Brut.* 39). Finally, Cicero's famous discussion of the *carmina* sung at early Roman banquets (carmina quae . . . in epulis esse cantitata a singulis convivis [*Brut.* 75]) seems to be echoed—and corrected—in the *Letter to Augustus*, where fathers and sons are now described as dictating, rather than performing, poetry as they dine (pueri patresque severi / fronde comas vincti cenant et carmina dictant [2.1.109–10]).

Despite Horace's reliance on the conventions of cultural chronology, the tensions between Rome and Italy that seem to be carried by the form

are absent, or, perhaps better, ignored in the epistle. Augustus's settlement of the affairs of Italy and Horace's reflection on a distinctively
Roman literary history are not made to interact or to undermine one another. The equality and equivalence between Italy and Rome evidenced in
the final odes of book 4 obtains here as well. While the ethnic or cultural
polemic that characterizes other chronologies is absent from Horace's,
polemic of another sort is central to the poem in question. The oppositions the poem articulates are not between two ethnic or cultural entities,
but between the literature of the past and a permanently expandable
canon of the present, and between mass culture and elite literature. How
these oppositions are portrayed and what, if any, relationship they might
have to the newly established Romano-Italic cultural unity are questions
to which we now turn.

Spectacle, Song, and Text

Over forty years ago, Antonio La Penna argued that the real target of
Horace's critique in the *Letter to Augustus* is not the antiquarian researches and preferences of figures like Varro, but the possibility of a
revived national theater.[31] La Penna pointed to passages in Suetonius and
Ovid that seem to hint of such a project, as well as to the evidence of the
Augustan building program. While it is certainly the case that drama occupies a major portion of Horace's attention in the letter, two details
complicate the scenario developed by La Penna.

In the first place, when Horace finally identifies two writers worthy of
unadulterated praise, one of them turns out to be Varius, who is best
known to posterity as the author of a tragedy, the *Thyestes*. Singular
praise of a tragedian patronized by the princeps scarcely accords with
opposition to plans for a national theater. In addition, during the course
of his discussion of the poet's usefulness to the community, Horace points
to his own composition of the *Carmen saeculare* for performance at the
Secular Games of 17 B.C.E. Neither theater nor public performance per se
would seem to be the target of Horace's negative criticism.

What does concern Horace about the present scene, at least as he depicts it, is the potential for performances that privilege spectacle and
music to displace the apprehension, whether in public or private, of carefully crafted verbal artifacts. The *Carmen saeculare*, whatever fanfare
surrounded its production, is described by Horace as prayer (*preces*
[2.1.133]), that is, a verbal production. It is this aspect that legitimizes it
as a cultural phenomenon. Plautus is criticized not for writing plays, but
for writing them poorly out of concern for money and popular success
(170ff.). The struggle of good writers to find an audience for their plays
is specifically articulated as a contrast between *ludi* and *scriptores:* if

Democritus came back to life, according to Horace, he would laugh to see the populace attentive to spectacles (*spectaret* populum *ludis* attentius ipsis / ut sibi praebentem nimio *spectacula* plura [197–98]), while writers narrate their stories to the proverbial deaf donkey (*scriptores* autem narrare putaret asello / *fabellam* surdo [199–200]). "What voices," Horace asks, "can overcome the ruckus that the theater itself produces?" (Nam quae pervincere voces / evaluere sonum, referunt quem nostra theatra? [200–201]). The assumption is that there are voices worth being heard, only not in the context of popular spectacle. When at last Horace turns directly to Augustus, it is with a request to pay at least some attention to those authors who seek readers rather than spectators (verum age et his, qui se *lectori* credere malunt / quam *spectatoris* fastidia ferre superbi, / curam redde brevem . . . [214–16]).

What troubles Horace about spectacle is that it interferes with the moralizing impact of poetry and that it appeals to the least common denominator within the population such as the "little people" (*plebecula*) who enjoy bears and battles (186) or the farmers of old whose love of Fescennine verse led them at times to intimidate their betters (et per *honestas* / ire domos impune minax [149–50]). Even the attack on the waxen images and shoddy epitaphs at the end of the poem, whether it alludes specifically to Varro's *Imagines* or to other works in the same style, may be seen as a poet's objection to rival, nonelite, and untraditional forms of cultural production.[32]

The elitism and exclusivity of Horace's defense of literature is hardly unique in ancient society. What distinguishes his argument is its appearance in a work that otherwise foregrounds cultural unity. At the moment when the tension between Rome and Italy is dissolved in both Horace's poetry and the public arena, the *Letter to Augustus* articulates a new set of oppositions, pitting elite against masses, literature against *ludi*, writing against performance. To express this development in concrete historical terms: no sooner has the population of Italy converged on Rome to elect Augustus pontifex maximus—an event remarked on in the opening of the epistle[33]—than Horace, and Augustus too, as it turns out, are seeking ways of keeping them at home.

Not long after the pontifical comitia of 13 or 12 B.C.E., Augustus abandoned the centuries-old requirement that citizens return to Rome for electoral assemblies and instead provided for voting throughout Italy, with ballots transferred to Rome for tabulation.[34] In the suggestive phrase of Nicolet, this reform, along with concurrent changes in the process of census-taking, "substituted for the mobility of people the mobility of documents."[35] Horace proposes a comparable development with respect to literature and does so in the context of a meditation on a new Italian cultural unity. Mass occasions such as *ludi* and performances or cultural forms that rely on visual and musical stimulation are to be discarded in favor of small elite gatherings, such as the *convivia* of *Odes* 4.15 or a literature composed for the attentive reader in the new libraries of the empire or at home. Like the electors throughout Italy, the literati will gather, but the community they share with others will be, in Benedict Anderson's famous description of modern nationalism, the "imagined community" of readers, not the all-too-visible community of spectators. Even the form of Horace's advice to Augustus reinforces his aim in this regard: according to Suetonius, the emperor asked to be included among Horace's *sermones*, or conversations. What he got instead was an *epistula*, or letter, a document crossing yet reinforcing the social and geographical distance between writer and addressee.[36]

HISTORY AND THE FUTURE

As an earlier chapter has argued, Latin literature, since its inception, is marked by a double movement between concealment and display. Like the records of scribes, whose role the poets partially assume, literature in an aristocratic empire is always to a large extent the property of the ruling elite. Sometimes it is to the elite's advantage to treat literature as a private possession, an enterprise of self-affirmation within the small circle of the aristocracy. At other times, literature is directed outward as a mark of social differentiation between those who have it, know it, and can comprehend it and those who cannot.

The conflicts between elites in the late Republic, with the jockeying for power between Romans and Italians, found expression in the cultural realm in debates over literary and cultural chronologies and canons. Resolution of the question, whose culture? in the form of an uneasy alliance of Roman and Italian allowed, or perhaps forced, another question to emerge: what sort of culture? Mechanisms for the consumption and distribution of literature that were appropriate for a Romanocentric enterprise were taxed by the expansion of the culture and of the reading community. Moreover, the broadening effect of unification ran the risk of producing a leveling effect as well—politically in the weakening of the traditional aristocracy, culturally in the development of what is perhaps best described as official popular culture.

Horace's late poetry, especially the *Letter to Augustus*, constitutes both a response to and an intervention in the broader discourse of his era. His assertion of the primacy of reading as a means of consumption, which implies a primacy of writing as a means of production, preserves the elite affiliations of literature while making possible a geographical and, by implication, cultural expansion of the provenance of the elite. Obviously he did not succeed (nor did he intend to) in persuading Augustus to abandon the *ludi* or other popular strategies as means of conveying power relationships within the city or throughout the empire. But he did manage to legitimize literature, in the later sense of an exchange between writer and reader, and to make it available as one means of social differentiation and cultural unification.

While for Horace the problem of literature emerges in the context of relationships between Rome and Italy, the solution he proposes has ramifications that extend far beyond ancient Italy in both time and space. Once the connection between performance and text, or between poet and traditional community, is broken, there is no easy way to localize the imagined community that replaces the real one. Here again, as throughout Horace's career, literature and politics describe isomorphic trajectories, for the moment of Italy's triumph in the ideology of the Principate is also, historically, the commencement of its decline as the focus of political energy. To cite Nicolet once again, the reorganization of Italy into administrative units led in time to its treatment as "but one province among many."[37] The substitution of the movement of documents for the movement of people gave impetus both to the administration of a pan-Mediterranean empire and to the proliferation of Latin letters well beyond the confines of either Rome or Italy.

As to the particular form that literature would take in Augustus's new world order, Horace's letter is ultimately both paradigmatic and prescient. Like *Odes* 3.30 and 4.15, so the letter to Augustus concludes by looking to the future of poetry, only this time it is a future with two opposed yet interrelated options: the "serious" literature of Horace and his self-chosen peers, or the mixed-media message to the masses of Varro and others. Far from seeking accommodation between them, Horace suggests that endorsement of bad literature is tantamount to obliteration, both for Augustus, whose fame depends on the ideals and capabilities of the artists and writers who surround him, and for Horace himself, in his capacity as literary celebrity. As he writes in the final words of the poem, and, possibly, the final words of his career,

> Nil moror officium, quo me gravat, ac neque ficto
> in peius vultu proponi cereus usquam,
> nec prave factis decorari versibus opto,
> ne rubeam pingui donatus munere et una
> cum scriptore meo capsa porrectus operta
> deferar in vicum vendentem tus et odores
> et piper et quidquid chartis amicitur ineptis

> I have no time for a favour that weighs me down,
> nor do I want myself exhibited
> as a waxen head or graced by shoddy verses;

I'd blush at so gross a tribute, find myself
cased with my author, coffined, carted down
to the backstreets where they peddle balm and spice
and everything that's draped in misused paper.

(Horace *Ep.* 2.1.264–70)[38]

In rejecting the vulgar memorialization consisting of waxen image and badly wrought verses, Horace expresses a preference for obliteration over bad handling and confounds the decline of artistic and literary standards with personal extinction. In so doing, he anticipates the recklessness of succeeding generations of cultural and literary purists who regard the subversion of their canon or reevaluation of their standards as cause for near-funereal grief.[39] But his act of making the *Letter to Augustus*, like all of his earlier work, available to a wider reading public, beyond that of its direct addressee or immediate performance context, is an expression of confidence both in literature's survival and in its inevitable, if ultimately unmanageable, participation in the construction of national and cultural identity.

To sum up: Horace's letter to Augustus can be read as an intervention in ongoing debates over Roman and Italian cultural identity and over verbal versus visual communication. It renews the tendency of Cicero, Vergil, and others to subsume Italian identity under Roman leadership, but links Rome's continuing hegemony to its elites' support of a dynamic, ever-revised literary tradition. It provides, in short, a blueprint for an imperial literature, one that will be complemented, as we see in a later chapter, by Ovid's use of poetry from exile to construct the appropriately colonialist subjectivity at home in Rome. In his efforts to secure a place for Latin literature among the privileged practices of Roman cultural hegemony Horace may have been more successful than in his bland acceptance of Italian-Roman harmony. As Andrea Giardina has recently argued, it is probably better to think of Augustus as having held in abeyance, rather than having resolved the tensions among local, Italian, and Roman identities.[40] But in his insistence on the social function of literary production, Horace joins Cato and Cicero before him in fashioning Latin literature as a medium that constitutes its own message of elite Roman dominance.

Chapter 5

WRITING AS SOCIAL PERFORMANCE

WHEN OVID in *Amores* 1.10 seeks to persuade his addressee to exchange sex for commemoration in his verse, he does so in part through an appeal to the immortality of literary fame. Being written down in a text can, in Ovid's view and that of many other ancient writers, help mortal humans transcend both temporal and geographical boundaries. When Horace accedes to Augustus's request to be preserved among his "conversations," or *sermones*, he does so in a letter, or *epistula*, thereby expressing through literary form one aspect of his advice to the emperor: in the new imperial context writing must take its rightful place alongside performance. Even Cicero, performer par excellence, knew the value of preserving the performance occasion through the written word; indeed, years after his successful expulsion of Catiline he was to regret his delay in publishing and circulating the written text of his orations.[1]

If circulating a written text, as opposed to delivering an oral performance, increases an author's renown by extending it in both space and time, it also runs the risk of disconnecting an author from his text and undercutting the importance of personal presence. Apart from any metaphysical anxieties such slippage between word and text may cause poets and theorists, there are serious practical and ideological ramifications as well, especially in the context of a traditional aristocracy. Aristocratic power depends on the presence of the aristocrat, and access to that presence is a crucial means of defining the status of others. Moreover, the conduct of an aristocracy depends upon the embedded nature of economic relationships. Decisions about the allocation of resources are based as much on considerations of power, status, and connections as on financial calculations of costs and benefits. The circulation of written texts has the potential to counter both the importance of presence and the embeddedness of economic relationships. Indeed, in the modern world, the circulation of texts is closely connected with an ideology of political freedom and with the possibility of financial gain. Texts have become commodities, and as such are both expressions of and contributors to a social system that reifies both people and resources. Given this tension between the circulation of written texts, with its implication of freedom and commodification, and aristocratic rule, we are naturally led to inquire whether Latin literature, precisely in its capacity as written text, might not undermine, rather than reinforce, the aristocracy that prompted its original invention.

As is clear from the discussion in previous chapters, writing, in the form of record keeping, surveillance, and command, is essential to aristocratic rule over an empire. But this is writing that is regulated by political authorities and completely embedded in asymmetric power relationships. As long as literature, even written literature, is distributed through the same channels, that is, among patrons and clients, within households or political factions, or in state-approved schools and *collegia*, then there is no intrinsic tension between it and aristocratic rule. But once literature is freed from such limited paths of circulation and becomes part of a market, then its potential as an independent source of authorization may be activated. The question then becomes, when we return to the more narrowly literary sphere, the following: does an author (for example, Ovid) upon releasing a text for publication and circulation through a literary marketplace inevitably undermine the aristocratic power he has sought to enhance and appropriate? When Ovid tells his mistress to abandon independence and self-interest for literary fame is he in fact weakening his own claim to authoritative status insofar as literary reputation is determined by disembedded market forces?

The question is one that interested many ancient authors, although to be sure they did not pose it in the same terms. Especially during the late Republic and early Empire, the contrast between embedded and disembedded versions of economic relations became manifest in the literary sphere in an expressed tension between authorial presence and written text. Authors struggled with the contrast between a desire to reaffirm aristocratic prestige and indeed acquire it for oneself, and the unseemly methods required to secure renown in a world that had long since moved beyond exclusive reliance on face-to-face communication. While each author who approached the issue did so in a distinctive way and from a distinctive perspective, certain common strategies can be identified, some textual, others more broadly social or institutional, and it is these strategies that are examined in this chapter. The general narrative that emerges is one marked by historical irony, for it appears that the more successful the Roman authors were in negotiating the tension between performance and text to the advantage of performance, the more opportunity they created for the emergence of an alternative elite that labored under no comparable anxieties concerning freedom and the word.

1. Admit Your Fears

Far from suppressing the contrast between performance and publication, Roman authors openly explore it. Horace's description of his first book of *Epistles* as a streetwalker is the most notorious case, but other passages, such as Propertius's lament over the waywardness of Cynthia, who is both his mistress and his book of poems, and perhaps even Catullus's reference to the "polish" of his *libellus*, which one scholar has likened to the self-adornment of homosexual prostitutes, betray similar concerns.[2] Ovid, writing from exile, is aware of the advantages to be obtained by written communication, yet his repeated references to his book's ability to go where he cannot go end up reinscribing the priority of author over text: Ovid's absence is exactly what the book is called upon to advertise and amend.[3] Horace and Seneca publish correspondences but hardly let their addressees get a word in edgewise. For them the letter is a device for self-exposure, but at a distance. Quintilian complains of works by others circulating under his name; his response is not to suppress them but to produce the real thing.[4] Cato the Elder objectifies his own speeches when he describes himself as willing to erase portions that contradict his opponent's arguments, but his remarks are sarcastic, since he of course expects the audience to understand that changing the written record does not alter what he actually said on a specific memorable occasion.[5]

The shared gesture that underlies these and other such passages is apotropaic. By talking about a problem, the writers hope to make it go away. Don't let my books replace me, Ovid implicitly beseeches the reader; don't accept the counterfeit Quintilian; don't reject my courtroom testimony; don't assume that I need to market myself to achieve renown. The reader is reminded of the materiality of the text only to have her or his attention drawn to the writer who authorizes it. Writers write, so they say, not to communicate ideas and certainly not to make money, but to direct attention to themselves and their performance. Pliny tells of the man who is so taken by the reputation of Livy that he travels all the way from Cadiz (ab ultimo terarum orbe) just to see him (statimque ut videat abesse).[6] Tacitus's Aper, who suffers no compunction over growing rich through speech making, tells essentially the same story, but makes sure the target is a poet and elaborates on the description of the author as object of admiring gaze: "As soon as the visitor sees him," declares Aper, "he leaves content, as if he had looked at a picture or a statue."[7] The point is not that the poet makes a spectacle of himself, for that would involve no dishonor, but that the lowly provincial (from Spain, or Asia, or even Gaul) enters into no relationship with him. He doesn't ask for a favor, or quake in terror, or shout in awe, or hire him as defense counsel. At least the statuelike Roman elder who stayed behind during the Gallic invasion had the aristocratic self-regard to strike the Gaul who plucked his beard, thereby prompting a heroic bloodbath.[8] Aristocrats are supposed to act, not be acted upon, which is why they must take preemptive action against the possible confusion of their texts with themselves.

2. Deny a Financial Motive

Aristocrats do not talk about money, except with one another. For this reason, despite the best efforts of indefatigable scholars we will probably never know whether or if or how much money Roman authors made through the sale of their books. It was probably very little, judging from the rudimentary nature of the distribution system.[9] To the extent that circulation benefited a poet financially, it was by bringing him to the attention of the kind of person who would make a good patron.[10] The poet stared at by Aper's tourist from the hinterland had the last laugh, as Vespasian gave him half a million sesterces.[11] Juvenal is annoyed, both at the size of the *sportula* the poet receives from the busy patron and at his inability to get the patron's attention to make the case for more.[12]

Yet apparently there were some who were not convinced by the poets' insistence on the purity of their motives. After mentioning Vespasian's liberality toward Saleius Bassus, Aper's skepticism toward poets' motives is understandable: he speaks of the "reputation and renown [of poets], before which alone they grovel, and which alone is the reward for their labor—or so they say. . . . "[13] Pliny expresses surprise and satisfaction that there are even booksellers at Lyons, much less that his works are doing well there: "I rejoice that my works are held in as high esteem abroad as in the city. At last I can rest assured now that the independent judgments of men in such diverse locations concur."[14] Martial gives us some sense of what those independent judgments sounded like, at least with respect to his own books. In one epigram, he apologizes for the sloppiness of the text, blaming it on the copyist who was totting up the lines, presumably for pay.[15] In another, he urges an acquaintance to come up with the five denarii the bookseller in the Agriletum is charging rather than have Martial supply him with a copy gratis.[16] To the potential buyer disturbed at the price of another of his books of epigrams, Martial cheerily remarks that the bookseller could have made a profit by selling it for half as much.[17] We might wish to conclude from passages such as these that ancient authors did not profit from the sale of their books, but what the texts in fact reveal is that ancient authors did not think it appropriate to talk about profiting from their books. They want their readers to believe that, unlike modern workers, they can eat prestige. To do so is a mark of their elevated status.

3. Maintain a Personal Relationship

The spread of writing as a means of preserving and communicating literature was largely dictated by forces extrinsic to literature. The increasing popularity of schools prompted a need for written texts.[18] In the Augustan age, Caecilius Epirota's novel use of the texts of living authors made it possible to become curricular material in your own lifetime.[19] Libraries served something of the same function, as Nicholas Horsfall has recently argued.[20] Augustus's development of Greek and Latin libraries meant a lot of "empty shelves on the Palatine"—a nice spur to producing something worth putting in writing. Then, too, the audience for literature refused to stay put. Merchants, soldiers, and government officials traveled the Mediterranean, and texts in writing were more likely to keep up with them than were authors (although some, like the poet Archias, evidently tried). Crassus's soldiers took pornographic literature with them on their Parthian campaign.[21] Martial has higher expectations (but only slightly) for Priscus, who, he hopes, will take along a copy of his *libellus* on the hunt.[22] Catullus is stuck in Verona with only one case of scrolls.[23] Cicero's letters follow his correspondents up and down the Italian peninsula and across the Mediterranean as well. Did he sometimes send copies of his speeches? or his philosophical works?[24] A certain Regulus did, for he had a thousand copies of a lugubrious work on the death of his son sent throughout Italy and the provinces. Pliny ridicules Regulus, but it is hard to tell exactly why: was a thousand too many? or was it just that the work seemed to have been written, as Pliny put it, not about a boy, but by a boy (non de puero scriptum sed a puero)?[25]

Perhaps the problem with Regulus is that he was too obvious. To send a thousand copies implies that there are not a thousand people who would have asked for copies once they knew they were available. Better to let the audience come to you. Asinius Pollio understood this, which is why he formalized the public recitation, or *recitatio*, early in the reign of Augustus.[26] Seneca the Elder says that Pollio was not comfortable with declamation (i.e., spontaneous and competitive speech making on set topics), so he sought literary renown through the public recitation of his own writings.[27] But the declaimers were social climbers, as their promoter Seneca must not not admit,[28] and participation in their activities would have been undignified for the ex-consul Pollio. The aim, however, of declamation was no doubt similar to that of recitation: to publicize the speaker and expose him to a network of influential listeners.[29] By reciting his compositions in public the author seeks to reclaim the authoritative presence that is in danger of being dissipated by the proliferation of writing. That he sometimes uses *recitatio* to prepare a work for further circulation via writing merely indicates his willingness to publicize himself through any means possible. Writing has become a necessity, but its influence can be obviated by new opportunities for personal contact. Even the library, which serves as storehouse for written texts, has a more sociopetal function than today: Lucullus's library, established in Rome in 73 B.C.E., was the location for cultural conversations as well as private reading.[30] And Pollio held his first recitations in the libraries he had placed in the Atrium Libertatis, site of the early archives of the Roman censors.[31]

Even writings that might seem to constitute depersonalized calls to political action and to take advantage of the liberating possibilities of written discourse tend on closer inspection to be instances of popular justice,
that is, personal attacks designed to intimidate the aristocratic opponent,
to console losers in political competition, or to inflame clients and followers to action.[32] Cicero's *Philippics* or the anti-Caesarian invectives are
examples of such tactics, but traces of other such scurrilous and ad homi-
nem writings abound, ranging from the inscribed sling bullets of the
Perusine War[33] to the dangerous *libelli* Otho burns as enemy forces
approach.[34] Yet with the possible exception of Cicero's claim to have
persuaded his nephew Quintus to change sides in the civil war via his
writings[35] and of T. Curtisius's use of *libelli* to stir a slave revolt under
Tiberius[36] such writings tended at best to preach to the converted. The
observation of E. J. Kenney rings true: "As an instrument for arousing
public opinion literature remained relatively powerless in large centralized societies until the coming of the printing press."[37]

4. Keep the Teachers in Line

Gellner tells us that "[a]t the base of the modern social order stands not
the executioner but the professor. . . ."[38] As guardian of identity, the
person behind the podium does as much to keep society in line as does
the person behind the gun.[39] The Romans were perhaps more inclined to
rely on executioners, or at least legionaries, but they understood the value
of professors as well. The first and perhaps most extended contact any
Roman would have had with literature was through his schooling.
Control schools and you would directly and indirectly shape the reading
habits of a generation of students. When confronted with the book market, however free it might be, former students would be predisposed to
choose in ways conducive to continuing aristocratic rule. Their selections
would be their own, but they would be nicely constricted by the old
school tie.

There are three ways to control a professor, and the Romans were
skilled at all: be him, buy him, or bully him. Livius Andronicus and Ennius tried the first. According to Suetonius they both taught school, in
Greek and Latin.[40] Years later Livius's version of the *Odyssey* was still a
staple in the curriculum[41] and Ennius's *Annales* were being discussed by
scholars and other aficionados.[42] Naevius, who apparently did not teach
school, was among those authors whose texts had not been circulated
much by the time of Crates' visit to Rome in 168.[43] Hence his *Bellum
Punicum* was available for the ministrations of Lampadio, who divided
the single *Carmen* into seven books.[44] Thus arrayed, it too was available
for further academic research and teaching.

Like Ennius and Livius, most teachers of literature, or *grammatici*, were far from highborn, a fact that made the large fees they sometimes collected that much more important to them. Like wage slaves everywhere, they could ill afford to offend their employers. Suetonius's work on the lives of the grammarians contains examples of professors who purchased their own freedom through the savings from their professional work. One such man, Staberius Eros, was the teacher of Brutus and Cassius.[45] The tutor of Augustus's children was paid 100,000 sesterces a year.[46] Remmius Palaemon, who earned 400,000 sesterces a year from teaching alone and a comparable amount from investments, regarded himself as the "judge of all poets and all poems."[47] The listing of such lavish sums reveals not just a certain wistfulness on the part of the archivist Suetonius, but also a recognition on the part of well-to-do Romans of the importance of keeping the professors on their side.[48]

Of course should the professors seek to free themselves from such influence or simply side with the wrong faction, there was always the option of banishment. In 161 B.C.E. the praetor was empowered to clear Rome of philosophers.[49] Similar action was taken against the *rhetores Latini* in 92 B.C.[50] The philosophers were again targets on several occasions during the early Principate.[51] Teachers were dangerous figures, not as fomenters of mass rebellion but as potential sowers of discontent among the elite and their would-be replacements. For whatever reason, the *grammatici*, or teachers of literature, seem to have gotten the point without being targeted for expulsion themselves. The curriculum they developed was painfully slow to absorb new authors and required them to be approached in a way that would have nullified whatever disruptive potential they contained within them.

5. TURN PAPER INTO STONE

Not all writing is disembedded. In fact, epigraphic writing, which was remarkably common in the ancient world, especially in urban areas, was deeply embedded, both physically and metaphorically.[52] It was difficult to move, or at least designed to remain in its original location; and it depended for its meaning on its relationship to a particular physical, social, and cultural context. A funeral inscription describes the occupant of the tomb to which it is affixed. A building dedication refers to the structure that it adorns. A dedicatory epigram marks the donor's relationship with the deity or cult honored in the locale in which it has been placed. The standard verb for the situating of an inscription or its monument is *loco*, that is, to place. And many a legal decree contains within it the instruction that it be posted in a much-frequented place: *celeberrimo loco*.[53] If the decree is not seen by enough people, its validity is at risk.

Inscriptional writing is long lasting, a consideration that constitutes the most obvious reason for its popularity as an analogue to literary writing. But other factors are also at play in the poets' allusions to the monumental or inscriptional nature of their texts: the embeddedness of inscriptions in a defined context, their availability to the public, their imperiousness, and, paradoxically, their evocation of the human voice.[54]

Consider the final poem of Horace's first lyric collection: *Odes* 3.30, the celebrated *Exegi monumentum*. The poet speaks of the fame and immortality he hopes to achieve through his poetic accomplishment and does so by developing a comparison between poetry and monument.

> Exegi monumentum aere perennius
> regalique situ pyramidum altius. . . .
>
> I have completed a monument more lasting than bronze
> built higher than the pyramids of kings. . . .
>
> (Horace *Odes*. 3.30.1–2)[55]

The reference to monuments situates Horace's claim with respect both to specific actions of the recent past and to the general cultural practice of constructing monuments and placing inscriptions on them. As Mary Jaeger has observed, the opening metaphor in this poem is the culmination of a set of references in the *Odes* to the building campaigns of Augustus and Agrippa, specifically the transformation of the Campus Martius from a field for exercise and assignation to the site of *monumenta* commemorating the achievements of the Roman nation and its leaders.[56] Horace locates his literary achievement among, and, to some extent, in competition with, the political achievements of his protectors. At a more general level, the ascription of monumentality to a collection of lyric poems is an attempt to assign to that collection the durability over time characteristic of stone monuments (such as the pyramids) and the bronze inscriptions often placed on them. As Corbier notes, bronze was the preferred medium at Rome for the publication of the most important and prestigious texts since it was regarded as especially durable.[57]

The durability Horace claims for his collection is of a particularly epigraphic sort, not just because of the allusions to *monumenta* and *tituli*, but because of his evocation of a recurrent theme of funeral inscriptions on Roman monuments.[58] As *Odes* 3.30 proceeds, it calls attention to the survival of the poet's reputation in, and in connection with, his place of birth in the vicinity of the river Aufidus. The Romanness of the other allusions in the poem, specifically the victory over Alexandria and the ascent of the pontiff, generate a contrast between Horace's location at the time his monument is constructed and his place of origin, exactly the contrast that characterizes many of the most striking Roman epitaphs, which call attention to the distance between the deceased's place of birth and place of interment. "Born at Tivoli, snatched by death at Aquileia," reads one;[59] "Rome is my homeland, my people hail from there,"[60] are the words inscribed on a tombstone in Armenia. That other poets played with this topos (e.g., Catullus 101 on the death of his brother, or the pseudo-Vergilian self-epitaph: "Mantua bore me, the Calabrians took me away, Naples holds me now")[61] is no argument against its epigraphical tone. Evocation of the topos is part of a general attempt on the part of Roman poets to assign to their creations preserved on paper the longevity and self-display characteristic of more public modes of writing.

Is this aspiration to permanence merely wishful thinking on the part of the poet, a lucky guess borne out by subsequent history? Or does Horace in fact offer the reader some reason to share in his self-confidence? The answer, again, is to be found in the references to inscriptions implicit in the poem and in the social context in which inscriptions function. An inscription is guaranteed permanence not just through the material on which it is written (indeed, ironically, bronze turned out to be one of the worst things on which to inscribe, since it was valuable and hence subject to reuse by succeeding generations);[62] equally if not more important is the context, physical and communal, in which the inscription is embedded. Horace alludes to the Capitoline and to the continuity of the pontifical rites associated with that site in part because they represent the permanence of the community for whom the monuments of Agrippa, Augustus, and others will be meaningful, and, by implication, the community that will supply the readers for Horace's poetry. He also alludes to the interplay between monument and community in the single verb *dicar*, on which the rhetorical movement of the whole ode turns. "I will be spoken . . .," he writes, meaning both "I will be spoken of" and "my texts will be recited." Much as at the end of book 4 of the *Odes* Horace projects his poetry into the future through the predicted survival of the Roman familial rites that form its occasion, so here he projects the future of his reputation and his poetry through its connection with the remembering Roman community. Even more specifically, the verb *dicar* reminds us that Roman inscriptions frequently exhorted the passerby to stop and read. By reading aloud, as was characteristic of the ancients, the reader quite literally speaks or gives voice to the one commemorated by the monument.[63] Thus the monumentality of Horace's accomplishment paradoxically is what guarantees its continuing vitality. But the paradox is no paradox at all if we keep in mind that the monument only functions properly in the context of a living, reading, interpreting community.

Horace's poetry ascribes to itself the power of inscriptions. It displays the author as does an inscription and it guarantees his longevity by placing him in a clearly defined yet potentially regenerative social context.

Both of these features characterize another well-known Latin poem, the dedicatory epigram of the Catullan *libellus*, one whose connection with inscriptions is equally strong, if not as widely recognized, as that of Horace *Odes* 3.30. In Catullus 1, as in the Horatian poem, the implied movement of attention is ultimately from the reader to the writer rather than the other way around. Written poetry, like spoken poetry, like inscriptions, works to make its subject present again as much as it seeks to communicate with its audience. The difference between Catullus 1 and Horace 3.30 in this area is chiefly a matter of degree, since Catullus advertises not just himself and his achievement but his social connections as well.

The poem enacts the dedication of Catullus's book of poems to Cornelius Nepos. As such, it recalls both dedicatory inscriptions generally and, more specifically, inscriptions that mark the dedicator's commitment to the dedicatee. The verb *dono* performs the dedication, while the description of the *libellus* as "having been given a smooth finish" (*expolitum*) characterizes it as the sort of prestige object appropriate for such an action: both high-quality books and marble statues receive this treatment.[64] The dedicatory aspect of the poem is maintained in the slight evocation of hymnic style (the repetition of the second person pronoun, *tibi . . . tu . . . tibi*)[65] and in the listing of the *erga* or accomplishments that justify the special honor bestowed on Nepos: that is, respect for Catullus's poetry and composition of the *Chronica*.

Mary Beard has described dedicatory inscriptions in temples, which testify to the dedicatee's commitment to patron or cult, as a process of "signing up for paganism."[66] The donor or dedicator expresses a public commitment which in turn marks him or her as affiliate of a prestigious group. More generally, anthropologists have noted that in traditional societies the circulation of prestige objects enhances the prestige of all involved.[67] In Catullus 1, the performance of a dedication to Nepos marks Catullus, whether ironically or not, as his affiliate and provides both men with a more privileged position in the public eye. In the penultimate line, this relationship is itself placed under the protection of a patron goddess (*o patrona virgo*) in another allusion to the extratextual process of ceremonial dedication. In other dedications, as in funeral inscriptions, one of the advantages sought by the dedicator is longevity, a longevity which, as we have suggested, derives both from the durability of the inscribed material and from the persistence of the community in which the inscription is situated. Catullus 1 fits this model well, for, as was indicated in chapter 4, the reference to survival "for more than one century" is a request to enter into the Italocentric cultural chronology characteristic of Nepos's work. Whereas Horace's lyric monument promises to outlast the pyramids through repeated reenactments by succeeding generations of Roman readers, Catullus's *libellus* seeks longevity through close attachment to Nepos and the cultural affiliations he embodies.

Viewed one way, the poem partakes of the characteristics of dedication of a prestige object, with the resultant display of author, patron, and text. At the same time, the poem, as lifeless written text, is necessarily dependent on other sources of meaning and vitality. Catullus signals an awareness of this fact precisely through his reference to the book of poems as a *libellus*.[68] Elsewhere in Latin (i.e., outside the set of texts that reinscribe Catullus's poetic ideals) *libelli* are ephemera: political pamphlets, shopping lists, and the like.[69] Their circulation on papyrus contrasts with the presumed longevity of marble and bronze inscriptions, and their placement on statues or affixed to walls as a form of prompt publication of political attacks or calls to action nicely captures in its opposition to the presumably elaborate rolls containing Nepos's *Chronica* (docti, Iuppiter, et laboriosi) the imagined relationship between Nepos and Catullus himself. For all its bravado the Catullan *libellus*, like the Catullan self, is a fundamentally dependent object. In poem 1, it draws upon and displays its connection with more stable sources of cultural authority and temporal persistence.

By describing their books of poetry in terms appropriate to inscriptions or public writing, Catullus, Horace, and other poets of the classical period undercut the dichotomy between paper and stone, or private and public writing, and seek to assign to their texts certain powers that they and Roman culture generally associate with inscriptions. The authorial persona, in its full social context, is displayed to passersby; longevity is secured; prestige is enhanced; and the community is indirectly reminded of the authority vested in remnants of the past. Perhaps most surprisingly, the association of written text with inscriptions secures the primacy of authorial presence, for just as epitaphs and dedications invite the "revoicing" of long-dead ancestors, so now the book hails the reader and commands his or her participation in the representation of the absent or deceased author. Thus the book, which might at first glance seem to signal the dislocation and diminution of aristocratic power, becomes a strategy for its reinscription and the "private" writing of literature demands acquiescence on the part of its reader with a force comparable to that of "public" writing on stone.[70]

There is a final dimension to the epigraphic analogy that must not be overlooked. For all that texts, both on scrolls and on monuments, articulate a wish to pass the boundaries of mortal existence, the choice to remember or forget is ultimately up to the living. The dead, as Lucretius observed, will not be around to appreciate the remembering of them that is occupying their descendants.[71] Vergil also understood this point, which is why in *Aeneid* 6 he assigned freedom from the endless cycles of death and rebirth only to those who in their lifetimes had been associated with a community that could through its continuity guarantee theirs.[72] This is one reason for Horace's connection of his lyric monument with the religious rites of the Roman pontiff: memory endures only as long as there is a remembering community. Even if the text survives, it is inconsequential without readers. If we are to understand the process of preservation through literature, then we must consider the motivations of the rememberers as well as of those who aspire to be remembered.

Here we find ourselves once again reckoning with the political and social advantages to be obtained by association with what Hobsbawm has called a "long-established cultural elite, possessing a written national literary and administrative vernacular."[73] By putting up monuments to deceased family members or friends and by circulating the texts of authors distant in time or space, survivors, like readers, seek to enhance their own prestige and to reaffirm their own connection with the authorizing elite of Roman society. By remembering they reaffirm the authority of the past and in so doing reassert their own authority over the present. This nexus of ideas explains why, in one of the few genuinely revolutionary texts in Latin, Horace's *Letter to Augustus* (*Ep.* 2.1), the writer can imagine the use of texts as wrapping paper in the spice market.[74] Just as he has denied the usefulness of past writings to the present, so he must acknowledge the possibility of such a determination on the part of future potential readers of his own work. But this is the exception that proves the rule, the case of a specialist who late in life is willing to be judged on what he regards as purely technical grounds. Otherwise writers, including Horace himself, are as happy to privilege the past as they expect their future readers to be.

6. KEEP AN EYE ON THE COMPETITION

Given the cohesiveness of the Roman system of literary circulation, in which writers and readers exchange recognition, regardless of the specific means of textual transmission (i.e., performance, purchase, inscription, or gift), we may well wonder how this system came into being and whether or how it underwent change. The passages discussed thus far in this chapter reflect a more or less stable system, with one innovation—public recitation—quickly incorporated into the general scheme. In fact, the means of producing and transmitting texts were not fixed in the Roman world, and stages in their evolution can be traced. Two developments deserve particular attention: the increased reliance on writing that characterized the period of imperial expansion, especially the second century B.C.E., and the competition between writing materials (papyrus versus parchment, roll versus codex) that characterized the postclassical period, especially the transition to Christianity. Perhaps the most significant lesson to be derived from a brief review of these developments is that, at least in the Roman world, social change was as likely to influence the direction of technology as the other way around. The written preservation of literature was a response to a variety of factors associated with the growth of the Roman Empire, while the adoption of the codex met the needs of a new, nonaristocratic sector of the reading population.

Early Latin literature, that is, the literature that replaced the songs of the *vates*, was, as argued in chapter 2, a literature of professionals. The plays and hymns composed by professionals such as Livius Andronicus, Plautus, and Ennius, were performed at civic festivals, and we assume, albeit without direct evidence, that works in other genres were read aloud at private gatherings and/or circulated in written versions through private channels. One other institution no doubt made use of written texts, and that was the school. While Plutarch's claim that the first "school of letters" was opened at Rome by Spurius Carvilius (i.e., late third century B.C.E.) probably refers to lessons for pay rather than schooling per se,[75] it seems likely that the same era that witnessed transformation in literary institutions saw major changes in education as well. Ancient tradition also reports that Ennius and Livius Andronicus taught (*docere*) in both Greek and Latin.[76] The coincidence of pedagogical and creative endeavors is worth reflecting on, for not only does it corroborate the view of literature as an essentially and not merely accidentally didactic and coercive institution, it also explains one means through which the texts of early Latin writers may have been preserved.[77] Indeed, one scholar has gone so far as to suggest that poetry was produced in the early era of Latin literature so that the teachers would have something to teach.[78] Whether this is the case or not, it is clear that teachers would have an interest in preserving written texts.

Another likely locus of textual preservation was constituted by the professional troupes of performers who would have needed the texts of Plautus and others as libretti for their paid performances.[79] The existence of groups of *Dionysou technitai* is attested for Greek-speaking Italy, and one assumes that comparable associations served a comparable function with respect to Latin productions. The establishment of the *collegium scribarum et histrionum* on the Aventine should probably be understood as the Latinization of the Greek guilds of *technitai*. While the preservation of texts is not specifically identified as one of the responsibilities of the collegium, it does not seem farfetched to imagine that the collegium in some way fostered this development, especially since both *scribae* and *histriones* would have had experience in record keeping (see chapter 2 above). Indeed, the phrasing used by Livy in describing the adoption of Livius Andronicus's hymn at the festival of 207 B.C.E. has led some scholars to infer that the text used had been employed on an earlier occasion and was resurrected for the new event.[80] If so, then the spectacular outcome of the festival, that is, the destruction of the Carthaginian army at Metaurus, would have taught all involved in the organization of the festival the value of a paper trail.

Another episode that provided the impetus toward the preservation of literary texts was the visit to Rome by the scholar Crates of Mallos in 168 B.C.E.[81] According to Suetonius, Crates' lectures in that year inspired certain members of his Roman audience to seek out and comment on texts that had not previously enjoyed wide circulation. Since the subject of Crates' lectures was grammar, and the Pergamene school, with which he was associated, took a particular interest in morphological peculiarities (as opposed to the Alexandrian school, which emphasized preservation of texts), it is not unreasonable to suppose that the texts resurrected in the wake of Crates' visit were characterized by linguistic difficulties or peculiarities. Moreover, the activities described in Suetonius's account chiefly consisted of oral presentation: the Romans imitated Crates by reading out and commenting on the texts that interested them.[82] Nonetheless, one aspect of this development appears to have been the copying and circulation of written texts. Thus Suetonius lists among the consequences of Crates' visit C. Octavius Lampadio's division of Naevius's *Punic War*, which had previously been written as a single uninterrupted text, into seven books. This divided version is reflected in later citations of the poem by book number.[83]

Another event of 168 is not always associated by scholars with the preservation and circulation of Latin texts, yet perhaps ought to be: the transfer of King Perseus's library to Rome.[84] This event marks the first reference to a Roman library; the persistence of the Greek loan word *bibliotheca* in Latin suggests that the institution, regardless of the date of its origin, was not native.[85] At other moments in ancient history (e.g., the creation of the Alexandrian Museum and the construction of the Palatine Library, as mentioned earlier) the development of a library served as an impetus not just for the collection of books already in circulation, but for the preparation of new books and copies of old books.[86] While there is no specific evidence linking the work of Lampadio and others on early texts of Latin literature to the arrival of Perseus's library, the two developments both reflect a high regard for the written literature of the past, one in keeping with Rome's transformation into an empire during this era.

Within a generation or two of the arrival of Crates the circulation of written texts is taken for granted by the satirist Lucilius. The fragments of his poetry show a concern with alternative spellings and peculiar word formations: interests of philologists, but interests that matter chiefly if a text is scanned visually.[87] More important, Lucilius invokes the soon-to-be-overworked topos of text as monument: in one fragment the poet refers to "illustrious pages" (claris cartis), transferring an adjective associated with the renown of aristocratic families (clarus) to the material means of preserving literature (carta, the Latin term for a "page" of papyrus text).[88] In another fragment the satirist observes, perhaps ironically, that "these monuments of your virtue are set out on pages" (haec virtutis tuae cartis monumenta locantur).[89] The juxtaposition of *monumenta* and *cartis* and the use of the technical term for the positioning of an inscription, *locantur*, may be intended to mark a contrast between Lucilius's faint praise of a character in his satire and the aristocratic monuments that have begun to spring up along the Appian Way. Regardless of tone or context, the fragment makes clear the expectation that literature consists of a written text and not just an oral performance and hints at the similarities, as well as the differences, between epigraphic and literary texts. Lucilius can thus be seen to anticipate the complex discourse of writing that characterizes Latin literature of the classical period and to enact at least one of the strategies by which writers of the classical period sought to maintain control of the written word, namely, identification of literature with monuments in stone.

In the postclassical period, the coexistence of text and performance persisted, but a new dynamic of writing emerged with the contrast between the papyrus roll and the parchment codex.[90] Eventually the parchment codex came to replace the papyrus roll as the primary means of written transmission of texts, especially among Christian authors. Reasons offered for the change are the relatively inexpensive nature of parchment as opposed to papyrus,[91] the possibility of preserving longer texts in a codex as opposed to a papyrus roll,[92] the special interest of the Christians in differentiating their Gospel from the Jewish roll,[93] and the greater convenience to the reader offered by the codex form, especially the ability to flip back and forth between pages as opposed to rolling and unrolling a long scroll.[94] Valid as these arguments and observations may be, they are limited in their explanatory power because they assume a uniformity in social function and context of reading and writing among different groups and at different periods of time within the Roman world.[95] The choice between papyrus and parchment or between roll and codex was not simply a matter of value-free technological alternatives but had economic, political, and social implications as well. In essence, the papyrus roll was appropriate for reading understood as a social phenomenon within a stratified community of writers, readers, reciters, and listeners, while the codex was characteristic of a more private, egalitarian, and—to return to our central concern—disembedded approach to reading and writing.

Use of the papyrus roll for literary texts is taken for granted by all pagan classical Latin authors. Yet many of these authors indicate awareness of other tools for writing. Catullus demands the return of his *codicilli*, that is, wooden tablets with wax surfaces that were routinely used as notebooks among the Roman elite.[96] Pliny the Elder, in a famous passage on the history and use of papyrus (*H.N.* 13.68–90), acknowledges the importance of both papyrus and parchment in preserving the records of humankind, although he gives pride of place to papyrus.[97] Martial seems to refer to the use of parchment in the production of deluxe or novelty copies of classical authors (Menander, Livy, Vergil) to be presented as gifts.[98] The material record corroborates and expands this picture of diverse technologies available simultaneously. Thus vellum or parchment documents datable to the early second century B.C.E. have been found on the site of a Roman fortress on the Upper Euphrates.[99] The discovery makes one wonder what sort of material Naevius's *Bellum Punicum* was preserved on before Lampadio divided the single volume into seven books. The exciting finds at the Roman imperial fortress of Vindolanda in Britain provide evidence of writing tablets of a type previously "almost entirely unknown—thin leaves of wood, written in ink with a pen."[100] As one of the scholars responsible for the decipherment and publication of these tablets puts it, "[t]he discovery underlines the crucial importance of establishing a typology of writing materials and their uses. These leaf tablets must have been cheap (or free) and easy to make. They completely undermine the argument that writing materials were available only to the well-to-do. . . ."[101] The tablets date to the period 90–115 C.E., not long after Pliny's paean to the preservative power of papyrus. Finally, the survival of a significant number of papyrus codices, including pagan literary texts such as the plays of Menander, with the earliest dated to the second century C.E., makes problematic the traditional associations of papyrus with roll and of codex with Christianity.[102]

The eventual displacement of papyrus rolls by parchment codices cannot be explained simply in terms of relative cost and ease of use; whose ease and whose cost are important factors. If the papyrus roll was associated with elite literature, it may be because the elites wanted it that way. And the displacement of the roll by the codex may be less a technological than a sociological development. Most scholars who discuss the prevalence of the papyrus roll as the favored means of transmitting pagan literary texts during the classical period comment on the inconvenience the roll poses to the reader. Some of this inconvenience is intrinsic to the roll itself, for example, the difficulty of cross-reference, the need for boxes or *capsae* for transporting rolls, the possibility of damage through friction. But some of the inconvenience is to be attributed to the mode of writing, which was often continuous with only occasional marks of punctuation and relatively rare use of headings and other readers' aids. The relative rarity of these aids is all the more striking given the fact that they did exist, were relatively systematic in nature, and can be found on a signifi-cant, albeit small, percentage of surviving texts from the classical pe-riod.[103] One is forced to inquire why the Romans did not make use of developments that were clearly available to them.

The answer would seem to lie, once again, in the social dimension of reading and writing. Since reading of literature was often carried out in less-than-private contexts—the schoolroom, dinner parties, *recitationes* —and done by specialized readers who had the opportunity to prepare in advance, then the conveniences that the modern reader, accustomed to solitary endeavor in the study or the library carrel, is in need of are not of such great importance to the ancients. Indeed, one might go so far as to argue that the material difficulties associated with gaining access to litera-ture, like the stylistic and linguistic difficulties, were convenient means of keeping literature in the hands of the well-to-do elite. Or, to put the same point in a less cynical way, the aristocratic context in which the reading of literature was conducted provided no impetus for the adoption of tech-nological innovations or alternatives.

A similar argument can be made with regard to expense. Sometimes luxury items are desirable precisely because they are expensive.[104] The papyrus roll may have been preferred despite the availability of the parch-ment codex or other materials because and not in spite of its costliness and consequent elitist connotations. Catullus's reference to the physical appearance of the book he dedicates to Nepos fits this argument, as does (paradoxically) Martial's experimentation with novel bookformats as in-dicated by the epigrams at the beginning of book 14.[105] In either case simplicity and thrift are antithetical to the enterprise of giftgiving.

If the aristocrats were by the very form in which literature was trans-mitted indirectly keeping it to themselves, individuals of lower rank were not without access to literary stimulation.[106] Public libraries would have provided some opportunities for those with access and leisure.[107] Inscrip-tions communicated not just regulations, but poetry as well. Mimes and plays as well as competitions at speechmaking would have reached a siz-able audience. Just what percentage of the population of the Roman em-pire could read is very much under discussion by scholars today.[108] The variety of communities contained within the Roman world makes it im-possible to describe reading as an exclusively elite activity.[109] Freedmen entrepeneurs,[110] village scribes,[111] military record keepers,[112] and stone-cutters,[113] not to mention personal secretaries, stenographers, and their teachers,[114] all enjoyed some degree of literacy and constituted a potential audience for imaginative literature of some sort. If the elite authors and the producers of deluxe editions ignored this audience (or pretended to) others may not have. The Christians in particular, who have long been associated with the production of codices, sought converts among precisely these sectors of the population.[115] And the codex, in turn, was better suited to what one assumes to be the less leisurely opportunities for reading available to the members of the various "subelites" (to borrow Keith Hopkins's term) of the empire.[116] Exactly the features that differentiate it from the papyrus roll—economy, portability, and ease of use by the nonprofessional reader—are the characteristics that would differentiate the needs of less elite readers from the opportunities available to their wealthier and higher-status contemporaries.

An instructive parallel to the development and proliferation of codices alongside other technologies of writing is perhaps to be found in the development and spread of the Coptic language alongside Greek and Latin in Roman Egypt during the first and succeeding centuries C.E.[117] Coptic, which originated with the transliteration of demotic Egyptian into the Greek alphabet, eventually came into widespread use as a means of communication among Egyptian-speaking subelites. It played an important role in the transmission of nonelite ideologies, but also in more mundane activities such as the recording of contracts and the maintenance of accounts. Clearly, readers were available who either could not or would not rely on Greek (the language of the most elite sector of the population in Roman Egypt) as a sole means of communication among Egyptian-speaking subelites. Coptic originated and persisted, to quote Keith Hopkins, "as a script of protest."[118] He continues, "[T]he invention and diffusion of a new script gives us a general insight into the educational level and ideological aspirations of lower social strata in a Roman province, of which we are usually ignorant, and which therefore we often choose either to underestimate or to ignore."[119] It may well be that the popularization of the codex, and in particular its connection with the antielite ideology of Christianity, is a technological development parallel to the linguistic development represented by Coptic. And indeed, in this context it should not surprise us to learn that many of the earliest surviving codices contain Coptic texts.[120]

The argument advanced here concerning the monopolization of certain modes of literary production and circulation and the subsequent emergence of countermodes would take much additional investigation and discussion well beyond the scope of this study. Yet if it turns out to be true, it would not be the last time in history that an elite was undermined by its own success. In the Roman world, the stability, prosperity, and sense of cultural unity fostered in part by the aristocratic project of Latin literature made possible a rise in educational level, however erratically, in large sections of the empire. In time, partly through collaboration with disgruntled members of the elite, partly through the ossification of the elite tradition, and partly through the emergence of alternative forms of communication, this subelite (or more precisely, this set of subelites) was transformed into the new interconnected elite of institutionalized Christianity, one that maintained its own sense of the past, its own artificial, fixed literary and administrative vernacular, and its own array of dominant and subaltern subjectivities.

To recapitulate the argument of this chapter: Latin literature continued its support of aristocratic hegemony in part through its ability to manage the tension between performance and writing to the advantage of performance. By calling attention to the problem, authors sought to negate it; by denying a financial motive they sought to resist the potentially liberating effects of commodification and the marketplace in favor of the continued privileging of aristocratic prestige; by controlling the channels of circulation they reinforced the importance of recitation; by doubling as "teachers" they predisposed their readership to make particular kinds of selection; by assimilating their compositions to inscriptional writing they sought to situate them within a living, remembering, validating community; and by privileging certain materials and technologies of writing they ensured literature's status as a prestige object. In short, in the Roman world, rather than liberating the subject, the written text extended over space and time his or her dependence on and attachment to the authorizing presence of the aristocratic performer. Written literature thus contributed powerfully to the amalgamation of Roman identity to subject status and helped to reconstitute the potentially free reader of the widely circulated literary text as a subject subject of an imperial regime.

Chapter 6

ROMAN WOMEN'S USELESS KNOWLEDGE

THE SCARCITY of writing by women should be regarded as one of the enigmas of the Latin literary tradition. Extensive evidence points to the existence of literate women, ranging in social status from stenographers and personal secretaries to aristocratic ladies of the highest rank, yet only scattered texts and references attest to the production of literature by women. With the growth of the Roman world, men were able to parlay the record-keeping function of the scribe and the advisory role of the "good friend" into the prestigious positions of poet and author. Women, it would seem, were stuck with the jobs of amanuensis, audience, and inspiration.

One possible reason for the survival of so few writings by women is what Amy Richlin has nicely described as the "triage of time."[1] Texts composed by women may simply have been regarded as less worthy of preservation than those composed by men. Yet if this is the case, it seems likely that the assigning of a low priority to women's writing began earlier rather than later in the trauma center of history. As James Zetzel has noted, in the case of Latin literature (as opposed to Greek, where the large and growing number of literary papyri creates a different dynamic of preservation), a text survives into the modern era because someone early on decided that it was worth preserving in a deluxe edition.[2] This characteristic of textual transmission does not in itself imply that a text's disappearance is always or exclusively due to disrespectful treatment in antiquity, but such treatment is certainly a possibility that needs to be considered in accounting for the relative absence of surviving writing by women.

Another way of explaining the contrast between women's literacy and women's writing would be simply to assign the scarcity of the latter to the generally repressive and patriarchal nature of Roman society. Such an observation, however, fails to account for the relatively greater availability of women's writing from equally or more severely patriarchal societies (e.g., Greece and early Christianity). In addition, to blame patriarchy is simply to state the obvious, thereby forestalling potentially more illuminating inquiries as to why patriarchy, especially of the Roman sort, should object to the development of women's literature, and how, in view of the literacy of women, it could keep them from producing literature.

Finally, a particular and straightforward tactic of exclusion can be acknowledged from the outset: women in ancient Rome were by and large denied access to the higher education available to men.[3] Yet even this consideration is less telling than it might seem at first glance, since in Roman education exposure to literary classics was a component of elementary as opposed to advanced schooling. The latter was devoted to rhetorical training preparatory to a career in public life and/or to specialized study of technical disciplines such as philosophy and law. Ovid's daughter (if such she was) may not have had the practice at declamation that so obviously shaped his poetry but he regarded her as very learned—*doctissima*—nonetheless in the things that mattered when it came to the writing of verse (see *Tristia* 3.7.31). And Martial, in an epigram belittling aristocratic pretensions of his era, expresses a wish for a simple home, fresh water, well-fed slave—and a wife who isn't particularly well educated (sit non doctissima coniunx [2.90.9]). One possible inference is that well-educated wives constitute a familiar problem among his readership.

As has been noted elsewhere in this study, it is a truism of political philosophy that where ideology fails to stabilize a social practice, force alone is rarely sufficient to do the trick. In the case of Roman women's silence, we need not minimize the role of force, in the form of destruction or nonpreservation of texts or denial of educational opportunity, to perceive the usefulness of exploring the ideological factors that both justified such acts of repression and functioned on their own as strategies of exclusion and silencing. In other words, the problem of Roman women's silence can be understood in terms of the intersecting issues of construction of female subjectivity (or lack thereof), invention of literature as a coercive institution, and patterns of aristocratic domination that characterized the Roman world. As the following discussion seeks to make clear, exploration of even a single word—in this instance, the poetic keyword *doctus*, in its differential application to men and women—can bring to light the complex ways in which literature interacts with other social practices to produce historical consequences of significant import.

Let us return, then, to the beginning, that is to say, to the institutionalization of literature as a written, professional, elite enterprise, in order to consider the ways in which literature constitutes itself as a male enterprise and situates women accordingly.

Ennius's description of the aristocrat's good friend lists the characteristics to be expected of an adviser and by implication of the literary products that constitute advice.[4] The first in a series of epithets applied by the poet to the good friend is *doctus*, an adjective that also figures prominently in the description of a wide range of females, human and divine, throughout Latin literature including the Muses,[5] the Cumaean Sibyl,[6] the mistresses of elegiac and amatory poetry,[7] Ovid's daughter,[8] the wife Martial prays not to have,[9] and various women aristocrats.[10] The use of the epithet *doctus/a* thus provides a window on the larger problem of women's literature at Rome, for if "learnedness" (or more precisely "doctitude") is a characteristic of the producer of literary advice and also a characteristic of women, then we may legitimately ask why learned women are not in turn authors.

When Ennius describes the good friend of the Roman aristocrat as *doctus* he means not only that the friend is wellinformed but also that he is capable of applying his knowledge in making judgments or offering advice about specific problems. He employs his knowledge in a hortatory context (suadet, line 278). Because of his understanding of the past (multa tenens antiqua, line 282) he is able to foresee the likely outcome of alternative courses of action, a point reinforced by the word *prudentem* (line 285), with its etymological reference to "foresight." In short, the *doctus vir* is both learned and discerning.

The association of the epithet *doctus* with discernment is implied in two other passages of Ennius as well. In one instance, *Annales* 250, *docta dicta*, or prudent sayings, are said to have been rejected in the mad rush to war, along with *sapientia* (wisdom or taste), the *orator bonus* (good, or aristocratic, orator), and *ius* (concern with what is right or just). In a second passage (*Annales* 15–16) the adjective *doctus* is apparently applied to Anchises, who is said to have received the gift of prophecy from his divine paramour Venus:

> Doctus†que Anchisesque Venus quem pulcra dearum
> Fari donavit, divinum pectus habere.
>
> (Ennius *Ann.* 15–16)

Otto Skutsch, the distinguished editor of the fragments of Ennius, obelizes the adjective *doctus* on technical metrical grounds, namely, that Ennius nowhere else lengthens through use of -*que* a syllable ending in a short vowel plus *s* that occurs in the fall of the foot. Whether the corruption, if it is one, occurred between the time of Ennius and the quotation of the line, with *doctus*, by Probus in the first century C.E., or occurred during the transmission of the text of Probus, we cannot tell. But it seems worth noting that the text of Probus, as preserved in the manuscripts, connects this passage of Ennius with Anchises' appearance in the sixth book of Vergil's *Aeneid*, where, as a figure in the Underworld, Anchises is represented as capable of providing his son Aeneas with both scientific knowledge or *doctrina* and a call to action based on an inspiring vision of the future.[11] Probus's connection of the Vergilian passage with the Ennian has to do with the ascription to Anchises of prophetic powers. Yet the assignment of the epithet *doctus* to one who has prophetic powers as a manifestation of his erudition nicely corresponds to the double significance of *doctus* identified in the Good Friend episode, that is, "learned" and "discerning."

The *Thesaurus Linguae Latinae* distinguishes uses of *doctus* with the meaning "knowledgeable" or "erudite" (cuiusvis doctrinae vel artis aut praeceptis aut usu peritus) from occurrences in which it means "shrewd," "discerning," or "prudent" (astutus, callidus, catus, prudens, sapiens).[12] In fact, these categories of meaning are, in Roman epistemology, two sides of the same coin. Ovid captures the ambiguity or, perhaps better, duality in a pun when, at *Fasti* 3.816, he asserts that anyone who has well-pleased Pallas will be *doctus* (qui bene placarit Pallada doctus erit): that is, such a person both will have shown discernment in giving the goddess her due and will enjoy knowledge as a gift of the goddess whose province it is. Cicero, Seneca, and other Roman moralists belabor the point that theoretical knowledge and/or erudition are incomplete unless made applicable to concrete situations calling for judgment or discernment. No doubt they argue this position as forcefully as they do because it is under attack from purveyors of specialized knowledge for its own sake (whom they usually identify as Greek). The view of the Roman moralists holds fast, and, indeed, throughout the history of Latin literature the decision to compose, especially to compose moral philosophy, in Latin, as opposed to Greek, implies acceptance of the inseparability of knowledge and advice, which in turn presupposes a connection between knowledge and discernment.[13]

In a passage from Cicero's *Brutus* that is key to understanding the connotations of the word *doctus*, Cicero takes the Ennian conception of knowledge as shading over into discernment a step further when he contends that right judgment, or discernment, implies the possibility of a knowledgeable account.[14] His specific concern is to explain how it comes about that the experts (*docti*) and the common people (*vulgus*) arrive at the same judgment as to what constitutes good and bad oratory. Cicero is of course defending his own popular success to an audience of cognoscenti who might be expected to regard it as evidence of inferior technique, but in so doing he articulates a view of the role of the *doctus* that is implicit in many other texts. The *doctus* and the *vulgus*, he asserts, will arrive at the same judgment, but the *doctus* will be able both to be more specific about that judgment (that is, the common people can tell good oratory from bad, but cannot tell better from best) and to explain how the relevant instance of good oratory came about. In addition, the learned evaluator—what Cicero calls the *doctus existimator* (*Brut.* 320)—has the advantages of alacrity and even of prescience. He can pass correct judgment on an orator at a single glance (uno aspectu [200]), and, as Cicero

indicates in a passage on the decline of Hortensius's oratorical skills, he
can discern the seeds of decline at an earlier stage (*Brut.* 320). With the
use of the word *existimator* at both 200 and 320, Cicero has brought us
back to the primal scene of aristocratic literary production, since, as was
argued in chapter 2, it is the need of the aristocrat to prepare himself for
evaluation and the potential of literature to provide both the preparation
and the evaluation that create the opportunity for the alien enterprise of
literature to assume a central role in Roman culture. In Cicero's *Brutus*,
as in Ennius's *Annales*, the appropriate evaluator of aristocratic conduct
is described as *doctus*. In these passages and others alluded to above, the
connection between evaluation and learnedness ultimately runs both
ways, for just as the best evaluator is one who is knowledgeable, so the
knowledgeable man's knowledge is useful precisely to the extent that it
can be enacted as evaluation.

The parallel between the Ennian situation and the Ciceronian can be
extended even further, for just as the knowledge and discernment of the
good friend ultimately entitle him to offer advice, so in Cicero's view
knowledge and discernment of oratorical practice are prerequisites for
the production of good oratory. Indeed, the true *doctus existimator* in the
Brutus is Cicero himself, who, at the end of a long career as a successful
orator, has earned the right to pass judgment on orators of the past and
to advise, evaluate, and exhort orators of the future.[15]

The association of learning with discernment and with prudent action
characterizes other fields of endeavor besides oratory. In *Aeneid* 6, for
example, the Cumaean Sibyl, who accompanies Aeneas through the Underworld, is described as *docta*. The reference is not to any generalized
knowledge about the past or present, but to her ability to bring her understanding of the Underworld to bear on the actions of her mortal companion: Aeneas, terrified by the sight of the Gorgon, Harpies, and other mon-
sters, would have assaulted them with his sword, had not his learned
companion (docta comes) "admonished him [*admoneat*] / How faint
these lives were—empty images / Hovering bodiless."[16] In a later and less
poetic version of Hell, the emperor Nero is reported to have prefaced his
musical performances with a speech to the judges stating, in effect, that
they, being wise and learned (sapientis et doctos), would know how to
evaluate his performance and act accordingly.[17]

But it is in passages referring to the production and judgment of poetry
that the term *doctus* is most frequently attested.[18] Indeed, in the context
of poetic evaluation the traditional Roman construction of the relationship between learning and performance nicely coincides with the Alexandrian ideal of the scholar-poet. A *doctus poeta* knows the poetry of the
past, knows how to write, and knows how to evaluate his own writing
and that of others. The Roman Alexandrians, it is true, do not share

Cicero's assumption that the *docti* and the *vulgus* will arrive at the same estimations, but this difference is attributable more to the distinctive contexts of the performance of oratory—geared to the public—and of poetry—composed for a select audience—than to any struggle over the meaning of *doctus*. In Cicero's view, as in Catullus's, being learned implies the ability and the right to pass judgment as well as the ability to create works that can stand up to the judgment of others among the learned.

Where Roman Alexandrianism does manifest an important difference from the Ennian and Ciceronian treatment of learnedness is in specifically raising the issue of learned women, or *doctae puellae*. Virtually from the outset of this sector of the Latin literary tradition, the potential of women to share in the three components of learning (i.e., knowledge, evaluation, and production) hovers about the male-authored text, like some Underworld ghost terrifying the brave yet naive poet-hero. In the world of Ciceronian oratory, the possibility of female learning or female performance scarcely needed to be taken seriously (although we do hear, not long after Cicero's death, of a reputable oratorical performance by Hortensius's daughter).[19] But in the narrower context of aristocratic poetry it takes a concerted effort to keep women from exercising all the perquisites associated with learnedness. Indeed, to the extent that poetry at Rome presents itself as the product of a sympotic environment the problem of the place of women intensifies, since it was characteristic of the Italian symposium, as opposed to the Greek, to include women as equal participants.[20] And so the poetry of Catullus, Propertius, Ovid, and others invokes the ideal of the *docta puella* precisely in order to regulate and marginalize her, turning the potential evaluator and competitor in the poetic sphere into a mirror that reflects the male's idealized self-image back upon itself. It is the poetry itself, independent of any external considerations of education, law, or status, that silences the female voice even before it can speak.

The *locus classicus* for this process of privileging the learned woman but only to the extent that her erudition redounds to the male's credit is poem 35 of Catullus. There a *Sapphica puella* (35.16), more erudite than a Muse (Musa doctior [17]), is presented as the one potential obstacle to the poet Caecilius's acceptance of Catullus's invitation to join him in Verona. The opening lines of the poem emphasize the mutuality of the relationship between Catullus and Caecilius: one is the other's *sodalis* (line 1), a peer and fellow in the comradeship of poets; each is expected to hear the thoughts of the other (quasdam volo cogitationes / amici accipiat sui meique [5–6]); the physical location of each is specified by name; and the indirect address of Caecilius via the apostrophe of the papyrus that will carry Catullus's poem conveys a respectful hesitation to issue a direct command to a peer. The relationship Catullus hopes to enact resembles the one he describes himself and Calvus as sharing in poem 50. But while in poem 50 the female goddess of retribution Nemesis is invoked as a figure outside the relationship between Catullus and Calvus who can punish the latter should he fail to reciprocate the former's poetic ardor, in poem 35 the human woman is the obstacle to the realization of the homo-social bond and, it would appear, to the completion of Caecilius's poem on Magna Mater, twice described as *incohata*, that is, begun but not complete (35.13, 35.18).[21] The *puella*'s status as *docta* characterizes her as learned and capable of evaluation (her passion for Caecilius being coincident with her reading of his incomplete poem) but the action that flows from her discerning judgment disables both herself and Caecilius. She is consumed by an out-of-control passion (impotente amore [12]) while he is stuck with an incomplete poem. Catullus' own poem alludes to Sappho's famous description of the symptoms of sexual jealousy, with special reference to heat and torpor, yet it ascribes them to the girl who has the benefit of Caecilius's presence rather than to Catullus, who, like Sappho, is in the position of observing a relationship of which he is not part.[22]

The redirection of Sapphic symptoms, from the observer to the observed, corresponds to the redirection of female erudition that characterizes this poem—and Roman Alexandrianism—more generally. Rather than facilitating male performance or generating a counterperformance in its own right, as might be expected from the Ennian and Ciceronian constructions of the *doctus*, the Catullan *docta puella* prevents the male from achieving his full potential. Her learned evaluation and the passionate outburst it provokes short-circuit the proper male-on-male process of *aestimatio* that Catullus regards as generative of the best, that is, his own, sort of poetry. As we shall see, this theme is repeated, albeit with variations, throughout the classical Latin tradition.

In the Propertian corpus, to choose a set of texts connected in theme and style to Catullus, the "doctitude" of the elegiac mistress is an expression both of the equivalent demands of love and poetry and of the separation of the poet-lover from run-of-the-mill mortals. Rather than holding the male back from his true poetic calling, as she does in Catullus 35, the *docta puella* of elegy keeps him from inauthentic choices of lifestyle and/or genre. Yet despite her success she is once again outsmarted by the male poet, for now instead of moving into a reciprocal relationship, as the traditional view of the interaction among *docti* would imply, she is situated as the upper half of an asymmetric master-slave arrangement, chiefly to be castigated as such. In the case of Catullus 35, female erudition leads to passion and inaction. In Propertius it prompts poetic activity and aspiration, but only on the part of the male poet. She will be his judge

(2.13a.11, 14), and his ability to meet her standards will be his primary claim to fame (1.7.11); but should she venture to approve of another, then the title of *docta* will be taken from her: nec dicet "Cinis hic docta puella fuit" ("nor will the passerby say 'this ash once was a *docta puella*'" [2.11.6]). The possibility of independent achievement, implied in the ascription of erudition, is held forth only to be withdrawn. The knowledge the *puella* possesses is rendered useless except insofar as it relates to the advancement of Propertius's own ambitions.

The Propertian management of the *docta puella* is perhaps clearest in poem 2.13, where the sequence of thought runs as follows:[23] It was Love that made me write the kind of poetry I write—learned, like that of Hesiod, Orpheus, and Linus, yet with the purpose of mesmerizing not trees or wild beasts, but Cynthia (sed magis ut nostro stupefiat Cynthia versu [2.13.7]). Of course, it's not a beautiful girl or one with noble ancestors I'm after; rather, I hope to have the pleasure of being read in the lap of a *docta puella* (me iuvet in gremio doctae legisse puellae [11]). With her as judge, I can dispense with conflicting assessment (confusa fabula [13–14]) on the part of the populace at large (populi [13]). I can even put up with the enmity of Jove. And so at the time of my death there will be no grandiose funeral fit for a nobleman or a foreign potentate (17ff.). Instead, my three books of poetry—and you—will be there, and inscribed on my grave will be two verses: "he who lies here dust and ash was once the slave of a single love" (qui nunc iacet horrida pulvis / unius hic quondam servus amoris erat [35–36]). Yet what's the point in living if you reject me? Too late will you lament me when I'm dead. In vain will you reciprocate my invitation when I'm a voiceless shade: how do you expect powdered bones to speak?[24]

The poem imagines an aristocracy different from the one that makes it possible for the historical Propertius to write his poetry. There will be a separation from the common people, but on the basis of erudition and taste as opposed to ancestry or appearance. Master and slave will be recreated, but in an erotic context only. A funeral will fix the reputation of the deceased, but the achievements celebrated will be literary rather than military or political. The parallels call attention to what is missing: the learned companion during life (i.e., Cynthia) has nothing to say, and the *laudatio* at death is spoken by the deceased himself. So complete is the absorption of the voice of the *puella* by the poet that even in his death she is silent because he is silent. To be sure, inasmuch as Cynthia is a fictional creation it is quite literally true to say that she will not be able to speak once her poet-ventriloquist is dead. But if she can be represented as calling the poet back, or perhaps, as I believe is implied by the word *revoco*, at last reciprocating his ardor, why can she not be imagined as speaking for herself? The possibility of mutual assistance implied in the identification of Cynthia as *docta* and by the funereal context with its opportunity for survivor's laudation is invoked only to be subverted. As lifeless text she has no blood to offer Propertius's ghost. As *docta puella* she has no voice through which to enact her knowledge.

By raising the issue of speech after death, elegy 2.13 looks forward to two of the most famous Propertian elegies, famous precisely because they envoice women. In elegy 4.7 the situation at the end of 2.13 has been reversed. Instead of Propertius dead and Cynthia speechless, Propertius is alive and well, and Cynthia, although dead, has found her voice, which she puts to good use rebuking Propertius for his faithlessness and dismissing her rivals from his household. In 4.11 the aristocratic Cornelia delivers her own funeral oration, justifying her behavior during her lifetime as worthy of her ancestors. That women are only allowed to speak at length once they are dead is an important, but by now unsurprising, feature of these poems. More striking is the fact that this delayed ventriloquism is also a characteristic of writers' relationships to other men. In those few instances in which words are put into the mouths of living men, either the strategy receives elaborate *apologia* (as in certain of Cicero's philosophical dialogues), or the aim of the *prosopopoeia* is to insult (as with Cicero's mockery of Clodius in the *Pro Caelio*), or the speaker in question is absent (as with the *Pro Milone*). To take on the voice of the living is a dangerous act. It poses aesthetic risks (will your mimicry be adquate?) but more important it constitutes a co-opting of the self-presentation of a fellow aristocrat, a "devoicing", that at least according to Cicero, constitutes one of the greatest insults possible in an honor-bound society.[25]

In the case of Roman love poetry, the postponement of female ventriloquism until after death (Cynthia and Cornelia in Propertius, various heroines in Ovid's *Heroides*) suggests that respect for another's voice may not be a gender-based phenomenon. Living women, like living men, are not envoiced in literary texts because at least to some extent they are capable of speaking for themselves. This explanation would accord with much that we know about the historical status of Roman women, as suggested at the outset of this chapter. Silence in a court of law or political assembly was taken for granted, but free and open speech in other settings seems to have been for Roman women, at least as opposed to Athenian, something of a matter of course. In this respect, then, poetry's postponement of female ventriloquism embodies the cultural knowledge of its originative context. Indeed, in one instance in which a living woman is ventriloquized, she appears as a writer, not a speaker. In the poem in question (Propertius 3.12) Aelia Galla is denied precisely the performance context that would have validated "her" verse as an authoritative exercise. Instead she appears as the "author" of a ghostwritten verse epistle in which she promises, not coincidentally, to remain faithful to her absent husband: vincit Penelopes Aelia Galla fidem ("Aelia Galla surpasses the fidelity of Penelope") are her final words.

The very fact that elegiac, and especially Propertian, poetry respects the protocol "don't speak for others until they're dead" makes the virtual absence of living female voices among the poets that much more striking a deviation from social practice and points to the possibility of an intentional intervention in the lives of women, a preemptive strike to prevent the development of independent and independently subjective female poetic voices. Elizabeth Harvey has argued with respect to the ventriloquism of Sappho perpetrated by male poets (specifically Ovid and John Donne) that "the suppression of actual feminine speaking enables and authorizes the fictional reconstruction of the (other) feminine voice, and ventriloquism thus functions as a poetic enactment of the mechanism of censorship at work within the broader cultural context. It is not in spite of the destruction of Sappho's verse, then, but partly because of it that she was so frequently acclaimed and imitated by subsequent poets. . . ."[26] A similar argument can be advanced with respect to Greek tragedy, where male citizens' assumption of the role of female heroines both responds to and reinforces the absence of female voices in the community. In the Roman context it seems that the poetry itself (or at least certain kinds of poetry and certain poems) is a mechanism of censorship more stringent than that found in the culture at large. Its redefinition, in the case of women, of the conditions for poetic creation works in opposition to other cultural factors that might have facilitated the development of female voices.

The struggle to silence learned women intensifies as the imperial period progresses in part because there are more learned women to silence and in part because the ability to command the attention of an audience is one of the few features distinguishing aristocrats from their competitors for social power.[27] Doctae puellae become important commodities in the symbolic economy and as such are subject to the same dynamic of sequestration and display that characterized Roman culture at least from the time of Cato. As human beings, as carriers of aristocratic bloodlines, as social actors with the potential to shape the distribution of resources, they are poised to enter into full partnership in the management of private and public affairs. Strictures on their public performance thus become more important even as they become more difficult to enforce.

The triple nature of male "doctitude"—learning, discernment, performance—is reinscribed in texts of this later period. For example, Martial at 4.86 exhorts his libellus to be pleasing to the learned Apollinaris. If he takes you to heart (si te pectore), if he takes you to mouth (si tenebit ore, i.e., reads you aloud), then you need not fear the jeers of the malignant, nor will you become wrapping paper (actually, a tunica molesta) for fish. If, on the other hand, Apollinaris condemns you, you'll be lucky to turn into scratch paper for student exercises. The learned judgment of Apollinaris has serious implications, and while he himself may not be depicted as a poet, nonetheless he is regarded as capable of reperforming the poet's text in a socially consequential way. In epigram 2.77 the bad practice of the versemaker Cosco is specifically contrasted with the successful epigrams of Martial, Marsius, and "the learned Pedo." Pedo's learnedness explains why he is capable of writing the kind of epigram which, as Martial puts it, although long needs no shortening.[28]

The ability of *doctae puellae*, like *docti viri*, to evaluate others' work and even to promulgate it is taken for granted by Martial's contemporaries. But as in the Augustan milieu, so in the later imperial context the parallel between men and women does not extend to the production of literature. When Pliny praises his wife to his mother-in-law (*Ep.* 4.19) he attributes the younger woman's literary inclinations not to her mother's rearing of her, nor to any teacher, nor to her own volition, but to her passion (*amor*) for himself. She puts Pliny's verses to the lyre but writes none of her own. She sits silently at his recitations, but takes in "with very eager ears" (avidissimis auribus [4.19.3]) the praises directed at him. Moreover, it is for precisely these reasons (his ex causis [4.19.4]) that Pliny predicts endless concord between the two of them, a mysterious harmony composed of his voice and her silence. Like Catullus and Propertius before him, Pliny situates the *docta puella* at the primal scene of poetic production, that is, the occasion of *existimatio*, but denies her any active role whatsoever.

In contrast to Catullus and Propertius, who share his tendency to silence learned women, Pliny articulates a justification for the passivity of the *docta puella*, specifically in letter 1.16 concerning Pompeius Saturninus and his learned wife. The letter in question praises the literary versatility of Saturninus, noting his skill in history, oratory, and poetry. With respect to his poetry, both the form and the content, we are told, resemble the works of none other than Catullus and Calvus. Immediately after this reference, Pliny proceeds as follows: "Recently he read to me some letters: he claimed his wife wrote them. . . . Whether they are his wife's, as he insists, or his own, as he denies, he deserves equal glory, either for composing them, or for taking so virgin a wife and returning her learned and accomplished" (uxorem quam virginem accepit tam doctam politamque reddiderit [1.16.6]). Sherwin-White, in his commentary on the letter, evades the striking sexual, educational, and economic implications of this phrase by pointing out that Roman women married young. This piece of information hardly accounts for Pliny's easy equation of sexual initiation with education or his articulation of the perfect interconvertibility of male potency, poetic acumen, and high return on investment within the exchange system that constitutes Roman culture. Saturninus takes a virgin out of circulation, educates her, then re-enters her, via her writings, into the public sphere, as a more valuable commodity.

The position of Saturninus's wife (who remains nameless in the letter) as both grammatical and physical object of her husband's actions is not the only explanation for her voicelessness. Underlying Pliny's language, which is blunt enough as it is, is an even coarser image. Saturninus, in Pliny's view, got himself a virgin and knocked some sense into her. By filling one of her orifices, he fills another as well, to such an extent that one cannot tell whether her words are her own or her husband's. Ovid expresses a similar notion in *Amores* 2.4 in the course of enumerating the "hundred reasons why he is always eager for sex" (centum sunt causae cur ego semper amem):

> sive es docta, places raras dotata per artes
> sive rudis, placita es simplicitate tua.
> est quae Callimachi prae nostris rustica dicat
> carmina: cui placeo, protinus ipsa placet
> est etiam quae me vatem et mea carmina culpet:
> culpantis cupiam sustinuisse femur:

> If you're *docta*, your artistic endowment delights me,
> if you're dopey, your naivete turns me on.
> One girl says Callimachus is a clod compared to me,
> I love her as she loves me
> Another finds fault with me and my poems:
> how I long to get between her thighs.

(Ovid *Am.* 2.4.17–24)

Once again, being learned implies the right to pass judgment: the transition in thought from the *docta puella* to the one who evaluates the poet's verse is seamless. Only this time the poet asserts his right to counter a negative evaluation by turning the judge into a sexual object. The passage looks forward to Pliny, explaining how Saturninus managed simultaneously to educate and to silence his wife, and backward to Propertius, whose desire to be read in the lap of the learned girl (in gremio doctae . . . puellae [2.13.11]) can now be seen in a new light. There reading substitutes for sex, just as here in Ovid sex counteracts a certain kind of reading.

The poetry of Ovid clarifies two final aspects of aristocratic literature's commitment to the silencing of women, namely, the connection with economic anxiety and the conditions under which envoicement might become possible. At *Ars amatoria* 2.277ff. Ovid invokes the familiar theme of the present day's privileging of gifts over poems:

aurea sunt vere nunc saecula: plurimus auro
   venit honos, auro conciliatur amor
ipse licet venias Musis comitatus, Homere,
   si nihil attuleris, ibis, Homere, foras.
sunt tamen et doctae, rarissima turba, puellae;
   altera non doctae turba, sed esse volunt
utraque laudetur per carmina; carmina lector
   commendet dulci qualiacumque sono.
his ergo aut illis vigilatum carmen in ipsas
   forsitan exigui muneris instar erit.

The golden age is now: from gold is the most abundant honor derived
   and by gold is passion procured.
So, Homer, you've come to your lover's surrounded by Muses—
   if you haven't brought a gift out you go
Yet there are learned girls, although few in number,
   and plenty unlearned, though willing to be.
Let both types be praised in song: you want the reader
   to praise your poems in soft moans
With either kind a poem worked out at night
   just might take the place of a tiny gift.

                                 (Ovid *Ars* 2.277–286)

Apart from confirming that reading can be both prelude and analogue to sexual intercourse, the passage aligns erudition, and all that it implies, with aristocratic disdain for tawdry wealth. *Ars* 3.551 takes the argument a step further by representing the exchange of song for sex as part of a religious economy in which the quest for cash is tantamount to sacrilege. "There is a god in bards," writes Ovid, "and they carry on commerce with the heavens. . . . It's a sacrilege to expect a price from learned poets—a sacrilege, alas, that no girl fears" (a doctis pretium scelus est sperare poetis).

We have come to expect from Ovid such knowing manipulations and to assume self-interest precisely where it is denied.[29] Yet it is also in the poetry of Ovid, of all places, that we encounter a silence in which a female voice can at last make itself be heard. The problem, from the standpoint of traditional Roman society, is that this silence is purchased at the cost of Ovid's exile. It is only in his isolation from the Roman world that he can begin to imagine certain aspects of that world in radically different ways. He must leave his culture in order to critique it. The poem in which the possibility of the contemporary female voice (as opposed to the myth-ical voices of the heroines of the *Heroides*) is encouraged rather than sub-verted is *Tristia* 3.7, addressed by Ovid to a young woman named Perilla, sometimes taken to be his stepdaughter. Just as Catullus marks his deference to Caecilius by having the papyrus containing his poetry request Caecilius's presence, so Ovid approaches Perilla indirectly, instructing his letter to speak to her on his behalf.

The similarity to Catullus 35 ends there, however, for now it is Ovid the poet who by his absence constitutes an obstacle to Perilla's creative endeavors. The verse epistle may find her among her books and remind her of the *studia communia* (common pursuits) she shared with her stepfather (11), but it fears (or rather Ovid fears, for partway through the letter's speech the voices of poet and poem merge) that Ovid's misfortune may be slowing her down. He had, after all, been critic and teacher of her literary endeavors and his absence, as well as his punishment for his scandalous *libelli*, explain her failure to compose (21ff.). Despite his distance from her, he performs his duty as friend and adviser and exhorts her to continue to write, but not in the manner of her father: *non patrio more*, (12). Perilla's verse must not teach anyone how to love (pone, Perilla, metum. tantummodo femina nulla / neve vir a scriptis discat amare tuis [29–30]).

The content of Ovid's exhortation to Perilla repeats motifs familiar from the elegiac lover's attempts to persuade his mistress: old age will ruin your beauty (33); possessions come and go (41–42); nothing remains except the products of talent (43–44). Only now, instead of composing a song of seduction designed to make a mistress succumb, the poet encourages Perilla to use her erudition to full effect in producing poems that, like his, will outlast Caesar and the grave. There are hints of the female ventriloquism and sexual possession that characterize other Ovidian productions, as when Ovid declares that it was he who led Perilla to the springs of the Pegasidae (15) and he who observed her talent in her tender virginal years (primus id aspexi teneris in virginis annis [17]). Yet these remarks can just as easily be construed as establishing the basis on which he, though not in fact her father, can speak to her as if he were. Moreover, the poem specifically does not anticipate Perilla's response, but limits itself to persuading her to break her silence. The closest we get to a description of the content of her poetry is reference to its avoidance of amatory instruction and its description as aristocratic occupation and sacred rite (bonas artes et tua sacra [32]). The two sources of authority, aristocracy and religion, that were invoked in *Ars amatoria* as means of securing a woman's silent acquiescence are here ascribed to the potential achievements of a female addressee.

The imaginative and moral transformation that permits Ovid to view Perilla in this new light costs him, in Eliot's words, "not less than everything." "Look at me," Ovid declares, "although I am bereft of home and country and all of you, although everything that can be taken has been, nevertheless I am companion and beneficiary of my own spirit [*inge-*

nium]: not even Caesar has rights over this. Though someone slay me with a sword, nevertheless my fame will endure. As long as Mars's victorious city Rome surveys the conquered world from on high, I will be read."[30] The future Ovid envisions is necessarily constructed from the remnants of the past: slavery, conquest, and domination he has not yet imagined away. Indeed, as we shall see in a later chapter, Ovid's poetry from exile facilitates in significant ways the late Augustan project of pacification of the provinces. But in one respect, at least, the new world that Ovid and Rome survey from their respective vantage points will differ from the old: in it women as well as men will break the silence of the grave through the survival of their own words.

Chapter 7

AN ARISTOCRACY OF VIRTUE

IN THE MATTER of birth as in other matters, Roman society of the early principate exhibits a tension between ideology and practice. Implicit in the Roman notion of an *ordo senatorius*, into which members are inscribed at birth, or in the distinctions between slave and free, *Romanus* and *municeps*, is a premium on beginnings of self, family, and nation. At the same time, the relative frequency of movement across what might appear to be rigid boundaries (slave/free, decurion/equestrian/senatorial) weakened the authority of beginnings, to the advantage of achievement, connections, and luck. This tension, which might have been expected to dissolve with the transition from one social system to another, was in fact perpetuated by the political stagnation and anachronistic modes of acculturation characteristic of the era. In contrast to the common view of the period as one in which all orders of society cowered before the mighty tyrant, politics during Seneca's lifetime (4? B.C.E. to 65 C.E.) might better be described as an equilibrium of balanced antagonisms between princeps, aristocrats, and arrivistes, while education promised social mobility to those most skilled at manipulating the symbols of a backward-looking and status-obsessed cultural tradition.

It is in this broader context of a competition or tension between the age-old authority of birth and the birth of new forms of authorization that the Senecan injunction to begin to live (*incipe vivere*) must be understood.[1] The readers of Seneca's dialogues and letters—like virtually all readers in the Roman world—would have been members of the economic elites, and thus would have benefited from certain aspects of the fixity and stratification of the Roman social system.[2] Yet as ambitious adolescents[3] or self-made adults[4] his audience could be expected to appreciate and capitalize upon opportunities to break free of the limits of birth and surpass the achievements of their predecessors. By posing the challenge of beginning to live, Seneca confirms and appropriates the very power that authorizes the reader's privileged existence while at the same time holding forth the promise of a life that transcends the limitations of each reader's beginning. Like authors more generally who seek the benefits of circulation of their texts without reduction in the authority of performance, so Seneca seeks to combine the advantages of tradition and innovation, of hierarchy and egalitarianism, through invention of an aristocracy of virtue. His treatises and letters, although intended for wide circulation, nonetheless advertise the intimacy of his relationship with his addressees and invite the reader to evaluate his own and his patients' ethical progress. He recreates the scene of *existimatio* familiar from early Latin literature and infuses it with an atmosphere of reciprocity whereby he evaluates the addressee while the readership evaluates his evaluation. Under the changing conditions of literary production, the performer has perforce become a writer; but Seneca also makes of the writer a performer, one whose claim on our attention consists not of surpassing the honorable, outer-directed achievements of his ancestors, but of living a certain kind of life. For all that its authority is located elsewhere than that of the traditional aristocracy of birth, Seneca's aristocracy of virtue ultimately faces social and political challenges comparable to those confronted by its rival.

While the social dimension of the Senecan philosophical project could be explored from any of a number of angles, it is through its representation of itself as a new beginning that we will consider it here. Roman society's paradoxical approach to beginnings—as locus of privilege and as problem to be overcome—is reflected in Senecan beginnings variously conceived. Whether we regard the "beginning" of a Senecan treatise as its origin in the literary and cultural tradition, its intervention in the lives of its readers, or simply the words with which it opens, the Senecan beginning manifests its ambivalence with regard to its own powers of authorization. Ultimately, as we shall see, Seneca seeks to escape the problem of beginnings in his own era by positing an ur-beginning, a beginning of beginnings, that authorizes and sustains precisely the contradictory project on which he is engaged. But first it will be useful to examine in some detail the Senecan beginning in its generic, cultural, and textual instantiations. Such an investigation will help to establish the ideological effect of Seneca's intervention in Roman culture and will inevitably generate a different account of Seneca's place in ancient culture than the one that emerges when he is viewed exclusively through the lens of Stoic philosophy.

The generic point of departure, or beginning, for the Senecan philosophical project is the traditional upper-class Roman performative genre of moral exhortation.[5] From a strictly generic standpoint, his works stand outside the mainstream of didactic literature (e.g., Hesiod, Aratus, Lucretius) characterized by address of a student by an expert instructor.[6] Moreover, while at times Seneca adopts the therapeutic posture characteristic of other Hellenistic philosophers, philosopher as doctor is but one of the many specialized expertises Seneca subsumes in his more distinctively Roman role of exhorter. By writing in Latin (instead of Greek, still the language of technical philosophy), by directly addressing friends and rela-

tions, by posing practical moral dilemmas and exhorting to new forms of
behavior, Seneca situates his treatises in the Roman hortatory tradition
and thereby claims for his own texts the authority both of exhortation as
a performance occasion and of the literary tradition (e.g., the treatises of
Cicero, the speech of Anchises, the *disticha Catonis*) dependent thereon.
His treatises lay claim to the authority of parental advice, mentor's guid-
ance, national and familial exempla, and self-interrogation in the presence of intimates—all conventional aristocratic modes of control over
thought, word, and action, in Rome as in other traditional societies.[7]
The social function of such exhortation is both to transmit the dominant
ideology in readily comprehensible form (i.e., create appropriate subjectivities for the maintenance of the social structure across time) and to
correlate specific instances of ethical choice with the general principles it
prescribes. The criterion of validation of exhortation is neither truth nor
beauty, but effect; hence in Seneca's case it is the origin of his project in
the (recreated) context of exhortation that legitimizes the relentless flow
of aphorisms, the shifts of stylistic register, and the logical contradictions
characteristic of his works.[8]

Even the arrogance of self-advertisement, damaging to Seneca's reputation in ancient as in modern times, has its beginning in his assumption
of the hortatory mantle. If effect is the measure of advice, where better to
seek it than in the person of the adviser? The Epicureans understood this
well, with their promulgation and circulation of letters of the master.
Seneca acknowledges it in his identification of the source of authority in
Demetrius the Cynic ("not a teacher but a witness of the truth is he")[9] and
in his reference to the enhancement of consolatory authority to be derived
from consoling oneself.[10] Thus the use of self as exemplum in Seneca's
philosophical works, especially his letters, is authorized by the performa-
tive/literary tradition in which he writes. At the same time, the generic
imperative toward self-exemplification is supplemented by the more
broadly social and political imperative to match, even outstrip, one's
predecessors.[11] Hence Seneca's claim to equal Epicurus in talent and influence,[12] the need to embrace and thereby restrict Demetrius,[13] the competitive urge, in the final texts, to advertise familiarity with the least compelling aspects of the Ciceronian exemplum.[14] The beginning of Seneca's
project in the Roman genre of exhortation is a circumstance whose presence is felt everywhere: no feature of the texts quite escapes it.

Yet escape, that is, an authentically new beginning, is precisely what
the text seeks. By writing in Latin instead of Greek and by opting for
exhortation, Seneca misses out on the opportunity to participate in the
technical debate of specialists. The hortatory mode itself, which Seneca
clearly differentiates from the exposition of dogma, does not readily lend
itself to lucid analysis of technical issues. Nevertheless, in numerous pas-

sages, from the meditation on time in *De brevitate vitae* to the analysis of the corporeality of the good in letter 106, Seneca struggles to develop a dogmatic approach within a hortatory framework, often signaling the shift by use of a key word or phrase such as *ratio* (reason), *scio* (to know), or *probo* (to prove). Whereas earlier philosophers had tried to minimize the role of exhortation—which they called *parainesis* in Greek—by making it subordinate to the articulation of philosophical dogma, Seneca reverses the implied status hierarchy, making technical argument and exposition but one component of his larger, culturally grounded project of exhortation.[15] Much like the emperor Augustus before him, who, as Andrew Wallace-Hadrill has recently argued,[16] sought to coordinate the separate, specialized expertises of law, philology, and antiquities in the interests of the Roman state, so Seneca seeks to subsume dogmatic philosophy in his cultural project of offering moral advice. The tensions and faultlines in Seneca's prose, sometimes ascribed to the drama of the soul's encounter with evil,[17] have a more mundane explanation as the predictable outcome of the writer's struggle against the authority of his own text's beginnings, a struggle that (not accidentally) parallels that of Seneca's insecure yet upwardly mobile readers. Seneca's treatises seek to maintain the privileges of their inception while denying the limitations that follow therefrom.

Given the inherent contradictions of the Roman social order and the ambivalence Seneca reveals toward the literary form he adopts, we should not be surprised to learn that the new beginning he proposes for his readers is equally ambivalent with regard to the social and cultural environment in which it is created. As Edward Said has observed, virtually all beginnings contain elements of that which they intend to disrupt or replace:

> It is, however, very difficult to begin with a wholly new start. Too many old habits, loyalties, and pressures inhibit the substitution of a novel enterprise for an established one. When the Old Testament God chooses to begin the world again he does it with Noah; things have been going very badly, and since it is his prerogative, God wishes a new beginning. Yet it is interesting that God himself does not begin completely from nothing. Noah and the ark comprise a piece of the old world initiating the new world.[18]

What God chooses, Seneca cannot avoid: the creation of a new life out of the materials of the old. A life that purports to be egalitarian, carefree, and at ease is in fact fashioned out of the political, aesthetic, and economic anxieties afflicting the very audience Seneca proposes to liberate. Although these anxieties are apparent throughout Seneca's treatises, our focus, once again, will be on their urgent expression at the (literal) commencement of Senecan texts.

The standard rhetorical strategy of the opening of a Senecan treatise—the claim to privileged knowledge—contradicts the repeated assertion that wisdom or virtue is available to all.[19] Seneca's insistence on his own expertise is to be differentiated from the didactic poet's advertisement of his own superiority to the addressee, for Seneca frequently includes his internal addressee among the ethical elite in opposition to a larger unspecified group of mortals who are invited to observe the dramatic interaction of Seneca and his friends. In *De providentia*, the cause of the gods, which Seneca will plead, is juxtaposed with the brief developed by doubting mortals (manente lite . . . causam deorum [*Prov.* 1.1]). At the outset of the *De brevitate vitae*, the greater part of mortals (maior pars mortalium) reveal their ethical ineptitude, in implicit contrast to the knowledgeable author.[20] In *De vita beata*, Gallio is informed that while all men desire the good life, they are blind to the means of achieving it [21]—the implication being that Seneca and Gallio are exempt from the company of the ethically sightless. Life, the passage continues, is not a simple country byway which anyone can traverse with ease, but a well-traveled highway whose very popularity is its danger. Along it moves the crowd leaderless as sheep, following rumor this way and that until their journey turns into a stampede in which each is led to destruction by others and in turn destroys those around him. In their behavior the masses of humanity simply repeat the political folly of the electoral assemblies who are surprised to hear the names of the candidates they have elected. Reliance on majority opinion, the reader is reminded, is the logic of the lowest in society.[22] Seneca and Gallio seek what is best (optimum [*Vit. beat.* 2.2]) and look forward to the fulfillment of the aristocratic dream of secure possession of eternal well-being (possessio felicitatis aeternae [*Vit. beat.* 2.2]). The distinction between the stampeding crowd and the followers of Seneca, soon to be secure in their permanent estate, is both a slur against the critics who prompt Seneca to defend his moral authority in the second half of the *De vita beata* and an assimilation of the philosophical life to the political prejudices of the rich and highborn. The idealized reader of Seneca's treatises, while ostensibly invited to learn more about the Stoic approach to providence, mortality, the good life, etc., is in fact put in the position of Cato's *existimatores*, called upon to evaluate the performance of the *vir bonus*. Virtue may create its own nobility, but it is a nobility that mimics the old aristocracy's strategies of theatricality and disdain.[23]

In a similiar vein the aristocratic obsession with orderliness and decorum revealed at the outset of *De ira* runs contrary to the numerous injunctions elsewhere in Seneca's writings against concern with appearance and style.[24] Anger, we learn at the commencement of the treatise dedicated to its management and elimination, is to be condemned because it violates the social norms of decorum and taste.[25] It cannot control itself (inpotens sui est),[26] forgets decorum (decoris oblita), ignores relations (necessitudinum immemor), persists beyond reason in its undertakings (in quod coepit pertinax et intenta, rationi consiliisque praeclusa), is set in motion by trivialities (vanis agitata causis), and is unfit for the investigation of the just and true (ad dispectum aequi verique inhabilis). The angry man is recognizable by his hideous appearance, which Seneca catalogues and anatomizes for the reader's edification. Gleaming eyes, red face, quivering lips, clenched teeth, bristling hair, forced breathing, crackling joints, groans and bellows, spluttering speech, pounding fists, and stamping feet make of anger a vice that is deformed as well as detestable (nescium utrum magis detestabile vitium sit an deforme [*Ira* 1.1.14]).

Only secondarily is the issue of anger's destructiveness raised, and then with a recurrent emphasis on its danger to the upper echelons of society. Anger causes murder and poisoning—and the auctioning of goods of leading citizens (principum sub civili hasta capita venalia, [*Ira* 1.2.1]). Anger destroys the notable foundations of noble cities, creates wastelands—and turns mighty generals into examples of bad fortune (memoriae proditos duces mali exempla fati [*Ira* 1.2.2]). When directed against large groups, it has led to the slaughter of assemblies, the butchery of the plebs—and the promiscuous condemnation of whole populations (in perniciem promiscuam totos populos capitis damna⟨tos⟩ [*Ira* 1.3.1]). It is anger's potential to destroy order, dissolve boundaries, and trample on hierarchies that makes it peculiarly dangerous and singularly inappropriate for members of the aristocracy. Thus, in the very act of condemning the reckless violence of Rome's dominant classes, Seneca reasserts their claim to privileged treatment.

In the area of economics, Seneca's evasion of the tension between birth and achievement is betrayed in a particularly striking manner. Philosophical *otium*, although proffered to the reader as a way of avoiding the risks and losses inherent in social and economic competition, merely opens space for reenacting the property owner's anxiety over loss of capital and for redeploying the contradiction between personal acquisition and aristocratic inheritance. From the opening of the collection of moral letters, Lucilius is commanded to lay claim to his birthright (vindica te tibi [*Ep.* 1.1]) and to seize control of the one possession that his truly his, namely time (omnia aliena sunt, tempus tantum nostrum est [*Ep.* 1.3]). Yet to do so he must involve himself in what Seneca calls the business of wisdom (sapientiae negotium, [*Ep.* 85.37; cf. 35.1, 68.9, 75.7]) and in the calculation of income and expenses (ratio mihi constat impensae [*Ep.* 1.4]). No matter how diligently the *proficiens* works, he cannot make headway against the dissipation of time's capital. He is reduced to poverty in spite of himself (causas paupertatis meae reddam [*Ep.* 1.4]). The most he can hope for is an augmentation of philosophical or ethical capital through the creation of memorable sayings (*Ep.* 64.8–10; 52.7–8). Even then, the capital will not be his to enjoy, for like a good paterfamilias he must leave behind more than he has received so that others will be able to enjoy the privileges of inheritance (sed agamus bonum patrem familiam, faciamus ampliora quae accepimus; maior ista hereditas a me ad posteros transeat [*Ep.* 64.7]).

Even the process of giving and taking advice is implicated in the revised economic order of the principate. What Cicero regards as an essential characteristic of friendship, namely, the unfettered exchange of frank advice,[27] is commodified in Seneca's relationship with Lucilius. "Here's a little something for the plus side"(lucellum [*Ep.* 5.7]). "I owe you another daily installment" (diurnam tibi mercedulam debeo [*Ep.* 6.7]). "This letter must be paid for" (pro hac epistula dependendum [*Ep.* 8.7]). Through the medium of language, social obligation is reassessed in financial terms. In the course of exercising his own prerogative as a retired statesman, cultural leader, and *amicus maior* to Lucilius, Seneca undermines the aristocratic code of *beneficia* by which the prerogative was initially assigned.

Sexuality offers a final perspective from which to explore the Senecan text's failure to liberate itself from its social and cultural origins and the strategies Seneca employs to mask the dependence of his new life on the material and psychological makeup of the old. For the Romans birth established a dividing line between the sexually privileged and sexually compelled, with freeborn men on one side and women and slaves on the other.[28] The special treatment of two marginal or transitional groups, freeborn youth and freedmen, reinforced the central divide: young *ingenui*, who as *pueri* might be mistaken for legitimate targets of sexual aggression, were protected by the identifying *bulla*, or phallic amulet, while freedmen, slaves by birth but free in status, could jokingly be described as performing sexual duties—*officia*—for their former masters.[29] Yet just as in the realms of economics, politics, and aesthetics, the transitional status of Roman society can be seen as authorizing new forms of behavior and creating modes of evaluation alternative to those established by an hereditary aristocracy, so in the area of sexroles and sexual behavior the possibility of a nonaristocrat's rise to power through sexual services,[30] the expanded opportunities for female participation in the economy and in court politics,[31] and the adoption on the part of the tyrants Caligula and Nero of sexually subversive practices such as crossdressing, incest, and homosexual marriage[32] created, at least at the upper levels of society, a new type of conflict between birth and achievement. As I have argued elsewhere, the elite sectors of Roman society in the late republic and early principate underwent a transition from a sex and gender system based on the principles of honor and shame associated with peasant societies to one more closely resembling that of contemporary urban centers.[33] The lurid accounts of sexual outrages that proliferate in the era are at least in part attempts to identify appropriate limits on behavior in an era of radical change.

Neither Seneca's text nor his reader escapes enmeshment in the sexual tensions and crosscurrents of the era. In a series of passages, the sexual prerogatives of freeborn males and the *verecundia*, or reserve, designed to veil those privileges from the less fortunate, are taken for granted as essential components of the Stoic dispensation. Thus the opening paragraph of the treatise on the constancy of the wise man (*De constantia sapientis*) informs us that there is as much difference between Stoics and other philosophers as there is between males and females (tantum interest Stoicos, Serene, et ceteros sapientiam professos interesse quantum inter feminas et mares). Each group is useful, but one was born to command, the other to obey (altera pars ad obsequendum, altera imperio nata sit). Some wise men seek to flatter and cajole (molliter et blande) like slave doctors (domestici et familiares medici); the Stoics, in contrast, take the manly approach (virilem ingressi viam), avoiding the pleasures of digression. The differentiation here, expressed in the sexual code words *molliter*, *blande*, and *virilis*, plays upon the contrasting sexual behaviors expected of the *cinaedi*, or sex slaves, of the Roman household and the businesslike Roman *pater*.[34] So too in *De providentia* Seneca reminds the reader that slaves are admired for their sexual forwardness (licentia, audacia), sons for their modesty and self-restraint (modestia, disciplina [*Prov.* 1.6]). The women who are lucky enough to be publicized beneficiaries of Seneca's advice owe their good fortune either to the inescapable bonds of motherhood (i.e., Helvia), or, in Marcia's case (*Consolatio ad Marciam*), to distance from the weakness of womanly spirit and a long-proven mental toughness (exploratum iam robur animi [*Marc.* 1.1]).

The discussion above of Seneca's transferral of contemporary economic concerns into the new life of the Stoic *proficiens* alluded to the economic rationalization of the supposedly liberal relationship between author and addressee. In the sexual realm, a similar conflict between the ideology expressed by the text and the behavior demanded of the reader encountering it becomes acute and involves not just the internal reader (i.e., the addressee of the treatise or letter), but the external reader as well (i.e., the audience, ancient and modern). To put it simply, while proclaiming the inherited values of upper-class male sexual conduct, Seneca sets in operation a mode of reading that requires the reader to be an accomplice in his own violation—a humiliating state of affairs according to traditional Roman sexual ethics.[35]

Here is Seneca's account of his own encounter with a text of Lucilius:

Librum tuum quem mihi promiseras accepi et tamquam lecturus ex commodo adaperui ac tantum degustare volui; deinde blanditus est ipse ut procederem longius. Qui quam disertus fuerit ex hoc intellegas licet: levis mihi visus est, cum esset nec mei nec tui corporis, sed qui primo aspectu aut Titi Livii aut Epicuri posset videri. Tanta autem dulcedine me tenuit et traxit ut illum sine ulla dilatione perlegerim. Sol me invitabat, fames admonebat, nubes minabantur; tamen exhausi totum. Non tantum delectatus sed gavisus sum. Quid ingenii iste habuit, quid animi! Dicerem 'quid impetus!' si interquievisset, si ⟨ex⟩ intervallo surrexisset; nunc non fuit impetus sed tenor. Compositio virilis et sancta; nihilominus interveniebat dulce illud et loco lene. Grandis, erectus es: hoc te volo tenere, sic ire. Fecit aliquid et materia; ideo eligenda fertilis, quae capiat ingenium, quae incitet.

I received your book as you had promised me, and I opened it at leisure with the intention of reading it. I wanted just to take a little taste, but it so charmed me that I decided to go further. Very nice it was, as you can tell from this: it seemed smooth, not like your body or mine, but at least at first glance like Livy or Epicurus. But then with such sweetness it seized me and dragged me off that I read it all the way through without taking a break. The sun called, hunger warned, clouds threatened—and still I swallowed it whole. This was beyond pleasure—it was ecstasy! What talent that thing of yours had, what spirit. I would say "what thrust" if it had ever settled down, ever risen up after taking a break. No, this wasn't thrust, it was endurance. Your way of fitting things together was manly and upright, yet still somehow charming and at times gentle. You're big, you're taut:[36] stay like that, keep it up! Oh, and your topic wasn't bad either. Keep picking a fertile one, the kind that will grab and arouse that talent of yours. (Seneca *Ep.* 46.1–2)

A remarkable passage. The writer begins as the controller, the subject of active verbs, the one who explores a new text at his convenience, and determines to sample only a portion. The text—which soon becomes indistinguishable from Lucilius himself—is smooth, like a beardless boy, not like a mature and hairy man. Then somehow the tables are turned, the controller becomes the controlled (note the switch to the accusative pronoun *me* and the passive participle *delectatus*, applied to Seneca). The only action left for Seneca is swallow it whole, drink it all down. Yet far from being humiliated by his "passivity" Seneca rejoices in what he has encountered—the force, the endurance that provide a pleasant surprise. Lucilius is congratulated on a job well done, and offered tips on preparing for the next encounter. Seneca the reader is not only penetrated by Lucilius the writer, but becomes a willing accomplice in the continuation and repetition of that act of intrusion.[37]

In the passage just discussed, the sexually subversive nature of the Senecan enterprise is muted by ascription of passivity to the author himself in the uncharacteristic role of reader. But can we doubt that the same process is initiated when an unsuspecting reader begins a Senecan text? *Arma virumque, Cynthia prima, Aeneadum genetrix*, the poets sing, fashioning an external reality, access to which authorizes the poet to continue. Cicero, too, imagines a world beyond the intercourse of writer and reader, one peopled with the likes of Q. Mucius augur (*Lael.* 1.1), resonant with the voices of Atticus, Quintus, and Marcus himself (*Leg.* 1.1), in which the interruption of the author's voice is cause for apology (*Fin.* 1.1). Senecan openings, in contrast, are invasive and unmediated: they situate the reader in a conversation already ongoing and refer to a world outside that defined by speaker and interlocutor only to deny its claims to validity.

Consider in this connection the beginning of the treatise on providence (*De providentia*):

> Quaesisisti a me, Lucili, quid ita, si providentia mundus ageretur, multa bonis viris mala acciderent. Hoc commodius in contextu operis redderetur, cum praeesse universis providentiam probaremus et interesse nobis deum; sed quoniam a toto particulam revelli placet et unam contradictionem manente lite integra solvere, faciam rem non difficilem, causam deorum agam.

> You have inquired of me, Lucilius, why it is, if the universe is directed by providence, that many evils befall good men. This would more appropriately be considered in the context of a work in which we could prove that providence presides over everything and that god is involved in our affairs. But since it is pleasing to pluck one small portion from the whole, and to resolve a single issue while leaving the rest of the brief intact, I will accomplish no difficult task, I will plead the cause of the gods. (Seneca *Prov.* 1.1)

Proclamation of the interlocutor's confidence in the author, clear articulation of a problem, implied dismissal of alternative solutions: such rhetorical strategies we might expect of any moral exhorter, ancient or modern, and can find paralleled throughout the Senecan corpus. More striking here is the absolute irrelevance of the external reader to description of the project at hand. It is Lucilius's question and Seneca's answer that together provide the opportunity for and set limits to the discourse that is to follow. As if to advertise this insouciance with respect to the reader, Seneca employs the impersonal verb *placet* (it is pleasing) without explicitly mentioning whose pleasure is served by the restriction of the treatise to one portion (*particula*) of a whole (*totum*).[38] Whereas conventional apostrophe, as found in hymns, or the dramatization of a figure from the past, as in Ciceronian dialogue, serves to draw a distant figure closer, to make familiar and apprehensible the sources of religious or ethical authority, Seneca's enstrophic play of *tu* and *ego* creates an inaccessible dialogue, inward directed and self-sustaining.[39] Yet for all its independence of the reader, the discourse between Seneca and his addressee intrudes itself upon us unapologetically and insists upon our cooperation in this very intrusion. To do otherwise, we quickly discover, is to side against the gods, to miss the moment of access, the window of opportunity, the *particula* that promises us insight into all the mysteries of the ethical universe.

The opening of the *De beneficiis* engages the reader in a similar interplay of part and whole, exposure and concealment, violation and seduction:

> Inter multos ac varios errores temere inconsulteque viventium nihil propemodum ⟨indignius⟩, vir optime, Liberalis, dixerim ⟨quam⟩ quod beneficia nec dare scimus nec accipere.[40]

> Among the many and various errors made by those who live rashly and without plan, my good man Liberalis, almost none would I call more unfitting than the fact that we do not know how to give or receive benefits.
>
> (Seneca *Ben.* 1.1)

Humans make many mistakes we learn, but only two types of error are to be of concern in this treatise. Why? What qualifies the writer to make this decision? By what criterion was the selection made? These issues are of no interest to the self-possessed voice of authority.[41] An opposition is established, or at least implied, between those who live rashly and those who do not (cf. the beginnings of *De brevitate vitae*, *De vita beata*, and *De providentia* discussed above), only to be dissolved in the first person plural *nec . . . scimus* ("we do not know . . ."). Are we, then, among the rash in need of correction? Or are we asked to take a stand with the one whose powers of discernment allow him not only to make corrections but also to decide what needs correcting? Before we can answer, even before the question is fully posed, we learn that the two categories are one, the arrogant intruder is nothing but a fellow sufferer, soliciting our empathy and companionship. Within a single sentence we have been insulted, disarmed, and seduced—a more concise version of the process of reading to which Seneca himself is subjected in letter 46. Thus the act of reading as Seneca describes it and initiates it requires of the reader a receptivity and engagement at odds with the conventional male sexual ideals of aggression and detachment promulgated elsewhere in the treatises.

Of the relationship between ideology and mythology Pierre Bourdieu has written that "unlike myth, a collective product collectively appropriated and consumed, ideologies serve particular interests which they tend to present as universal interests, common to the whole group."[42] Of Stoicism more particularly, the Roman historian Brent Shaw has argued that its proponents seek to generalize "the traditional idea of values and good behaviour, once restricted to a narrow elite of the city . . . as a good for everyone. . . . Stoicism was thus cosmic social metaphor positing a Divine Economy, in which everything and every person had its proper place and function." Shaw is unwilling to go as far as Bourdieu and the Marxist analysts on whom Bourdieu relies and suggests instead that Stoicism, *qua* ideology, rather than serving as a weapon "in the unique possession of certain individuals or groups," provides "external signposts or referents shared and used by various, even divergent, social groups."[43] Shaw's stricture may be applicable to Stoicism conceived of as a timeless, or at least trans-temporal system, but it is surely not farfetched to regard the particular version of Stoicism inscribed by Seneca as functioning as a weapon, both offensive and defensive, in the hands of the class by whom it has been appropriated. Seneca's performance, via writing, of a new kind of virtue seeks to create the conditions for the reproduction of a social and political elite that is at once Rome centered and capable of communicating across great expanses, landed and mercantile in its sources of wealth, wanton and reserved in its sexual ethics, and committed to the authority of both birth and achievement. His works both express and mediate the contradictions that sustain the sector of the population for and about whom he performs.

In this capacity, his philosophical works make exactly the universalizing gesture predicted by Bourdieu, for they present the contemporary tension between birth and achievement as characteristic of human civilization from its outset. By implication, then, the Senecan text assimilates the elite Roman's vested interest in preserving his privileges to the interest of the whole of human society, past and present. This linkage between a chronological and sociological fraction, on the one hand, and the whole of humanity, on the other, is most clear in letter 90, concerning the end of the Golden Age and the commencement of philosophy, and the immediately succeeding letters, which elaborate on the association between Senecan philosophy and the originary force of desire. Thus we may conclude our survey of Senecan beginnings—generic, cultural, and textual—with a brief consideration of yet another type of beginning, one that we may call either cosmic, following Shaw, or mythological, following Bourdieu.

The apparent aim of letter 90 is the rejection of the Posidonian claim that philosophers invented the arts or technologies of human society during the Golden Age.[44] Posidonius's position is to be rejected because the arts he ascribes to philosophers are trivial and/or subject to ethical misuse, and because there could not have been philosophers in the Golden Age, since there was (by definition) no desire in that era, hence no room for the exercise of virtue, which it is the function of philosophy to instill.

In other words, Seneca criticizes Posidonius's claim concerning philosophers' invention of arts in the Golden Age through an analysis, expressed or implied, of philosophy, of the other arts of human society, and of the meaning of the Golden Age.

In the context of his criticism of Posidonius, Seneca develops a positive account of philosophy and its origins. Philosophy, we learn, is active and involves achievement; hence, according to Seneca, it cannot have been part of the effortless lifestyle of the Golden Age (quamvis egregia illis vita fuerit et carens fraude, non fuere sapientes, quando hoc iam in opere maximo nomen est [*Ep.* 90.44]). The best thing about philosophy is precisely that one does not stumble upon it by chance (sapientia quod in se optimum habet perdidisset, inter fortuita non esse [90.2]). Passages of this sort display an explicit privileging of achievement, a strategy that serves the immediate purpose of the argument against Posidonius, but also makes a more general claim about the nature and significance of philosophy. Yet despite the attempt to link philosophy to the self-fashioning tendencies of the ethically upwardly mobile, its real claim to authority, in this letter and those that follow it, seems to be its connection with the originary force of desire. Philosophy would not exist if there were no desire. And, concomitantly, it would seem, philosophy is available to human beings, from the outset, as a potential therapy of desire. The Golden Age came to a conclusion when vice insinuated itself (subrepentibus vitiis [90.6]) and avarice thrust itself onto the scene (inrupit . . . avaritia [90.36]).[45] In an era without vice, there was also no wisdom or philosophy. "Through ignorance of affairs were those men innocent. But there is a great difference between choosing not to sin and not knowing how to sin" (ignorantia rerum innocentes erant; multum autem interest utrum peccare aliquis nolit an nesciat [90.46]). The end of the Golden Age, not the Golden Age itself, marks the commencement of human civilization through the agency of desire. And so philosophy cannot have come into existence until the time at which desire had prompted the transition from the Golden Age to human history. By assigning philosophy to the Golden Age, Posidonius has not only ascribed a laborious project to an age of inertia; he has also ascribed a remedy for desire to an era in which desire does not yet exist.

Philosophy's intrinsic connection with desire is reinforced in succeeding letters in which it is described as mimicking in the individual soul the techniques that desire once deployed against the Golden Age and continues to deploy in each succeeding generation. In mimesis of desire's inruptive force, philosophy lays hold of the emotions (adfectus ipsos tangunt [94.28]), takes the listener by force (vim praeceptorum, occursus . . . sapientium [94.40]), and penetrates more deeply (altius penetrat [94.44]). If desire instead creeps in and seduces, then philosophy, too, can press itself upon the chest (paulatim descendit in pectora [94.40]) and insinuate virtue (insinuanda virtus [95.35]). Such language, particularly in the context of advice to separate oneself from the mob (94.69–74), gain control of one's own affaris (liberet, potestate [91.21]), and become a new incarnation of the traditional *vir bonus* (95.69ff.), reinforces both the paradoxical sexual implications of the Senecan project and the cosmic connection between philosophy and desire.

Posidonius's position concerning the place of wise men in the Golden Age had been a strongly elitist one; according to him, the arts of human life, vulgar as well as noble, had been invented by sages during the Golden Age. Seneca resists that elitism by emphasizing the effort involved in philosophy and its availability to all. Yet in so doing, he relies on a distinction between philosophy and the vulgar arts and reenacts Posidonius's aristocratic gesture by privileging philosophy on the basis of its origin. What appears to be an acknowledgment of the claims of achievement is undercut by a rhetorical focus on beginnings. Seneca transforms and mythologizes the anxieties of his immediate audience into the originary tensions between the Golden Age and history, and nature and desire. "If the gods had made wisdom a common good and we were born prudent, wisdom would have lost what it possesses best in itself" (nam si hanc quoque bonum vulgare fecissent et prudentes nasceremur, sapientia quod in se optimum habet perdidisset . . . [90.2]). "Inclined toward philosophy, but not in possession of it, are we born, and even among the best, until you civilize them, there is the material of virtue, not virtue" (ad hoc quidem, sed sine hoc nascimur, et in optimis quoque, antequam erudias, virtutis materia, non virtus est [90.46]). The distinction between the good and the vulgar or the best and all the rest frames a letter that otherwise describes philosophy as a matter of effort or achievement. Here, as throughout Seneca's writings, an aristocracy of virtue supplements, even as it purports to supplant, the age-old aristocracy of birth.

Chapter 8

PANNONIA DOMANDA EST:
THE CONSTRUCTION OF THE IMPERIAL SUBJECT
THROUGH OVID'S POETRY FROM EXILE

Empire follows Art and not vice versa.
—William Blake

THE POET OVID was a prime beneficiary of Rome's hierarchical and imperialistic social order. Scion of a leading family of Sulmona, he had the opportunity to choose between a political and an artistic career, with either one offering expanded opportunities in the relatively peaceful first half of the reign of Augustus. His success as a poet who moved in the highest circles of the elites has been taken by later generations as indicative of the promise of Augustanism, while his exile in 8 C.E., ostensibly at the behest of Augustus himself, has signified for many the tyrannical impulses that lay behind the enlightened facade of the early principate. Ovid's career epitomizes in advance the benefits and costs the Roman principate laid out for successive generations of its elites.

Ovid's career, or, more precisely, the turn it took with his relegation to Tomis, is both a sorry consequence of Roman imperialism and an enabling condition of its continuation. This is not to say that the Roman empire would have fallen if Ovid had been allowed to remain in Rome. But something like Ovid's exile poetry had to be produced if Roman readers were to be constructed as appropriate subjects of an imperial regime. Both the *Tristia* and the *Epistulae ex Ponto* do the important ideological work of fostering empathy for fellow Romans abroad, disdain for the non-Roman peoples who threaten the stability of the imperial system, and a patronal attitude toward those who are to be absorbed. They present dependency and subjection on the part of Roman reader and barbaric Tomitan alike as the necessary condition for enjoyment of the benefits of the imperial system. Like later colonization narratives that legitimize the enterprise of colonialism while absolving the writer and the reader from responsibility for the violence that sustains it, so Ovid's laments from exile and dispatches from the contact zone of Pontus sentimentalize his own and his readers' involvement in the project of Roman imperialism. At the same time, the persistent sentimentalization of Ovid's exile by scholars and other writers serves as a reminder of the continuing hold of Romantic ideology on students of classical Rome. If, as has been recently argued, Romanticism itself is a product of the encounter between dominators and dominated, then the contemporary return to the figure of Ovid in exile, that is to say, to Ovid in direct contact with the victims of Roman imperialism, may be taken as symptomatic of the crisis of Romantic models of literature and literary intepretation.

DISPATCHES FROM THE CONTACT ZONE

Let us turn first to the issue of readers and writers, that is, to the performative status of the Ovidian text. As we saw in earlier chapters, Roman writers routinely privilege direct communication between author and audience. The written text points to the absent author and/or becomes a script for a new performance in a real or imagined environment of face-to-face contact. The empire's need for communication across space and time is interpreted by the writer as an opportunity to extend his renown. Just as the empire locates its authority in the permanent settlement of Rome, so writers locate the text's authority in the allegedly stable *ego* of the author. Literature regularly presents itself as if it were being performed at an exclusive gathering of friends or, in the case of letters, seeks to recreate the colloquy of friends under necessary if temporary conditions of separation. For Horace, the portable intimacy of the written text is what makes it a useful complement to mass spectacle as a form of nonviolent regulation of imperial subjects. For Seneca, in writing the *Epistulae Morales*, the fiction of separation from Rome, either on the part of the writer or on the part of the addressee, both justifies the outpouring of moral exhortation and demonstrates the political soundness of the potential enemy of the emperor who presents himself as exclusively occupied with private affairs, too mobile and self-absorbed to serve as focus for any conspiracy real or imagined.

The Rome-centered nature of most literature of the late republic and early empire reflects the general principle that in imperial or colonial systems the metropolis imagines itself as constructing the periphery rather than acknowledging that it is the periphery that constructs the metropolis, both objectively through its expropriated resources and figuratively in that there need to be clearly defined margins in order for a center to be a center.[1] But occasionally events on the periphery become sufficiently unstable to impose themselves on the attention of the center. Such was the case at Rome in the years leading up to and immediately following the relegation of Ovid. A revolt by the Pannonians and disturbances among other peoples of the northern frontier required the presence of both Augustus and his adopted son Tiberius, and coincided with famine, depopulation, and social unrest on the homefront.[2] The provinces organized by Augustus in the Balkans and the Danube basin—Illyricum, Pannonia, and Moesia—were notoriously unstable; the situation posed threats to the steady supply of resources from the area, to communication between Italy and the east, and to the well-being of the imperial heartland. Moreover, the human and material cost of the thus far unsuccessful campaigns against the peoples of the area must have raised questions at home both about the importance of the enterprise and about the competence and legitimacy of the Augustan regime.[3] In this context Ovid's laments and letters from Tomis condition the Roman audience to acquiescence in authorization from afar while continuing to assert the priority of Rome-centered modes of discourse. While from the standpoint of the relegated Ovid the experience of writing in Tomis is represented as consolation for the separation from Rome and the sole means for securing a return, for the Roman audience the laments and letters constitute a paradoxical reassurance of the possibility of maintaining one's Romanness in the farthest reaches of the empire and of the need for making precisely the sort of sacrifice imposed on Ovid if the pleasures of life in Rome are to continue. Horace's *Letter to Augustus* sought to enshrine the place of literature as written text among the tools of the new imperialism by contrasting writing with the *ludus*, or playful spectacle. Ovid's writings from afar, he tells us, are performed before a full theater at home, a use he claims not to have intended, but for which he is grateful nonetheless, since it keeps his name from falling into oblivion (*Tr.* 5.7.25–30). Writing, which implies distance, and spectacle, which implies immediacy, have merged in the same way that the edges of the empire and the center are to be merged into a single political, social, and psychic unit.

Ovid's identification of Rome as the sole source of both artistic and political authorization is more readily apparent in the letters (*Epistulae ex Ponto*) than in the laments (*Tristia*) despite the temporal priority of the latter. Letters, by their very form, openly acknowledge the geographical gap between writer and audience. These particular letters encode spatial separation as separation in social status as well, inasmuch as Ovid identifies and addresses prominent political and artistic figures whom he hopes can prevail upon the emperor to recall him to Rome, or at least grant him a more hospitable place of relegation than Tomis. But the *Tristia* too construct a relationship between author, addressee, and reader that serves the aristocratic and imperial aims of Roman literature more generally as well as fitting the needs of the immediate political situation. As the passage from *Tristia* 5.7 referred to above suggests, Ovid the writer can no longer control the use to which his texts are made once they are committed to writing and circulated to a wider readership. Throughout the *Tristia* Ovid avoids identifying his addressees, with the exception of Augustus and members of Ovid's own family. The poems seek to recreate the sympotic circle or *sodalicium* that is the implied audience of most Latin poetry, yet as a circle whose membership is not to be advertised to the broader readership beyond. Indeed the density of references to *sodales*, that is, fellow symposiasts, is virtually unprecedented in Latin literature.[4] In a sense, all the readers of Ovid's poetry are reduced or elevated to membership in the inner circle. This condition, which might be seen as empowering the writer and freeing him from the traditional obligation under which his predecessors have labored, is instead figured by Ovid as a kind of death. Indeed, immediately preceding the passage in which he refers to the performance of his works in the theater, he expresses his desire to be dead and for his shade (*umbra*) to be apart from his current wretched place of abode.[5] Writing, he reports, is what keeps him alive, yet under conditions of separation from Rome and the aristocratic circle that constitute social death.

Rather than accepting the new conditions under which he lives and writes and seeking new sources of authorization or inspiration, Ovid prefers to legitimize his compositions from exile by reference to the social structures that have traditionally authorized and rewarded literary production. The *existimatio*, or analysis of worth, is reproduced by Ovid in the highly charged context of the funeral *elogium*. In *Tristia* 4.10, he explicitly recreates the traditional context for the defense of the dead, in this case delivering the *elogium* on his own behalf before his ancestors (specifically his father and mother [4.10.81]) and his contemporaries (ad vos, studiosa, revertor / pectora [*Tr.* 4.10.91–92]). The presentation is construed in legal terms (crimina, foro, acta), with not just vindication but triumph over rivals the sought-after outcome (non minor illis / dicor [127–128]). Such moves are familiar in Latin literature from its inception,[6] yet the circle of *existimatores* is here definitively expanded and transformed to encompass the whole world (in toto . . . orbe [128]) of potential readers (legor [128]; candide lector [132]). The potentially free reader of the exile poetry, disconnected from Rome by geography or ethnicity or status, is situated firmly in the traditional circle of evaluators, not replacing them but supplementing them. Indeed, the entire poem in question is constructed with reference to its own status as written object, but more as inscribed epitaph than as waxen tablet. It opens with a near-citation of an earlier passage in the *Tristia* which Ovid has explicitly described as fit to be his epitaph (ille ego fuerim tenerorum lusor amorum [*Tr.* 4.10.1]; hic ego qui iacuit tenerorum lusor amorum [3.3.73]), recapitulates the achievements of the speaker's life, and employs the epigraphical convention of noting the difference between birthplace and resting place: *Sulmo mihi patria est* [4.10.3] versus *hic ego* [4.10.111]. In addition, key passages mimic the rhetorical structures of epitaph, with the summary of Ovid's literary achievements expressed in a couplet marked by tricolon with unit-final perfective form of the verb (multa quidem *scripsi*, sed quae vitiosa *putavi* / emendaturis ignibus ipse *dedi* [*Tr.* 4.10.61–62]), and a final address directed to the anonymous reader (iure tibi grates, candide lector, ago [4.10.132]).

In the poem that constitutes the entirety of book 2 of the *Tristia*, Ovid also defends himself, this time directly to Augustus, and in so doing again makes use of a conventional literary and argumentative strategy: reference to authorizing exempla. Indeed, the entire second half of the poem consists of a long list of authors, past and present, Greek and Latin, whose writing has not been assumed to reflect their personality (as Ovid wants us to believe his has) and whose subject matter has not been deemed offensive by the political powers that be. It is a peculiar poem, all but insisting on Ovid's fitness to be incorporated in a list of authors whose only common feature is not having suffered the same fate as Ovid. What the poem ends up doing, rather than making a case for Ovid's recall to Rome or transfer to a different site of relegation, is calling attention to the contrast between the fanciful and escapist nature of much of Rome's literary and cultural tradition and the grim realities facing the emperor. If in fact Augustus has relegated Ovid for his poetry, then it is Augustus, not Ovid (or at least not the Ovid of this poem), who takes poetry seriously, who regards it and its creator as worth the time and effort to respond to not via intermediaries, but directly, in his own words.

Ovid describes Augustus's role in his relegation as follows:

> nec mea decreto damnasti facta senatus,
> nec mea selecto iudice iussa fuga est.
> tristibus invectus verbis (ita principe dignum)
> ultus es offensas, ut decet, ipse tuas.

> You did not condemn my deeds through a decree of the senate
> Nor was my exile ordered by a designated judge.
> Inveighing with grim words (worthy of the princeps)
> You yourself, as is fitting, avenged the insults to yourself.

(Ovid *Tr.* 2.131–34)

The passage identifies Augustus as the initiator of the relegation, thus justifying the direct appeal to him that is book 2. It also establishes a relationship of reciprocity between Augustus and Ovid that operates in two stages: Ovid insults Augustus, prompting Augustus's revenge (stage one); and Augustus's revenge, taking the form of *tristia verba*, prompts Ovid's composition of his own *tristia verba*, in the form of the five books of the *Tristia* (stage two).[7] Augustus's words of condemnation are described not as harsh (dura) or severe (severa) or judgmental (rigida), but as grim, even regretful, much like Ovid's experiences and poetry in Tomis. Psychologically and rhetorically we may regard Ovid's choice of adjective here as skillfully giving the emperor an opportunity to back down, to alleviate both his and Ovid's dejection. Politically, the use of the term *tristia* to describe both the emperor's speech and the poet's poetry reveals what Philip Hardie in referring to the end of the *Metamorphoses* has called the "ineluctable collusion" between poet and princeps.[8] The shift from offensive to defensive military strategy, from expansion to consolidation both at home and abroad, calls for grim words and grim action on the part of princeps and poet alike. Ovid's argument from tradition cuts both ways, suggesting on one reading that no poet should ever be condemned for what he writes, but on another that the new circumstances of the late Augustan principate call for a new kind of poetry. *Tristia* 2 is in essence a self-referential defense of the political correctness of Ovid's past and current poetic projects.[9]

DESCRIBE AND CONQUER

The reader of Ovid's exile poetry is invited to turn her or his attention to the periphery of the empire, to understand that what happens there matters at Rome, even though what happens there derives all significance from its relationship to Rome. What she or he sees, apart from the figure of the lamenting poet, is very different from what a contemporary historian or archaeologist "sees" in assessing the information available today concerning Ovid's place of exile, Tomis, modern-day Romanian Constanza. So great is the gap between the reality of Tomis and Ovid's representation of it that some scholars have been prompted to hypothesize that Ovid's exile is an enabling fiction, much like his love affair with Corinna in the *Amores* or his pose of erotic expertise in *Ars amatoria*.[10] Without arguing the issue of fiction versus reality one way or the other, we may legitimately ask to what end Ovid describes Tomis and the experience of exile as he does.

The answer would seem to lie in the passage from which the title of this chapter is drawn. In the apologia to Augustus, *Tristia* 2, Ovid suggests that Augustus may not even have read the poetry for which he was supposedly condemned inasmuch as too many other more pressing issues occupy his attention, among them the taming of Pannonia and Illyricum; the defeat of Raetican and Thracian arms; the proper handling of Armenia, Parthia, and Germany; not to mention the guardianship (tutela) of the city via laws and morals. The litany of responsibilities recalls Horace's apology to Augustus in *Epistle* 2.1 for distracting him from management of Italy with a discourse on poetry, and raises the likelihood that this poem, like Horace's, specifically responds to the immediate political context in its discussion of appropriate and inappropriate literature, as has already been suggested above. But it is surely no accident that the territories of the northeast, that is, those contiguous to Ovid's place of exile and connected to Moesia in their military management, are the ones that receive pride of place. Pannonia, like other new Augustan provinces, must be tamed, and Ovid's poetry seeks to prepare tamed and tamers alike for the process.

Consider his representation of the Getans, the indigenous people who share Tomis with the longtime Greek population (dating to the city's foundation as a colony of Miletus in the seventh century B.C.E.) and the more recently arrived Romans (the region was subjugated by Lucullus in 72 B.C.E., revolted in 62, and was retaken by Crassus in 29–28). Getans first appear in Latin literature in the comedy of Terence, where the name Geta is assigned to a slave character in both the *Phormio* and the *Adelphoe*. Like "Syrus" or "Phrygia," "Geta" enters the Latin language in reference to a people regarded as suitable for enslavement by civilized Greeks and Romans. Yet in 29 B.C.E., it has been argued, a number of Getans were enrolled as Roman citizens by Crassus,[11] while Ovid describes an occasion on which Getans resident in Tomis are invited to express their loyalty to the new emperor Tiberius[12] (more on this important passage below). In other words, the Getans were but one of many peoples of the Roman *imperium* whose individual status fluctuated between inferiority and something approaching legal parity. Where there had been subservience there is now potential partnership; where there had been uniform inferiority there is now the differentiation between loyal and disloyal tribesmen.

The description of others and of The Other has attracted a great deal of attention in recent years among scholars of antiquity as well as of later periods. But it is worth remembering that not every outsider is conceived of as a polar opposite to the insiders. By and large it is true that Greeks, especially those in democratic cities, were inclined to stereotype barbarians as effeminate, inert, and ruled by tyrants, characteristics they sought to expel from their own psychic and social lives.[13] At crucial moments in history, Romans picked up on these stereotypes and put them to their own use. Thus, Vergil plays upon Orientalist anxieties in his depiction of the forces surrounding Antony and Cleopatra, but also in his careful delineation of characters such as Aeneas and Ascanius who evoke Augustan ideals. The god Apollo seems to have been called upon both by Vergil and by Augustus to validate the strength and masculinity of political leaders who called for a restriction of the vendetta and the enjoyment of the fruits of *otium*.[14]

Ovid's handling of the inhabitants of the Black Sea region is very different, as indicated by what he includes as well as by what he omits. What he omits, by and large, is the high degree of Hellenic culture attested to by the longtime Greek colonies, Tomis a leader among them. The one clear reference to Tomis's Greek foundation paradoxically points to its continuing "barbarian" traits: according to *Tristia* 3.9 the city received its name from Medea's murder and butchery of her brother Absyrtus as a delaying tactic against her pursuing father. One would never imagine from Ovid's account that Tomis boasted a gymnasium and richly decorated civic buildings, that its epitaphs give evidence of its inhabitants' familiarity with Euripides, Theocritus, and other Greek authors, or that it served as religious and civic center of the five Greek city-states in the immediate Danube delta.[15]

Instead, Tomis is depicted by Ovid as materially and culturally bleak. As a physical space, it lacks the cultivation of the Italian countryside: few orchards or gardens, fields subject to abandonment due to intermittent attack, bitter cold for a long period of the year (see especially *Tr.* 3.10 and 3.12). The inhabitants of Tomis are neither dangerous nor particularly prone to violence—just underdeveloped: few know Greek (in all likelihood a false claim), fewer still Latin. They acknowledge the authority of spear-wielding chieftains and have at best a rudimentary legal system (*Tr.* 5.7). Their clothing ranges from the savage (*Tr.* 5.7) to the outlandish (*Tr.* 4.6.47). All these details emphasize Ovid's isolation from his fellow Tomitans while at the same time making clear their need for the civilizing influences of Rome. Without Roman protection they run the risk of being overrun by enemy tribesmen who cross the frozen Danube and ravage the countryside. Without the presence of Ovid, they show no signs of acquiring the attributes of civilization on their own. Scholars have rightly noted the extent to which Ovid invokes earlier descriptions of northern barbarians, particularly Scythians, in his description of the Getae as well as of the enemies from across the Danube who threaten them and their Roman overlords.[16] The emphasis on prolonged cold and the nomadic lifestyle it requires and enables links Ovid's account to those of Herodotus, Vergil, Horace, and others before him. There is some debate over Ovid's aims in assimilating the real-life inhabitants of the Danube delta to the mythicized Scythians of earlier literature, yet the discussions by and large neglect the political implications of the process. Through his redeployment of traditional stereotypes, Ovid communicates to his audience a sense of the familiarity and hence assimilability of the Pontic peoples. In contrast to European representations of their New World encounters, wherein, as Stephen Greenblatt has argued, a sense of wonder constitutes the primary response to new peoples and places,[17] in Ovid's exile poetry the chief marvel is the poet himself. What is surprising is that he, alone of all his profession, finds himself in such a situation. The isolation of the figure of civilization reminds the reader of the labor still required in the pacification of places like Tomis.

A similar effect is achieved by another device much noted yet little interpreted by scholars, namely, Ovid's insistence on the immediate threat posed by barbarian peoples whose homelands are in fact far removed from Tomis. As Gareth Williams puts it, "It is scarcely credible that, as Ovid claims, tribal forces from throughout the vast geographical area of Thrace, Scythia, and Moesia are all active in the immediate vicinity of Tomis."[18] Williams argues that the "unreality" of Ovid's account is meant to be noted by "the sophisticated reader." But to what end? The peoples in question may not have threatened Tomis, but they were disruptive of Roman rule more generally. By personalizing and rendering immediate the threat they pose, Ovid invites his reader to reflect on the instability of Roman rule throughout the region. Indeed, his requests, based on both the cultural bleakness and the physical vulnerability of Tomis, for removal not to Rome but to a safer place of exile, up the ante in the struggle between Rome and its enemies, making it a combat between all of civilization and all of barbarism. While Ovid is not willing to acknowledge the extent to which Tomis is a Greek city when he is decrying it as a wasteland, nonetheless he places it in the front line of the struggle between civilization and barbarism when it comes to arguing for his and its protection. It is the *ultima terra* (*Tr.* 3.4.52), that is, the last piece of territory submissive to Roman rule. The phrase he uses to describe the relationship between town and countryside at Tomis could serve as a motto for the emerging imperial policy of pacification within secure boundaries: *nil extra tutum est*, nothing beyond is safe (*Tr.* 5.10.17).[19]

In Greek colonization narratives, the new arrivals are frequently described not as conquerors and colonists, but as exiles from the homeland. As Carol Dougherty has argued, the crimes with which they are charged displace the violence of encounters between colonists and natives onto an earlier stage of the narrative.[20] For Ovid, the events in Tomis are almost entirely a matter for negotiation among Romans. From his perspective, and that which he invites his intended audience to share, his arrival in Tomis is the result of an unspeakable and apparently unforgivable mistake. He has been officially relegated (i.e., allowed to retain his citizenship, his property, and his income), but he assimilates his status to that of other refugees and exiles (*profugus* at *Tr.* 5.4.49; *exul* at *Tr.* 1.1.3, *Tr.* 4.1.3, etc.). From the perspective of the Tomitans, the arrival of Rome's most famous poet, no doubt laden with possessions and retinue, may have had a different appearance. And indeed, those who could read or hear Ovid's poetry might well have been confirmed in their initial suspicions. His letters advertise connections with some of the highest-ranking aristocrats at Rome, such as Fabius Maximus and the sons of Messalla Corvinus, with the client prince of Thrace, with poets, orators, military men, and consuls.[21] His disdainful descriptions of the inhabitants of the Pontic region as barbaric, subhuman, uncultivated, are only occasionally tempered by references to their kindnesses to him. He praises Vestalis for slaughtering in battle Getans, members of the same population Ovid elsewhere describes himself as living among without barrier (nullo discrimine) and celebrates Cotys, the Thracian prince, for writing poetry that shows no traces of his ethnic origin (carmina testantur, quae, si tua nomina demas, / Threicium iuvenem composuisse negem [P. 2.9.51–52]).

And yet the Tomitans honor Ovid with a crown and immunity from taxes,[22] honors granted other benefactors of cities in the Pontic region, as inscriptional evidence indicates.[23] Are we to imagine them as developing a fondness for the Roman Muses? Or did they suppose that such a well-connected guest offered them a link to the center of Roman power? Ovid describes himself as assuming a significant role in a public ceremony marking the Tomitans' allegiance to the new emperor not long after the death of Augustus. On this occasion, according to P. 4.13.25ff., he at last delivered a poem in Getic. Its content is depicted as nothing less than praise of the deceased emperor, hope for the well-being of his successor, and recognition of the role Livia played in the transition of power between the two. The reference to the Getic poem provides an indirect means for Ovid to indicate his own loyalty to the new regime, indeed to suggest his willingness to make a special effort to mark the occasion of Tiberius's ascension to power. It also marks the interesting if brief giving of voice to the Getae. As Ovid tells the story, after he had delivered his poem of praise, reading it himself all the way to the last sheet of papyrus, one of the assembled Getans declared, "Since you write these things about Caesar, you ought to have been restored by (or to?) the command of Caesar." ('scribas haec cum de Caesare,' dixit / 'Caesaris imperio restituendus eras'[P.4.13.36–37].) The sentence may indicate sympathy for the poet and hope that he will be granted his fondest wish; but it can also be taken to say, in effect, since you feel that way, too bad you can't leave. Indeed, Ovid invites us to interpret the unnamed Getan's comment in precisely this manner, since in the next poem of the collection (the antepenultimate poem of the final book of the Epistulae), he reports that the Tomitans had become irritated with his complaints about their homeland, and that anger had been aroused in public as a result of his poems (talia suscensent propter mihi verba Tomitae / iraque carminibus publica mota meis [P. 4.14.15–16]). Ovid attempts to assuage the natives' emotions by claiming that it is their locale, with its bad climate and continuing danger, that he has lamented and not the inhabitants or their gracious acceptance of him. The episode reads like the inverse of Propertius's farewell poems to Cynthia (*Elegies* 3.24 and 3.25) in which his abandonment of her as a poetic topic corresponds to the death of his affection for her. Here the end of the exile cycle of Ovid's poetry corresponds to a different kind of relationship with the Tomitans: a poem in Getic, interest in his Latin poetry by the inhabitants, and an explanation, of sorts, for his eagerness to get away from them. The explanation makes no sense, of course, since there seems little reason to believe that Tomis is any longer in grave danger and the frigidity of the climate had been grossly exaggerated from the outset. What is figured by the two poems is an emerging process of negotiation between relocated metropolitan elite, represented by Ovid, and local leaders. Ovid's poetry thus embodies in its implied personal narrative a political narrative as well, one that must have been familiar in many communities as Rome sought not merely to conquer but also to tame the far reaches of her empire.[24]

What is more, the reference to the so-called *Geticum libellum* advertises the potential role of poetry and poets in the process of pacification. As D. M. Pippidi notes, Ovid asks us to believe that he delivered not a speech but a poem, not at a recitation or other cultural event but at an assembly that Getans attended carrying their weapons and dressed for battle.[25] Tacitus, I believe, appreciated the strangeness of Ovid's account, for he echoes this passage in his description of Germanicus addressing the legions in Germany, on exactly the same historical occasion, that is, the transfer of power from Augustus to Tiberius (*Ann.* 1.34.4–6). Tacitus makes the context more appropriate—a general addressing his troops—and the outcome more ominous; Ovid's Getans respond to his speech with a long murmur, *longum murmur*, in Getic no less, *Getico in ore* (*P.* 4.13.36), and rattle their heads and quivers to show approval, while Germanicus's audience of soon-to-be-rebellious legionaries greet the part of the speech that praises Augustus and Tiberius with silence or at best a mid-sized murmur (silentio . . . vel murmure modico [*Ann.* 1.34.6]). Tacitus's revision allows us to see the humor in Ovid's tale (most of it, to be sure, at the Getans' expense) while at the same time exposing the extent to which Ovid depicts himself as having taken on the burden of poet as acculturator. Like most jokes, this one has important elements of both truth and aggression contained within it.

FOREIGN BODIES

Encounters between dominant and subordinate cultures have consequences for both sides of the exchange. Rome's expropriation of Greek literature, philosophy, and art redefined Roman culture in fundamental

ways. Europe's attempt to incorporate large sectors of the Americas and
Africa changed political and social relations within Europe. Ovid represents the impact of the colonized on the colonizer as anxiety about the
linguistic and literary corruption of the latter.[26] Repeatedly in the exile
poetry he voices concern and/or apology for the lowered quality of his
poetic output. Sometimes he refers this decline to the negative impact of
his misfortunes, using general terms such as *mala* or *dolor* to describe the
unfavorable psychic, cultural, and material conditions under which he
labors. On other occasions he is more pointed in his reference to the effect
of being surrounded by no one but Tomitans. In summarizing his poetic
output at *Tristia* 3.14, he describes the three books of the *Tristia* composed by then as "children who have inherited my contagion," *nati con-
tagia nostra secuti* (3.14.17). From the standpoint of the Romans he is
corrupted, marked, infected as one whose error profoundly displeased
the emperor. But he and his poetic children are also infected as a result of
their contact with the Tomitans. As he indicates later in the same poem,
he is fearful that Getic meters and Pontic words have been incorporated
in his Latin writings (3.14.47–50). To be sure, nothing of the sort has
happened, and it does not take a particularly "sophisticated reader" to
ascertain as much. Ovid's aim here is not to deceive the unwary reader or
to undermine his own authority as a reporter of his condition in Tomis.
Instead, he concentrates in a concern about language, which after all is of
special interest to himself and his circle, the anxieties about intercultural
contact that absorb the attention of colonizers everywhere.

If contact with Getans contaminates Ovid's poetry, longing for his
family and friends emaciates him with homesickness (*Tr.* 4.6.42) while
the unhealthful elements of Tomis—earth, water, wind, and air (*Tr.*
3.8.23)—combine to produce a generalized and chronic indisposition.
Body and soul, creator and creation suffer equally, each becoming a metaphor for the other (*Tr.* 3.8.25–28, 5.13.3). Corresponding to the images
of sickness, as both corroboration and result, are claims of sterility. Se-
verus's period of *otium* is fertile, productive, Ovid's is not (*P.* 4.2). Ovid's
book of poetry, like its author, is *infelix*, unlucky, but also unproductive
(*Tr.* 1.1.4). Behind the reference to sterility is a complex associative pattern, one that asks us to regard poetic production as the result of intercourse between poet and audience, poet and subject, or one poet and
another. Bereft of an audience, including the supportive company of fellow poets, and uninspired by his Pontic surroundings, Ovid can only, in
his own words "till a dry shore with a sterile plow," *siccum sterili vomere
litus aro* (*P.* 4.2.16). Williams tries to connect the image with a trio of
passages on plowing in Ovid's *Heroides* and the poetry of Propertius and
sees in the very possibility of making such a connection, once again, evi-

dence of Ovid's fertile genius standing in contradiction to his claim of lost ingenuity. This may well be, but in context, the passage seems to be concerned with more than just poetic intertexts. Plowing is a metaphor throughout ancient literature both for sexual intercourse and for writing.[27] Ovid's evocation of the sexual aspect is graphic here and helps to explain the application of the image to writing as well. Writing by himself, applying pen to paper, is a sterile process in contrast to the practice of composition and correction in the company of friends. It is an unproductive application of the poet's *ingenium*, one forced upon him by circumstances beyond his control. As he writes at *Epistulae ex Ponto* 1.5.30–34, again in context of a declaration of poetic infertility,

> An populus vere sanos negat esse poetas,
>   sumque fides huius maxima vocis ego,
> qui, sterili totiens cum sim deceptus ab arvo,
>   damnosa persto condere semen humo?

> Or is the populace right to deny that poets are sane
>   and am I the greatest evidence of this claim,
> Since, even though I've been tricked so often by the sterile field,
>   I persist in planting my seed in toxic soil?

Unlike Triptolemus, the mythical founder of agriculture, who is depicted at the outset of *Tristia* 3.8 as releasing seed into soil as yet unfamiliar with it, Ovid pointlessly deposits his seed, over and over, in pernicious soil—the literal territory of Pontus and the figurative poetic *materia* of his Pontic exile. If, as Duncan Kennedy observes, Ovid earlier represents his amatory elegies and in particular the *Ars amatoria* as a sex act culminating in simultaneous orgasm of man and woman, writer and reader alike, here Ovid regards his poetry in exile as more closely akin to the sin of Onan who spilled his seed upon the earth in vain. No wonder that he describes the first three books of the *Tristia* as having been created without a mother (de me sine matre creata / carmina [*Tr.* 3.14.13–14]). The Tomitans among whom Ovid dwells are either unwilling or unable to play the compliant female to his phallic potency.[28]

Writing on his own, dwelling in a barren land, living among unattractive and uncultivated Tomitans: each aspect of Ovid's situation reinforces the others in its negativity. The answer to his problems consists either in being transferred to a more receptive site of relegation where, presumably, it will be possible to find or create a community in which poetic exchange thrives, or to recreate such a community through the poetry he writes in Tomis. Ovid asks for the former but accomplishes the latter. Both in the *Tristia*, where he engages in elaborate self-dramatization and constructs unnamed, unknown readers as a surrogate *sodalicium*, then again in the *Epistulae ex Ponto*, where he employs the more conventional strategy of including poets among his addressees and poetry among his chief topics of discussion, Ovid recreates from afar the conditions of poetic creativity, of fertility, he had known at Rome. By insisting on the difference between this long-distance community and the one he had known at Rome, Ovid demonstrates his loyalty both to individual *sodales* and to the traditional institutions of Roman culture. Yet by continuing to produce poetry, despite his relegation, he demonstrates and enacts the transferability of Roman institutions to an alien context. Naming the source of the contagion—that is, isolation from Rome—becomes the most effective cure.

White Man's Burden

With respect to later instances of imperialism, D. K. Fieldhouse has written that "[t]he basis of imperial authority was the mental attitude of the colonist. His acceptance of subordination—whether through a positive sense of common interest with the parent state, or though inability to conceive of any alternative—made empire durable."[29] A comparable claim can be made with regard to the agents of Roman imperialism—soldiers, administrators, and culture workers alike—especially as the Roman system was transformed during the Augustan age from what Conrad's Marlow called "merely a squeeze" to a colonial system of pacification backed up by an idea, namely, the superiority of Roman culture to that of its subject populations.[30] Early Augustans, such as Vergil, had articulated—whether unambivalently or not is beside the point here—the idea of Roman superiority, of the habit of peace Rome could impose on the world. A work like the *Aeneid* can also be read as representing in part the habits of self-sacrifice imperialism imposes upon its leading figures, whether Aeneas or Augustus. It works at one level to condition the Roman reader to accept the loss of certain aspects of republican political and social institutions in exchange for the putative benefits of a stable imperial system. Through its central movement of lamentation it distances the author and reader from their responsibility in the losses generated by imperialism while foreclosing the possibility of resistance on the part of the defeated. Ovid's exile poetry takes the accommodationist function of literature one step further, for it now dramatizes the more immediate cost to the individual Roman required to make personal sacrifices in the interests of maintaining both the supremacy of the emperor and the stability of the empire while at the same time it makes of the poet and his plight the subject of lament. Far from repudiating Augustus or those around him, Ovid's *Tristia* and *Epistulae ex Ponto* acknowledge the legitimacy of their dominance and invite its extension over other peoples as well. The more the poet laments his personal loss of Rome, with all its cultural, material, and social attractions, the more he reminds the reader of what is at stake in the enterprise of pacification she or he is invited to support.

The self-pitying dimension of Ovid's poetry has been criticized by some scholars and explained away by others. But the underlying assumption in each instance is that too much lamentation is undignified and unmanly, that it is indicative of what we might call character flaws. The political function of lament, as of much else in Ovid's exile poetry, is overlooked. The reason for this omission would seem to be that lamentation is a familiar, even comfortable pose within the dominant strain of classical literary criticism, as was discussed in the opening chapter of this study. To critique the lamentation, nostalgia, and sentimentality of much of Latin poetry is to rethink the very foundations of one's own practice as critic and perhaps especially as classicist; even Schiller objected not to Ovid's pose of lamentation, but to his lamentation over an unworthy subject. Hence a posture of disengagement and of sadness at the world's failure to live up to expectation, one born of the late Romantics' description of themselves as cast out of Eden, persists even to this day. Indeed, it can be illustrated, perhaps not surprisingly, in the most recent studies of the exile poetry of Ovid. Thus Peter Green, who fully understands the gap between Ovid's description of Tomis and the complex Geto-Grecian culture that must have prevailed there for centuries before the arrival of the Romans, nonetheless elects to interpet these mystifications in terms of a speculative psychodrama: Ovid's account of his illness is "over-emotionalized," his description of Tomis reflective of "psychological ambivalence." Augustus's choice of place of exile shows "a certain sadistic appositeness." Residence at Tomis "rubbed the poet's nose in the rough and philistine facts of frontier life, the working of the *imperium* which he has so lightheartedly mocked."[31] What such remarks overlook is the simple fact that we would be able to make no such claims had Ovid not chosen to write and to write as he did from exile. The psychological narrative is an epiphenomenon of the literary text, not the other way around.

Gareth Williams goes even further in trying to rescue an autonomous and sentimental Ovid, one who playfully resists, through shrewd application of the intertext, the political implications of his own text. Yet like many critics who insist on the ambivalence or impudence of the Ovidian text he does not consider the implications of writing anything at all or inquire what else the poet might have written. To explain away the eulogistic dimension of *Metamorphoses* 15 or the imperialist function of *Tristia* and *Epistulae ex Ponto* simply on the grounds that some passages can be read in more than one way—what passages can't?—is to ignore the fact that the poet could have said nothing. But in Williams's case, the attempt to vindicate Ovid of his text's embeddedness in its material and social context goes even further, inasmuch as it has the poet say what he has not. Thus central to Williams's assertion of Ovid's "impudence" with respect to the emperor is his interpretation of *Tristia* 2.225–34, the passage in which Ovid intimates that Augustus, preoccupied with the concerns of a troubled empire, has not had the opportunity to study the poetry for which he has been relegated. On Williams's reading the passage is a panegyric for Augustus's achievements some twenty to forty years earlier, a panegyric that is "undercut" by the historical fact that these regions are unstable at the time of Ovid's writing.[32]

A closer reading suggests that the passage is better described as an agenda than a laudation. The present tense is used throughout, and the force of the gerundive, *domanda*, is unambiguous: Pannonia must be tamed. Ovid mixes items that currently require the emperor's attention (the Pannonian revolt, troubles in Rhaetica and Illyricum) with examples of past successes (e.g., the recovery of the Parthian standards), all to suggest the onslaught of demands on the emperor's time and energy. His declaration earlier in the same poem that "sacred law forbids that anyone born of Latin blood endure barbaric chains as long as the Caesars survive" echoes the justifications of imperialist ventures from the war against Mithridates to the American invasion of Grenada. And his pronouncement that Pannonia must be tamed—*Pannonia est domanda*—far from constituting an ironic reference to an earlier campaign by Augustus, calls to mind the elder Cato's declaration against another enemy that took none too kindly to Roman control: *Carthago delenda est*. It is important to understand that irreverence toward the person of Augustus does not in itself constitute resistance to the principate, to Roman social structures, or to the imperialist enterprise that sustains Rome's prosperity and preeminence. Indeed, Ovid's wary partisanship— praising Augustus, while introducing just enough critique to protect himself in case the winds of power shift[33]—reinforces the traditional structures of exclusion and oppression by reducing politics to infighting among the elites. We see a similar move on Ovid's part in the finale of the poems from exile, where Ovid at last describes himself (famous poet, Roman citizen, property intact) as a gladiator whose body has no more room to accommodate blows: *non habet in nobis iam nova plaga locum* (*P.* 4.16.51–52). Like the competitors in the arena whose foreignness is both a visible sign of Rome's ability to command the human resources of its empire and a challenge to the manly dignity of Rome's warrior elite for and by whom the games are orchestrated, so Ovid in Tomis is a figure of both shame and glory, one who valorizes the very power of which he proclaims himself a victim.[34]

Duncan Kennedy has remarked in a justly celebrated essay entitled " 'Augustan' and 'Anti-Augustan': Reflections on Terms of Reference," that "[t]he politics of Augustan poetry is inextricably linked with the politics of talking about it."[35] As I have tried to argue throughout this book, the politics of talking about Augustan poetry, indeed of talking about classical Latin literature more generally, is by and large a politics of nostalgia and evasion: nostalgia for a realm of the aesthetic untainted by the vulgar concerns of social and material existence, and evasion of the exploitative political and economic practices that could bring such an ideal to realization, if only for the few. In opposition to these strategies, I have tried to practice what Edward Said describes as contrapuntal reading—an approach that observes the antitheses between text and context, or one text and another, and describes how they interact with one another. As Said puts it, "In reading a text, one must open it out both to what went into it and what its author excluded."[36] This sort of reading is particularly challenging in the case of Ovid's exile poetry, for it requires us to question our "natural" sympathy for the victim of an emperor's outrage, to question the innocence of a mere poet in exile seeking the consolation of the Muses in his loneliness. But this is exactly how literature works its ideological magic, by making us believe in the inevitability of its own enabling fictions. Cicero constructs a version of prior Roman aristocratic interaction and asks us to believe that this is what Roman tradition looks like. Ovid writes poetry from exile and leads us to assume that it could not have been otherwise, either the exile or the poetry. The "innocent naturalist," of whom Pratt writes, differentiates himself, if only by implication, from the "guilty conqueror."[37] Sometimes the counterpoint occurs within the text itself; the alternative or suppressed voice does indeed make itself heard. But these occasions are few and far between, and their power can only be appreciated when we have attended to literature's habits of accommodation, mystification, and consolidation with as little evasion or nostalgia as our own subject position makes possible.

Near the outset of this book I observed that the research university is a Romantic institution in both historical origin and recurrent temperament. Here it is useful to recall that the institution that set the pattern for the modern research university, that is, the University of Berlin, was founded by Wilhelm von Humboldt shortly after and as a continuation of his brother Alexander's journey of exploration in Latin America. That is to say, the European university came into being at least in part as a way of mastering the New World, of ordering the reality of the new in accordance with the epistemological and social protocols of the old. As Pratt notes, the writings of Alexander von Humboldt and other naturalists seek to substitute for the peasant knowledge of indigenous peoples the supposedly objective knowledge of European science. Their work shares with that of their contemporary poets and novelists a tendency to sentimentalize the landscape of the colonies—both internal and external in the case of Romantic poets—through careful visual description and through benign neglect of the human presence. Both naturalists and poets seek to differentiate themselves from conquerors who can be constructed as truly to blame for whatever ills have befallen the countryside and its inhabitants. Romanticism, like the university, thus becomes an expression of the European bourgeois subject's need to absolve himself/herself of responsibility for conquest while enjoying its benefits.

One need look no further than Keats's famous ode, "On First Looking into Chapman's Homer," to sense the power of Pratt's insight connecting Romanticism, scientific exploration, and imperialism, for while the poem purports to describe the speaker's discovery of the magnificence of Homer's poetry through his encounter with Chapman's translation, it draws heavily on metaphors from colonial conquest, as well as the sense of sight, from its opening verses, "Much have I travelled in the realms of gold / And many goodly states and kingdoms seen," to its climactic comparison of the reader of Chapman to "stout Cortez" who "with eagle eyes / . . . stared at the Pacific . . . / Silent, upon a peak in Darien." The reader at home has an experience as intense as that of any explorer without incurring the costs, to explorer and explored alike, associated with exploration. He sees with what Pratt calls "imperial eyes [that] passively look out and possess,"[38] in this case both the wonders of the New World and the splendors of antiquity. Yet far from accepting responsibility for the enterprise of colonialism, he displaces the experience from the British conquest of, say, Jamaica or the Atlantic seaboard, to the earlier Spanish assault on the kingdoms of Mesoamerica, routinely depicted by English writers as having gold as its aim, in contrast to their colonists' allegedly more honorable aims.[39] The poem was published in 1816, during the course of Simon Bolivar's wars of liberation, to which the British offered some support in order to annoy their enemies the French, whose conquest of Spain had catalyzed the Creole uprisings in Central and South America as well as the United States, whose insatiable hunger for territory was already pressing heavily on the former Spanish colonies. While the poem makes no explicit reference to these contemporary events, it resonates with the Creole propagandists' depiction of Latin America as a place of natural wonder in need of ordered management by Europeans—but up close.[40] And of course it shares with von Humboldt in his descriptions of his travels, and with much of the leadership of the new republics, a veritable suppression of the perspective of the millions of non-European inhabitants of the region. Only Cortez "and all *his* men [emphasis mine] / Looked at each other with a wild surmise. . . ." The ode is both a reaction to the history of colonial conquest and a contribution to a developing discourse that will legitimize colonialism by other means (i.e., "scientific" knowledge at home, Creole-dominated republics abroad).

When we return to Rome we find a similar combination of scientific inquiry and poetic sentimentality, of response to historical developments and ideological groundwork for new imperial enterprises. Scientific inquiry is manifest most clearly in the *Historia naturalis* of Pliny the Elder, whose work has rightly been described as a stocktaking, or inventory, of Roman conquests.[41] But it is worth remembering that Pliny was preceded in this enterprise by Aristotle, the famed tutor of Alexander the Great, and by Posidonius whose work in any of a number of scientific fields— not least ethnography—attracted the attention of Roman politicos and poets alike. Ovid occupies a special place in this history of imperialist appropriation, since, like Keats, he can, in the early stages of his career, survey the Roman colonies from afar and work to separate himself from those who conquered them, while later, like von Humboldt, he also encounters the territories firsthand. What he writes from Tomis is by no stretch of the imagination a natural history, yet, as I have tried to argue in this chapter, it has much the same effect of representing the non-Roman world as there to be tamed by the Romans and their civilized subjects. And as with von Humboldt, whose representation of the Latin American landscape proved so useful to the inheritors of the Spanish colonial tradition, so it is perhaps not surprising that Ovid's sojourn in Tomis continues to absorb the attention of contemporary beneficiaries of Rome's self-proclaimed civilizing mission.[42]

NOTES

INTRODUCTION

1. For the context of literary performance in the Roman world, see F. Dupont, *L'invention de la littérature: De l'ivresse grecque au livre latin* (Paris 1994), and "*Recitatio* and the Reorganization of the Space of Public Discourse," in *The Roman Cultural Revolution*, ed. T. Habinek and A. Schiesaro (Cambridge, 1997), pp. 44–60.

2. This summary formulation of Williams's approach rephrases the remarks of F. Nostbakken, "Cultural Materialism" in *Encyclopedia of Contemporary Literary Theory*, ed. I. Makaryk (Toronto, 1993), pp. 21ff. Nostbakken's article gives relevant bibliography and briefly discusses the relationship between cultural-materialist and new-historicist approaches to literature.

3. W. B. Michaels, "The Victims of the New Historicism," *Modern Language Quarterly* 54 (1993): 110–20. For an example of just such a conflation directed against a classicist, see R. F. Thomas, "The 'Sacrifice' at the End of the *Georgics*, Aristaeus, and Vergilian Closure," *Classical Philology* 86 (1991): 211–18. In analyzing the reactions prompted by resistant readings of canonical texts I have been aided by the observations of W. B. Carnochan, *The Battleground of the Curriculum: Liberal Education and the American Experience* (Stanford, 1993). Carnochan argues that the recent focus on the content of reading lists revives Matthew Arnold's program of replacing religious with secular dogma, in contrast to the equally venerable, if less well-publicized, position of Arnold's near-contemporary John Henry Newman, who defended study of the classical humanities not as making students better people, but as preparing them to face the world in all its intermingled beauty and corruption.

4. E. Said, *Beginnings: Intention and Method* (New York, 1985), p. 34 (passage quoted in full in chapter 7).

5. D. Kennedy, "'Augustan' and 'Anti-Augustan': Reflections on Terms of Reference," in *Roman Poetry and Propaganda in the Age of Augustus*, ed. A. Powell (Bristol, 1992), pp. 26–58; quotation from p. 29.

6. For an introduction to Polanyi's thought, see G. Baum, *Karl Polanyi on Ethics and Economics* (Montreal, 1996); also J. R. Stanfield, *The Economic Thought of Karl Polanyi* (Basingstoke, Hampshire, 1986).

7. On inheritance, see E. J. Champlin, *Final Judgments: Duty and Emotion in Roman Wills, 200* B.C.–A.D. *250* (Berkeley, 1992), and C. Paulus, *Die Idee der postmortallen Persönlichkeit im römischen Testamentrecht*, Schriften zur Rechts-Geschichte 55 (Berlin, 1992). Sumptuary regulations are discussed in chapter 2, with bibliography.

8. It is interesting to note that in the 1996 *Directory of College and University Classicists in the United States and Canada*, three times as many scholars list a

primary interest in "Women in Antiquity" as in "Gender Studies." And "Feminist Theory" is outnumbered by "Women in Antiquity" ten to one.

9. J. F. Lyotard, *The Postmodern Condition: A Report on Knowledge*, trans. G. Bennington and B. Massumi (Minneapolis, 1989).

CHAPTER ONE
LATIN LITERATURE AND THE PROBLEM OF ROME

I know of no comprehensive history of the study of Latin literature and/or Roman culture in the United States or any other nation. Much information on the role of Classics more generally in American history can be gleaned from M. Reinhold, *Classica Americana* (Detroit, 1984), and from C. Richard, *The Founders and the Classics* (Cambridge, Mass., 1994). E. Vance, *America's Rome*, 2 vols. (New Haven, 1989), esp. vol. 1 on classical Rome, considers the use to which American "writers, painters, and sculptors" put what they "saw and experienced" in Rome, especially during the nineteenth century (p. xix). Vance's concern is chiefly with nonacademic uses of Rome, and with classical Rome as mediated through the encounter with Roman ruins and Italian landscape. His observations find a close parallel in Nicholas Purcell's remarks on European Romantics and their reaction to the Roman ruins, e.g., "The contrast between the complete world evoked by the ancient authors and its dilapidated vestiges is vital to the poignancy of the experience" ("The City of Rome" in *The Legacy of Rome: A New Appraisal*, ed. R. Jenkyns [Oxford, 1992], 421–453; quotation from p. 451). For European responses to Rome in the nineteenth and early twentieth centuries, see also *Palimpsests: Receptions of Rome 1789–1945*, ed. C. Martindale and C. Edwards (Cambridge, forthcoming), the contributors to which seek to correct the notion that only Greece had a legacy in northern and western Europe during the period in question. On the particular issue of the preference for Greece over Rome, see the very helpful essay by F. Turner, "Why the Greeks and not the Romans in Victorian Britain?" in *Rediscovering Hellenism: The Hellenic Inheritance and the English Imagination*, ed. G. W. Clarke (Cambridge, 1989), 61–82. Turner's observation that the apparent distance between ancient Greece and contemporary Britain made Greece easier to appropriate than Rome parallels my conclusions concerning American classical studies (but not American popular culture) and Greece vs. Rome. The social and ideological implications of the institutionalization of classical studies are treated by R. S. Turner, "The Prussian University and the Concept of Research," *Internationales Archiv für Sozialgeschichte der deutschen Literatur* 5 (1980), 68–93, and "The Bildungsbürgertum and the Learned Professions in Prussia 1770–1830: The Origins of a Class," *Histoire Sociale/ Social History* 13 (1980), 105–135. On the ideology of classical studies, see also G. Bandelli, "Le letture mirate" in *Lo spazio letterario di Roma antica*, ed. G. Cavallo et al. (Roma, 1989), 2.361–397. In developing my own historicizing account of Latin literary studies I have been influenced by G. Graff, "The University and the Prevention of Culture," in *Criticism in the University*, ed. G. Graff and R. Gibbons (Evanston, Ill., 1985), and G. Graff, *Professing Literature: An Institutional History* (Chicago, 1987). Although not specifically concerned with university life, T. J. Jackson Lears, *No Place of Grace: Antimodernism and the Transfor-*

mation of American Culture 1880–1920 (New York, 1981), provides a useful framework for reflecting on the social role of Classics in modern American culture. Lears describes the dialectical relationship between American progressivism and the retrospective cultural forms favored by certain sectors of the American elite. On Latin in the American schools, see M. Reinhold, "The Latin Tradition in America," *Helios* 14 (1987): 123–39. On recent developments in Latin studies, especially in the United States, see M. Santirocco, "Latin as a Scholarly Discipline," *Helios* 14 (1987): 17–32. As it turns out, the factors Santirocco identifies as characteristic of revitalized *Latinitas*, namely, a historicity that frees poetry from social dependence and a brand of intertextuality that neglects ideology, both point toward the continuation of the opposition between literature and culture this chapter is designed to critique. Santirocco is right to acknowledge that there is a type of historicism that grants to literature the power to "create reality, as ideology" (p. 22), but his examples of such work in Latin all consist of the aestheticization of the political as opposed to the politicization of the aesthetic. See also the discussion of Santirocco's paper by D. Selden, "Textual Criticism," *Helios* 14 (1987): 33–50.

On the work of Martin Bernal concerning the role of racism and anti-Semitism in the formation of classical studies see the discussion in note 2, below. An earlier version of this chapter was published in *The Interpretation of Roman Poetry: Empiricism or Hermeneutics?*, ed. K. Galinsky, Studien zur klassischen Philologie 67 (Frankfurt am Main, 1992), pp. 227–42.

1. M. Bernal, *Black Athena: The Afroasiatic Roots of Classical Civilization*, 2 vols. (New Brunswick, N.J., 1987, 1991).

2. The quotation is from R. E. Norton, "The Tyranny of Germany over Greece?: Bernal, Herder, and the German Appropriation of Greece," in *Black Athena Revisited*, ed. M. Lefkowitz and G. M. Rogers (Chapel Hill and London, 1996), p. 405. Norton otherwise rightly objects to Bernal's misrepresentation of some of the work of Herder. Other contributors to the volume who criticize Bernal's historiography make similar concessions. Richard Jenkyns, in an attempt to defend some of Bernal's British targets through reference to their narrowly factional political allegiances (as if being a left-wing atheist automatically inoculates one against racism), still grants the broader version of Bernal's thesis, e.g., in his statement "I also agree that in the nineteenth century the externalist pressures upon the study of Greece were abnormally strong: Hellas was admired, even worshiped, as a means of satisfying certain cultural needs" ("Bernal and the Nineteenth Century," pp. 411–20; quotation from p. 413). M. Liverani, in the most sympathetic of the group of comments on Bernal ("The Bathwater and the Baby," pp. 421–27), severely criticizes Bernal's methods and rhetoric while granting that "[t]he logical structure of the first volume of *Black Athena* is built on a syllogism whose accuracy I fully concede. The major premise is that scholarship (historiography in particular) is influenced by the scholar's sociopolitical background. The minor premise is that the ancient history of the eastern Mediterranean was construed by European scholars living in imperial times and countries. The conclusion is that their work was biased by imperialism and is now in need of thorough revision" (p. 422). G. M. Rogers ("Multiculturalism and the Foundations of

Western Civilization," pp. 428–43) rejects what he regards as Bernal's "monolithic picture of racism and anti-Semitism," without offering more than a series of scattered observations to replace it. As for the overall importance of Bernal's work, I am inclined to share Liverani's judgment: "A truly progressive strategy of research would ... work ... with a self-consciousness derived from a critical appreciation of how sociopolitical conditions influence schoalrship. Though Bernal's *pars destruens* (destructive element) is a contribution to multicentered scholarship, his *pars construens* (constructive element) poses an insurmountable obstacle to scholarly progress" (p. 424). As for the attempt to minimize the importance of Bernal's work by suggesting that the true origins of classical studies are in the researches of the Alexandrians, there is something of an air of desperation about the claim. No serious historian of education can deny the importance of the invention of the modern research university in the early nineteenth century, whatever earlier antecedents it may have had at various points and in various locales during the preceding millennia. Moreover, it is hard to understand how identifying oneself with the courtiers of the Ptolemies is supposed to make the contemporary classicist more comfortable than is being linked with early nineteenth century anti-Semites.

3. Winckelmann lived from 1717 to 1768. His *History of Ancient Art* appeared in 1764. B. de Montfauçon, *L'antiquité expliquée et représentée en figures* appeared in five volumes from 1719 to 1724. For calling the contrast between the two to my attention I am grateful to Daniel Selden. With respect to Winckelmann, see the concise remarks of R. Pfeiffer, *A History of Classical Scholarship From 1300 to 1850* (Oxford, 1976), p.170: "Only in the emulation of earlier masterpieces could new ones be created. Roman culture now appeared to be no more than an approach to that of Greece."

4. Bernal, *Black Athena*, vol. 1, p. 214.

5. Ibid.

6. The periodization of Romanticism, in Germany and elsewhere, is a topic of some controversy. I follow the terminology espoused by V. Nemoianu, *The Taming of Romanticism* (Cambridge, Mass., 1984). On the continuing importance of Romanticism as a feature of contemporary culture, see *Romanticism*, ed. with introd. by Cynthia Chase (London and New York, 1993), and F. Pyle, *The Ideology of Imagination: Subject and Society in the Discourse of Romanticism* (Stanford, 1995).

7. F. Schiller, *Aesthetical and Philosophical Essays*, ed. N. H. Dole (London, Berlin, New York, 1902) vol. 5, p. 212 (the essay dates to 1798).

8. Schiller, part one, p. 296.

9. Cited in F. Schiller, *On the Naive and Sentimental in Literature*, trans. with introd. by H. Watanabe-O'Kelly (Manchester, 1981), p. 12.

10. Watanabe-O'Kelly, p. 16, following P. Szondi, "Das naive ist das Sentimentalische. Zur Begriffsdialektik in Schillers Abhandlung," *Euphorion* 66 (1972): 174–206. For Goethe's attitude toward the Greeks, see H. Trevelyan, *Goethe and the Greeks* (Cambridge, 1941). Trevelyan's study also contains a section on Goethe's attitude toward Rome, which he summarizes thus: "In so far as it was not Greece it was nothing, and in many ways it was very far from being Greece" (pp. 124–25).

11. P. Alpers, "Schiller and the Modern Idea of Pastoral" in *Cabinet of the Muses: Essays in Classical and Comparative Literature in Honor of Thomas G. Rosenmeyer*, ed. M. Griffith and D. Mastronarde (Atlanta, 1990), 317–31.

12. D. O. Ross, *Virgil's Elements: Physics and Poetry in the Georgics* (Princeton, 1987), p. 3.

13. Schiller, "Naive and Sentimental," pp. 291–92. D. Feeney, *The Gods in Epic: Poets and Critics of the Classical Tradition* (Oxford, 1991), p. 385, employs similar language to praise the decidedly un-naive poet Statius: "It is astonishing how Statius contrives to channel so many of the poem's currents of energy together into the climactic moment of the brothers' duel. . . . The duel displays the crescendo and termination of the Furies' action, the abnegation of Jupiter and the celestial powers, the rout of Pietas—and it prepares for the disappearance of the allegorical narrative mode itself. The sense of escalating competition over the brothers' fate becomes quite overwhelming, making this one of the greatest moments in the poem."

14. Nemoianu, *The Taming of Romanticism*, p. 14.

15. Ibid. p. 40.

16. Z. Yavetz, "Why Rome? Zeitgeist and Ancient Historians in Early 19th Century Germany," *American Journal of Philology* 97 (1976): 276–96; Pfeiffer, *History of Classical Scholarship from 1300 to 1850*, pp. 184ff.; H. Berthold, "Barthold Georg Niebuhr und J. W. Goethe über die Geschichte Altroms," *Klio* 60 (1978), 569–579; K. Christ, *Römische Geschichte und deutsche Geschichtswissenschaft* (Munich: Beck, 1982), pp. 35–42.

17. Niebuhr, *Römische Geschichte*, translated in F. Stern, *The Varieties of History* (New York, 1973), p. 52.

18. Ibid.

19. Ibid.

20. Niebuhr, p. 51.

21. On Gildersleeve's life and contribution to American classical studies, see the collection of laudatory essays in *Basil Lanneau Gildersleeve: An American Classicist*, ed. W. Briggs, Jr., and H. Benario, *American Journal of Philology* Monographs (Baltimore, 1986); the biographical article by Briggs in *Classical Scholarship: A Biographical Encyclopedia*, ed. W. Briggs, Jr., and W. M. Calder III (New York and London, 1990), pp. 93–118; and *The Letters of Basil Lanneau Gildersleeve*, ed. W. Briggs, Jr. (Baltimore, 1987).

22. Bernal, *Black Athena*, vol. 1, p. 209.

23. B. L. Gildersleeve, "A Southerner in the Peloponnesian War," originally published in *Atlantic Monthly* 80 (Sept. 1897): 330–42; reprinted in *The Creed of the Old South* (Baltimore, 1915; New York, 1979), pp. 53–103.

24. Gildersleeve, "A Southerner in the Peloponnesian War," p. 73.

25. Gildersleeve, "The Limits of Culture," in *Essays and Studies Educational and Literary* (Baltimore, 1867, 1890), pp. 3–40. Quotation from pp. 39–40.

26. W. W. Briggs, Jr., "Basil Lanneau Gildersleeve at the University of Virginia," in *Basil Lanneau Gildersleeve*, ed. W. Briggs and H. Benario, pp. 10–20; quotation from p. 15. Briggs goes on to note, "Certainly he may have needed a pocket Goethe less than a pocket Homer, for he appears to have nearly everything the German master wrote committed to memory."

NOTES TO CHAPTER ONE

27. "The Creed of the Old South," first published in *Atlantic Monthly* January 1892, reprinted in Gildersleeve, *The Creed of the Old South* (Baltimore, 1915; New York, 1979), pp. 7–52. The episode referred to in the text is described on pp. 12–15.

28. Gildersleeve, "Maximilian: His Travels and his Tragedy," in *Essays and Studies*, pp. 451–96; see esp. p. 480. The essay in question was originally composed in 1868, according to an authorial note in the edition of 1890.

29. The eulogy of Julian is to be found in "The Emperor Julian," which was originally published in *Southern Review* of 1868 and is reprinted in *Essays and Studies*, pp. 355–98.

30. Gildersleeve, "Maximilian: His Travels and His Tragedy," p. 494.

31. Nemoianu, *The Taming of Romanticism*, p. 40. Compare Purcell's account of the Romantics' reaction to Rome of their era: "How could sense be made of the vivid contrast between the desolation of the present and the evidence of the prosperity of the area in Roman times?" ("The City of Rome," p. 447).

32. Gildersleeve, "On the Present Aspect of Classical Study," in *Essays and Studies*, pp. 500–8 (essay dated to 1886; quotation from pp. 507–8).

33. On the significance of the Hegelian view of language for the institutionalization of language study in American universities, see the brief discussion by G. Graff, *Professing Literature* (Chicago, 1987), pp. 28ff.

34. Gildersleeve, "A Southerner in the Peloponnesian War," p. 24–25.

35. "Maximilian," p. 481.

36. Ibid.

37. Ibid., p. 487.

38. Ibid., pp. 487–88.

39. Ibid., p. 487.

40. Ibid., p. 488.

41. Gildersleeve, "On the Present Aspect of Classical Study," p. 504.

42. J. Higham, *Strangers in the Land* (Westport, Connecticut, 1963, 1981), pp. 13ff.

43. D. Bushnell and N. Macaulay, *The Emergence of Latin America in the Nineteenth Century*, 2d ed. (New York, 1984), p. 3: "[T]he generic designation 'Latin' America, though apparently first used by the Colombian publicist José Maria Torres Caicedo in 1856, was quickly taken up and promoted by French ideologues in an effort to stake out for France a partial claim to what Spain and Portugal had founded." Cf. A. Ardao, *Genesis de la idea y el nombre de America Latina* (Caracas, 1980), cited by Bushnell and Macaulay. There is a slight, but revealing, misrepresentation of the term's origin in the glossary that opens *The Cambridge Encyclopedia of Latin America and the Caribbean*, 2d ed. (Cambridge, 1992): "Latin America—the expression first came into use in France just before 1860. . . ." For further reflections on "Latin" America in its relationship to classical Rome, see T. Habinek, "*Pax Colombiana*: Simon Bolivar, Augustus Caesar, and the Future of the Universe" (unpublished).

44. Gildersleeve's letters are peppered with insults based on the national origin of his target, for example the "slowness of Englishmen" (to D. C. Gilman, December 20, 1875) and the "want of personal cleanliness of Orientals" (to D. C. Gilman, June 30, 1880). Gildersleeve's view of unique national characteristics

formed part of his public discourse as well: he argued for the likelihood of a significant American contribution to classical philology on the grounds that "[a]n audacious, inventive, ready-witted people, Americans often comprehend the audacious, inventive, ready-witted Greek *à demi-mot* while the German professor phrases, and the English 'don' rubs his eyes, and the French savant appreciates the wrong half" (Gildersleeve, "University Work in America and Classical Philology," in *Essays and Studies*, pp. 85–123; quotation from p. 105).

45. This issue is explored throughout Reinhold, *Classica Americana*.

46. Obviously I am not referring to work that relies on analogies to Greek cultures in acccordance with accepted comparative methodologies. Nor do I deny—far from it—that the study of Greek literature and culture has developed in directions far different from those outlined by Gildersleeve and others of his era. Indeed, it is one of the paradoxes that pervades classical studies that at least until recently Romanists were more likely to cling to a Romantic version of Greece than most Hellenists. On the Hellenization of Latin studies see also Santirocco, "Latin as a Scholarly Discipline."

47. B. Knox, "The Serpent and the Flame," *American Journal of Philology* 71 (1950): 379–400, reprinted in *Virgil: A Collection of Critical Essays*, ed. S. Commager (Englewood Cliffs, N.J., 1966), 124–42.

48. S. Commager, *The Odes of Horace: A Critical Study* (New Haven, 1962).

49. E. Curtius, *Europäisches Literatur und lateinisches Mittelalter* (Bern, 1948), and V. Pöschl, *Die Dichtkunst Virgils* (Innsbruck, 1950). English translations were published in 1953 and 1962, respectively. On Curtius's aims, see F. Lentricchia, *Criticism and Social Change* (Chicago, 1983), pp. 127–28. On Pöschl, see W. R. Johnson, *Darkness Visible* (Berkeley, 1976).

50. D. Daiches, *The New Criticism*, Aquila Essays 5 (Portree, Scotland, 1982).

51. R. Fowler, *Literature as Social Discourse: The Practice of Linguistic Criticism* (Bloomington, 1981), p. 55.

52. Commager, *Virgil: A Collection of Critical Essays*, pp. vii, viii.

53. Graff, "The University and the Prevention of Culture," p. 72.

54. Commager, *Virgil: A Collection of Critical Essays*, p. 2.

55. My interpretation of the "literary" turn in postwar Latin studies contrasts sharply with that of R. Bolgar, "Latin Literature: A Century of Interpretation," in *Les études classiques aux XIXe et XXe siècle: Leur place dans l'histoire des idées*, Entretiens Fondation Hardt 26 (Vandoeuvres-Génève, 1980), pp. 92–126. For Bolgar, the concern with new methods of literary analysis is evidence of Latin studies' attempt to reconnect with the larger culture. My point is that Latinists focused on precisely the new methods least likely to achieve such reconnection.

56. Gildersleeve, "The Limits of Culture," p. 8.

57. T. Habinek, "Sacrifice, Society, and Vergil's Ox-Born Bees," in *Cabinet of the Muses: Essays in Classical and Comparative Literature in Honor of Thomas G. Rosemeyer*, ed. M. Griffith and D. J. Mastronarde (Atlanta, 1990), pp. 209–24.

58. *Classics: A Discipline and Profession in Crisis?*, ed. P. Culham and L. Edmunds (Lanham, Maryland, 1989). The tenor of most of the discussions in the volume suggests an affirmative answer to the title question. In the same vein, see D. Damrosch, "Can Classics Die?" *Lingua Franca* 5 (Sept./Oct. 1995): 61–66.

For a different view, see K. Galinsky, *Classical and Modern Interactions: Post-modern Architecture, Multiculturalism, Decline, and Other Issues* (Austin, 1992), pp. 154–70.

59. I agree with the recommendation of James Halporn that history of scholarship take precedence over the history of scholars (see J. Halporn, "Foreign Scholars in American Classical Education," in *Classics: A Discipline and a Profession in Crisis?*, 305–15, at p. 315, citing Anthony Grafton). My concern here with Mickiewicz and Michelet, as with Gildersleeve, is with the exemplary nature of their discourse, rather than with personal biography.

60. "To Joachim Lelewel" and "On Romantic Poetry" cited and discussed in H. Weintraub, *The Poetry of Adam Mickiewicz* (The Hague, 1954).

61. From the report of the Faculty of Letters, University of Lausanne, to the Swiss Council of Public Instruction, quoted in *Adam Mickiewicz: Poet of Poland. A Symposium*, ed. M. Kridl, Columbia Slavic Studies (New York, 1951), p. 220. We may usefully contrast Brigg's description of Gildersleeve as "a strict teacher, barely forgiving of errors" (Briggs, in *Classical Scholarship: A Biographical Encyclopedia*, p. 108).

62. Report of the Director of the Cantonal College at Lausanne to the Rector of the University, quoted in *Adam Mickiewicz*, p. 221.

63. Although Mickiewicz himself, it should be noted, hoped for Jewish participation in the emancipated Polish state and spent the last months of his life organizing a Jewish legion to fight on the side of the Ottoman Empire during the Crimean War. On the complicated question of Mickiewicz's attitude toward Jews, see A. Duker, "Adam Mickiewicz and the Jewish Problem," in *Adam Mickiewicz*, pp. 108–25, and S. Scheps, *Adam Mickiewicz: Ses affinités juives* (Paris, 1964).

64. Nemoianu, *The Taming of Romanticism*, p. 151, seems to be making a comparable point. See also M. Dudli, *Pushkin, Mickiewicz, and the Overcoming of Romanticism*, Stanford Honors Essays in Humanities 18 (Stanford, 1976).

65. G. R. Noyes, *Poems of Adam Mickiewicz*, translated by various hands (New York, 1944), p. 385.

66. J. Michelet, *Histoire romaine*, 2 vols. (Brussels, 1840). Quotation from vol. 1, p. xv. My translation here and throughout. Subsequent page references appear parenthetically in the text.

67. Bernal, *Black Athena*, vol. 1, p. 341.

68. Niebuhr, as translated in Stern, *Varieties of History*, pp. 50 and 51.

69. Michelet had published translations of portions of Vico's work in 1829, two years before the first printing of *Histoire romaine*.

70. Bernal, *Black Athena*, vol. 1, p. 33.

71. See note 43, above. The French tendency to appropriate Roman models, during the ancien régime, the Revolution, and again under Napoleon III, accounts in part for British philhellenism during the nineteenth century: see F. Turner, "Why the Greeks and Not the Romans in Victorian Britain?"

72. *Lettre à sa Majesté l'empereur Napoléon III sur l'influence française en Amérique par Un homme de la race latine* (Paris Ledoyen) dated 25 December 1858; quotation from p. 6; my translation.

73. C. Milosz, "Mickiewicz and Modern Poetry," in *Adam Mickiewicz*, pp. 57–65, discusses the thesis of Ludwik Fryde, whose work *The Classicism of Mic-*

kiewicz was left incomplete at the time of his murder by the Nazis. For a brief glance at Polish classical studies in the twentieth century see *Zur geschichte der klassischen Alterumswissenschaft der Universitäten Jena, Budapest, Krakow*, Wissenschaftliche Beiträge der Friedrich-Schiller-Universität Jena (Jena, 1990).

74. On philology as a weapon of exclusion and the philological seminar as a means for controlling access to classical studies, see R. S. Turner, "The Prussian University and the Concept of Research."

75. H. Lloyd-Jones, *Blood for the Ghosts: Classical Influences in the Nineteenth and Twentieth Centuries* (London, 1982), p. 10.

76. Graff, "The University and the Prevention of Culture," and Lentricchia, *Criticism and Social Change.*

77. Halporn, "Foreign Scholars in American Classical Education."

78. A. Bloom, in *The Closing of the American Mind* (New York, 1987), is quite open about his affiliation with the Hellenocentric project of a later generation of German professors; while at least some proponents of multiculturalism subscribe to an Edenic view of primitive or folk cultures unsullied but for their contact with the West.

79. Fowler, *Literature as Social Discourse*, p. 10.

80. T. Pavel, *Fictional Worlds* (Cambridge, Mass., 1981), p. 141.

CHAPTER TWO
WHY WAS LATIN LITERATURE INVENTED?

Useful background material for this chapter includes the discussion of archaic Greek musical culture in G. Nagy, *Pindar's Homer: The Lyric Possession of an Epic Past* (Baltimore, 1991), and L. Kurke, *The Traffic in Praise: Pindar and the Poetics of Social Economy* (Ithaca, N.Y., 1991), and the attempt to relate archaic Roman culture to comparable models of development in N. Zorzetti, "The Carmina Convivalia," in *Sympotica: A Symposium on the* Symposion, ed. O. Murray (Oxford, 1990), pp. 289–307, and "Poetry and the Ancient City: The Case of Rome," *Classical Journal* 86 (1991): 311–29. The recoverable evidence concerning the early period of Latin literature is analyzed by E. Gruen, *Studies in Greek Culture and Roman Policy*, Cincinnati Classical Studies, n. s. 7 (Leiden, 1990), and *Culture and National Identity in Republican Rome*, Cornell Studies in Classical Philology (Ithaca, N.Y., 1992). Gruen's analysis is followed closely by S. Goldberg, *Epic in Republican Rome* (Oxford, 1995). To the extent that Gruen and Goldberg are interested in the politics of the earliest Latin literature, it is chiefly to deny the partisan affiliations of specific poets and texts. They may well be correct, but their investigations leave open the question of early Latin literature's intervention in broader conflicts over social and political authority, conflicts considered in the present chapter. On the question of the relationship between the invention of a literary tradition and the construction of cultural identities, a number of recent works in anthropology, political science, and literary criticism have proven useful, particularly J. Kautsky, *The Politics of Aristocratic Empires* (Chapel Hill, 1982); B. Anderson, *Imagined Communities* (Ithaca, N.Y., 1983); E. Gellner, *Nations and Nationalism*, New Perspectives on the Past 1 (Oxford, 1983); A. Giddens, *The Nation-State and Violence* (Cambridge, 1985); E. Hobsbawm, *Nations and Nationalism since 1780: Programme, Myth, Reality*

(Cambridge, Eng., 1990); T. Eagleton, F. Jameson, and E. Said, *Nationalism, Colonialism, and Literature*, with an introduction by S. Deane (Minneapolis, 1990); R. Helgerson, *Forms of Nationhood: The Elizabethan Writing of England* (Chicago, 1992); and S. Gruzinski, *The Conquest of Mexico: The Incorporation of Indian Societies into the Western World, 16th–18th Centuries*, trans. E. Corrigan (Cambridge, 1993).

1. The focus on Greek models and the consideration of the Roman experience in isolation are characteristic of otherwise excellent recent studies such as the works of Gruen listed above and G.-B. Conte, *La letteratura latina* (Florence, 1987), available in English as *Latin Literature*, trans. J. Solodow (Baltimore, 1994). Characteristic is the remark of Goldberg, *Epic in Republican Rome*, p. 50: "Latin literature was Andronicus' to begin."

2. On Greek-Roman interaction prior to the third century B.C.E., I have found G. Maddoli, "Contatti antichi del mondo latino col mondo greco," in *Alle Origini del Latino: Atti del Convegno della Societa Italiana di Glottologia*, ed. E. Vineis, Biblioteca della Societa italiana di glottologia (Pisa, 1982), arguing from linguistic evidence; and T. P. Wiseman "Democracy and Myth: The Life and Death of Remus," *Liverpool Classical Monthly* 16 (1991): 116–24, helpful and concise. The articles of Zorzetti (mentioned in the headnote to this chapter), which are of paramount importance, seem undecided with respect to the relevance of Greek "influence" upon early Rome. On the one hand, Zorzetti acknowledges and cites important work on the prevalence of Greek material remains in early Italy; at the same time, his analysis of archaic Roman musical culture makes use of Greek cultural forms as analogies to rather than sources for the early Roman situation. For my purposes, it is reconstruction of the Roman scene, and not its antecedents, that is of most importance. For Roman attitudes toward Greek culture see the works cited in note 64, below.

3. As implied by Zorzetti, "The *Carmina Convivalia*" and "Poetry and the Ancient City."

4. For the broad social and economic changes resulting from Rome's victory in the Second Punic War and subsequent imperialist expansion, see A. H. McDonald, "Rome and Italy in the Second Century B.C.," *Cambridge Historical Journal* 6 (1939): 124–46; "Rome and the Italian Confederation," *Journal of Roman Studies* 34 (1944): 11–33; A. J. Toynbee, *Hannibal's Legacy*, 2 vols. (London, 1965), esp. vol. 2; M. K. Hopkins, *Conquerors and Slaves*, Sociological Studies in Roman History 1 (Cambridge, 1978), esp. pp. 48–56 and 99–114; E. Frézouls, "Rome et les latins dans les premières décennies du IIe siècle av. J.-C.," *Ktéma* 6 (1981): 115–32; E. Gruen, *The Hellenistic World and the Coming of Rome* (Berkeley, 1984) esp. pp. 288–315; E. Gabba, "Rome and Italy in the Second Century B.C.," in *Cambridge Ancient History*, 2d ed. vol. 8: *Rome and the Mediterranean to 133 B.C.* (Cambridge, Eng., 1989), pp. 197–243; and S. Dyson, *Community and Society in Roman Italy* (Baltimore, 1992).

5. R. E. Smith, "The Aristocratic Epoch in Latin Literature," in *Essays on Roman Culture*, ed. A. J. Dunston (Toronto, 1976), pp. 187–223, calls attention to the aristocratic nature of early Latin literature. Whereas he sees this element as merely reflective of social reality, I prefer to focus on its role in the construction of that reality.

6. Zorzetti, "The *Carmina Convivalia*" and "Poetry and the Ancient City." T. Cole, "In response to Nevio Zorzetti," *Classical Journal* 86 (1991): 377–82, and C. R. Phillips III, "Poetry Before the Ancient City: Zorzetti and the Case of Rome," *Classical Journal* 86 (1991): 382–89, expand on and respond to the work of Zorzetti in constructive ways. On the prehistory of Latin literature, see also the essays in *Studien zur vorliterarischen Periode im frühen Rom*, ed. G. Vogt-Spira, Scripta oralia 12 (Tubingen, 1989). While useful, the papers collected by Vogt-Spira overemphasize the divide between oral and written cultures at the expense of other relevant distinctions between archaic Roman literary culture and the literature of the late third and early second centuries B.C.E. J. von Ungern-Sternberg, "Uberlegungen zur frühen römischen Uberlieferung im Lichte der oral-Tradition-Forschung," and D. Timpe, "Mündlichket und Schriftlichkeit als Basis der frührömischen Überlieferung," both in *Vergangenheit in mündlicher Überlieferung*, ed. J. von Ungern-Sternberg and H. Reinau, Colloquium Rauricum 1 (Stuttgart, 1988), consider the verifiability of the information about early Roman history that can be traced to oral tradition as well as the continuing interrelationship of written and oral "history" at Rome. G. Gianotti and A. Pennacini, *Le lettere e la società di Roma antica* (Torino, 1982), refer to the literary and other productions of the pre-Hannibalic period as features of "cultura gentilizia." T. P. Wiseman, *Remus: A Roman Myth* (Cambridge, 1995), passim, but esp. pp. 129ff., emphasizes the place of drama in pre-Hannibalic Rome.

7. On the Roman symposium, see in addition to Zorzetti, "The *Carmina Convivalia*," the important discussion by F. Dupont, *L'invention de la littérature de l'ivresse grecque au livre romain* (Paris, 1994), who distinguishes between the dining (*cena*) and drinking (*commissatio*) aspects of such gatherings. For archaeological evidence pertaining to sympotic gatherings in early Italy, see A. Rathje, "The Adoption of the Homeric Banquet in Italy in the Orientalizing Period," in *Sympotica*, ed. O. Murray (Oxford, 1990), pp. 279–88; and, on a later period, O. Murray, "Symposium and Genre in the Poetry of Horace," *Journal of Roman Studies* 75 (1985): 39–50. The continuing importance of *sodalitates* to the understanding of later periods of Latin literature is touched upon in chapters 6 and 8. Cole, "In Response to Nevio Zorzetti," and Wiseman, *Remus*, both supplement Zorzetti's emphasis on sympotic poetry in archaic Rome by calling attention to the evidence for a significant pre-Hannibalic tradition of Roman drama.

8. Zorzetti, "The *Carmina Convivalia*," p. 295.

9. On writing in early Rome, see, for example, G. Colonna, "Le iscrizioni strumentali latine del VI e V secolo a.C.," in *Lapis Satricanus*, ed. C. M. Stibbe et al. (The Hague, 1980), pp. 53–69; von Ungern-Sternberg, "Überlegung zur frühen römischen Überlieferung," esp. pp. 227–41; T. Cornell, "The Tyranny of the Evidence: A Discussion of the Possible Uses of Literacy in Etruria and Latium in the Archaic Age," in *Literacy in the Roman World*, Journal of Roman Archeology Supplementary Series 3 (Ann Arbor, 1991), pp. 7–33. Also on the association of writing with political power at an early period in Italian history, see G. Colonna, "«*Scriba cum rege sedens*»," in *Mélanges offerts à Jacques Heurgon: L'Italie préromaine et la Rome républicaine*, Collection de l'École française de Rome 27 (Rome, 1976), pp. 187–95. For more general reflections on literacy and power in the Roman world, see the essays by A. Bowman and

G. Woolf in *Literacy and Power in the Ancient World*, ed. Bowman and Woolf (Cambridge, 1994).

10. On the *collegium* on the Aventine, see N. Horsfall, "The *collegium poetarum*," *Bulletin of the Institute of Classical Studies* 23 (1976): 79–95, with modifications concerning the social position of scribes in N. Horsfall, "Statistics or States of Mind?" *Literacy in the Roman World*, Journal of Roman Archaeology Supplementary Series 3 (Ann Arbor, 1991), pp. 59–76; also A. Romano, *Il collegium scribarum*, Pubblicazioni del Dipartimento di diritto romano e storia della scienze romanistica dell'Università degli Studi di Napoli Federico, II.3 (Naples)—not yet available to me. The ancient testimonium concerning the collegium is Festus 446 Lindsay: itaque cum Livius Andronicus bello Punico secundo scribsisset carmen quod a virginibus est cantatum, quia prosperius respublica geri coepta est, publice adtributa est [et] in Aventino aedes Minervae in qua liceret scribis histrionibusque ac dona ponere; in honorem Livi, quia is et scribebat fabulas et agebat.

11. Zorzetti, "Poetry and the Ancient City," describes the *vates* as figures engaged in the reformation of pre-political (i.e., pre-state) rituals. This identification of the *vates* meshes nicely with my argment that the defeat of the *vates* represents the development of "literature" as an enterprise of the state broadly conceived as opposed to its being a by-product of the ritual performances of the aristocratic *sodalitates*. In other words, the transition from literature as performance to literature as text is at Rome less an evolution, as seems to be the case in many Greek city-states, than an imposition. On the gradual shift from performance to text in Greek history see now G. Nagy, *Poetry as Performance: Homer and Beyond* (Cambridge, 1996); also Dupont, *L'invention de la littérature*. In general it is helpful to read Zorzetti's theories concerning archaic Rome in terms of the more highly articulated and richly documented work of Nagy on archaic Greece, especially the opening chapters of *Pindar's Homer*.

12. Gruzinski, *The Conquest of Mexico*.

13. Cole, "In Response to Nevio Zorzetti," also calls attention to the availability of professionals in surrounding communities of Italy as a reason for the transition between what I am calling pre-Musaic and Musaic cultures. Phillips, "Poetry before the Ancient City," p. 385, usefully asks why "the elite so readily yielded its erstwhile prerogative" in musical culture: my argument is that under the changing circumstances of Hannibalic and post-Hannibalic Rome the professionalization of literature actually made its management by the elites an easier task.

14. The passage in question reads: poeticae artis honos non erat: si quis in ea re studebat aut sese ad convivia adplicabat, grassator vocabatur (*Carmen de moribus*, fgm. 2 Jordan). On guests performing at *convivia*, see Cic. *Tusc.* 4.3: gravissimus auctor in Originibus dixit Cato morem apud maiores hunc epularum fuisse, ut deinceps qui accubarent canerent ad tibiam clarorum virorum laudes atque virtutes.

15. For the view that Cato is differentiating between genres of poetry, see Gruen, *Culture and National Identity*, pp. 71–72. My interpretation is supported by Cic. *Tusc.* 1.3, where Cicero goes on to differentiate sympotic poetry, of which Cato approves, not from epic poetry per se but from Nobilior's taking of client poets into his province with him.

16. Nagy, *Pindar's Homer*, pp. 17–51.

17. On the politics of writing, see chapter 5 and the works cited there, especially W. V. Harris, *Ancient Literacy* (Cambridge, Mass., 1989), and the essays collected in *Literacy in the Roman World*. My analysis of the passage from Cato discussed in the text expands upon the brief remarks of Zorzetti, "Poetry and the Ancient City," 322.

18. Gruen, *Studies in Greek Culture and Roman Policy*, p. 92.

19. T. Habinek, *The Colometry of Latin Prose*, University of California Studies in Classical Philology 25 (Berkeley, 1985), pp. 187ff.

20. Gruzinski, *The Conquest of Mexico*.

21. O. Skutsch, "On Three Fragments of Porcius Licinus and the Tutiline Gate," *Bulletin of the Institute of Classical Studies* 17 (1970): 120–23. See also H. Mattingly, "L. Porcius Licinus and the Beginning of Latin Poetry," in *Tria Lustra: Essays and Notes Presented to John Pinsent*, ed. H. D. Jocelyn and H. Hurt, Liverpool Classical Papers 3 (Liverpool, 1993), pp. 163–68.

22. G. Nagy, "Hesiod," in *Ancient Writers: Greece and Rome*, ed. T. J. Luce (New York, 1982), vol. 1, pp. 43–74.

23. Cicero's chronology at *Brutus* 72–73 continues to be subjected to a lesser degree of skepticism than the Accian chronology he seeks to repudiate. For a concise presentation of the problems attendant upon Cicero's chronology of early Latin literature, see A. E. Douglas, *M. Tulli Ciceronis Brutus* (Oxford, 1966), pp. 62–64.

24. L. R. Taylor, "The Opportunities for Dramatic Performances in the Time of Plautus and Terence," *Transactions and Proceedings of the American Philological Association* 68 (1937): 284–304.

25. A. H. McDonald, "Rome and Italy in the Second Century B.C.," *Cambridge Historical Journal* 6 (1939): 124–46.

26. A. H. McDonald, "Rome and the Italian Confederation"; A. Astin, *Cato the Censor* (Oxford, 1978), pp. 54–55 and 319–23.

27. Toynbee, *Hannibal's Legacy*, vol. 2, pp. 128–64; Gabba, "Rome and Italy in the Second Century B.C."

28. On the relationship between colonization and Latinization, see E. Pulgram, *The Tongues of Italy* (Cambridge, Mass., 1958), pp. 264ff; Harris, *Ancient Literacy*, pp. 175–284; and the brief remarks of M. Durante, "Evoluzione storica del rapporto tra lingua e dialetti in Italia" in *Lingua, Dialetti, Società: Atti del Convegno della Società Italiana di Glottologia*, ed. E. De Felice, Orientamenti linguistici 10 (Pisa, 1979), pp. 13–29, relative to the failure of classical Latin to develop regional dialects. On linguistic diversity and linguistic contact in early Italy, see in addition to the above: A. Budinzsky, *Die Ausbreitung der lateinischen Sprache über Italien und die Provinzen des römischen Reiches* (Berlin, 1881); A. Borst, *Der Turmbau von Babel: Geschichte der Meinungen über Ursprung und Vielfalt der Sprachen und Völker*, Bd. I, *Fundamente und Aufbau* (Stuttgart, 1957), pp. 139–40 and 152–58; N. Pounds, *An Historical Geography of Europe* (Cambridge, 1973); R. Lazzeroni, "Contatti di lingue e di culture nell'Italia antica," in *La cultura italica: Atti del Convegno della Società Italiana di Glottologia*, Orientamenti linguistici 5 (Pisa, 1978), pp. 91–102; E. Campanile, "La diaspora italica: Implicazioni storico-culturali di fatti linguistici," *La cultura italica*, pp. 103–20; G. Devoto, *The Languages of Italy*, trans. V. Katainen (Chicago, 1978).

29. Campanile, "La diaspora italica."

30. in coloniam, mercules, scribere nolim, si trium virum sim, spatiatorem atque fescenninum. For interpretation, see R. E. A. Palmer, *Roman Religion and Roman Empire* (Philadelphia, 1974), p. 177.

31. qui Obsce et Volsce fabulantur, nam Latine nesciunt (175 Ribbeck). See B. Rawson, "Theatrical Life in Republican Rome and Italy," *Proceedings of the British School in Rome* 53 (1985): 97–113, who discusses the other passages cited in this paragraph as well.

32. On immigration and urbanization during this period, see Gabba, "Rome and Italy in the Second Century B.C.," pp. 212–21.

33. Lucilius 1034ff. Marx; discussed by Rawson, "Theatrical Life."

34. A. Meillet, *Esquisse d'une histoire de la langue latine* (Paris, 1928), pp. 108–9. Cf. L. Palmer, *The Latin Language* (London, 1954), p. 83; G. P. Shipp, "Greek in Plautus," *Wiener Studien* 66 (1953): 105–12; and R. MacMullen, "Hellenizing the Romans" *Historia* 40 (1991): 419–38 with further bibliography.

35. Meillet, *Esquisse*, pp. 108–9 (my translation).

36. Devoto, *The Languages of Italy*, pp. 89–90.

37. On Terence's language as *purus sermo*, see conveniently S. Goldberg, *Understanding Terence* (Princeton, 1986), pp. 170–202.

38. See A. Traglia, "Sulle origini della lingua letteraria latina," in *La formazione delle lingue letterarie*, ed. A. Moreschini, Biblioteca della Società Italiana di Glottologia 8 (Pisa, 1985), pp. 109–12.

39. On the persistence on non-Latin substrata in dialects of modern Italy, see Pulgram, *The Tongues of Italy*, p. 281; T. deMauro, *Storia linguistica dell'Italia unita*, Nuova edizione (Bari, 1970); Devoto, *The Languages of Italy*; and A. L. Lepschy and G. Lepschy, *La lingua italiana* (Milan, 1981).

40. Gellner, *Nations and Nationalism*, p. 127. On linguistic complexity and social differentiation at Rome, see W. M. Bloomer, *Latinity and Literary Society at Rome* (Philadelphia, 1997).

41. Hobsbawm, *Nations and Nationalism since 1780*, pp. 37–38. On language and literature as constitutive of national identity, see the other works cited in the headnote above. On an ancient situation with some similarities to the one sketched here, see the discussion of Coptic in K. Hopkins, "Conquest by Book," in *Literacy in the Roman World*, pp. 133–59.

42. On aristocratic recruitment, see J. Powis, *Aristocracy*, New Perspectives on the Past 2 (Oxford, 1984), esp. pp. 19ff. On the state's need to provide for reproduction of the conditions of production, see the classic essay by L. Althusser, "Ideology and Ideological State Apparatuses: Notes towards an Investigation," in *Lenin and Philosophy and Other Essays*, trans. B. Brewster (New York, 1971), pp. 127–86, with elaborations and modifications pertaining to the Roman situation in E. Gunderson, "The Ideology of the Arena," *Classical Antiquity* 15 (1996): 113–51. The role of literature in acculturation in archaic Greece has been widely discussed: see, for example, C. Calame, *Les choeurs des jeunes filles en gréce archaïque*, 2 vols. (Paris, 1978); also L. Kurke, "Pindar's *Sixth Pythian* and the Tradition of Advice Poetry," *Transactions and Proceedings of the American Philological Association* 120 (1990): 85–108. With respect to the Roman context we might imagine the pre-Musaic *carmina* as carrying forward the project of aris-

tocratic ideological reproduction in the absence of "Musaic" literature but for the quick emergence of rival sources of social authority, and thus, one hypothesizes, rival strategies of reproduction and acculturation.

43. On ascribed vs. achieved status, see M. Sahlins, "Poor Man, Rich Man, Big-Man, Chief: Political Types in Melanesia and Polynesia," *Comparative Studies in Society and History* 5 (1963): 285–303, adapted to classical context by W. Donlan, "Reciprocities in Homer," *Classical World* 75 (1981/82): 137–75, and B. Qviller, "The Dynamics of Homeric Society," *Symbolae Osloenses* 56 (1981): 109–55.

44. On the etymology of *aestimare/existimare*, see A. Ernout and A. Meillet, *Dictionnaire étymologique de la langue latine*, 4e éd. (Paris, 1979), p. 13, and E. Benveniste, *Le vocabulaire des institutions indo-européennes* (Paris 1968), vol. 2, pp. 121–28. On *exemplum*, see Benveniste, vol. 1, pp. 85–86. Festus 23 Lindsay describes an *aestimata poena* as one that sets a relationship between money and animals: aestimata poena ab antiquis ab aere dicta est, qui eam aestimaverunt aere, ovem decussis, bovem centussis, hoc est decem vel centum assibus. For other earlier equations of money and animals, see E. Peruzzi, "Le origini della monèta à Roma," in *L'Etrusco e le lingue dell'Italia antica*, ed. A. Moreschini, Biblioteca della Società italiana di Glottologia 9 (Pisa, 1985), pp. 39–52. The link between *aestimatio* and *exemplum* is made explicit at Festus 72 Lindsay: Exemplum est quod sequamur aut vitemus. Exemplar ex quo simile faciamus. Illud animo aestimatur, istud oculis conspicitur. D. Schmandt-Besserat, "From Accounting to Written Language," in *The Social Construction of Written Communication* (Norwood, N.J., 1988), pp. 119–30, associates the use of exempla with the shift "from accounting to written language." Z. Yavetz, "*Existimatio, Fama*, and the Ides of March," *Harvard Studies in Classical Philology* 78 (1974): 35–66, discusses the elements that contributed to the acquisition of a good or bad *existimatio* in the late Republic. He notes the relative rarity of the noun in early Latin, but ignores related uses of the verb *existimare*. Yavetz also expresses some puzzlement over the relationship between *fama* and *existimatio*; but it is my impression that the etymological force of each persists well into the classical period, with *fama* being what people say *(fari)* about you and *existimatio* being their evaluation *(ex + aestimare)* of you. The two will often overlap and may even coincide, but they remain distinct concepts. In general Yavetz seems to go astray by trying to read modern concepts of "public opinion" into the ancient evidence rather than letting the ancient concepts, practices, and institutions emerge from the texts that encode them.

45. Examples in G. Lodge, *Lexicon Plautinum* (Leipzig, 1924; reprinted Hildesheim, 1971), vol 1, p. 563.

46. On the socioeconomic context of *De agricultura*, see in particular Astin, *Cato the Censor*, pp. 240–66. Astin rightly emphasizes Cato's own interest in agriculture as a moneymaking proposition and surveys controversy both ancient and modern over Cato's allegedly hypocritical behavior in this regard. He also rightly notes the social dimension of Cato's privileging of agriculture. Astin does not, however, inquire why agriculture should be socially privileged or why this privileging should be invoked at the outset of the treatise. Similiar problems afflict Humphreys's intemperate critique of Meyer in S. C. Humphreys, "War, Imperial-

ism, and the Early State: A Comparative View," in *Staat und Staatlichkeit in der frühen römischen Republik*, ed. W. Eder (Stuttgart, 1990), pp. 293–302, responding to J. C. Meyer, "From a Turkish Village to Republican Rome: Ideology, Mentality, and Control," in the same volume, pp. 258–77. Meyer finds an instructive parallel to Cato's attitude in contemporary preindustrial villages where wealthy people are often "eager to dissociate themselves in words and material symbols from the market economy," which may well be a source of their wealth. Humphreys challenges the appropriateness of Meyer's economic model but misses Meyer's larger point that the ancient sources, such as *De agricultura*, are ideological rather than descriptive. Thus her assertion (pp. 297–98) that "the pursuit of wealth by archaic elites seems to arise from their commitment to traditional values" begs the question of the origin of those "values" and the sources of their authorizing power at any given moment in history. Of course, as Gabba notes with respect to Cato's treatise ("Rome and Italy in the Second Century B.C.," p. 205), there is a contradiction within the text in that "the Catonian farm as thus depicted [i.e., dependent on slave labor and substantial capital investment] certainly appears to conflict with the ideology expressed in the prologue, which harks back to the model of the small, self-sufficient peasant farm. Gabba claims that the contradiction is "resolved by the timocratic nature of Roman and Italian society." My point is that texts like the *De agricultura* make it possible for such timocracy to flourish.

47. See the articles by Zorzetti cited in the headnote to this chapter.

48. The selections in this paragraph are from Polybius 31.23.9–12 (Loeb translation).

49. Ennius *Annales* 268–86. I rely on the interpretation of O. Skutsch, *The Annals of Quintus Ennius* (Oxford, 1985), pp. 447–62. E. Badian, "*Nobiles Amici*: Art and Literature in an Aristocratic Society," *Classical Philology* 80 (1985): 341–63, claims that the consul in the passage under consideration held office during the First Punic War. On the passage see also T. Habinek, "The Politics of Candor," *Apeiron* 23 (1990): 165–85. Recently, S. Goldberg, *Epic in Republican Rome* (Oxford, 1995), pp. 121ff., has also linked this passage to the role of the literati in early Rome. He denies that the "good friend" is in a servile relationship to the nobleman and suggests that the passage is indicative of Ennian poetry's "countervailing power." I agree, but on condition that we accept that this description is Ennius's self-interested representation of the way poetry ought to be (or indeed, ought to have been, since the episode is placed at least a generation prior to Ennius's description of it). It seems worth noting that when Vergil refers to this passage at *Aen.* 11.820ff. in the fateful exchange between Camilla and Acca, he specifically describes the latter as *ex aequalibus unam*, perhaps signaling the distance between the asymmetric relationship described by Ennius and the more egalitarian arrangement of Camilla and her companions.

50. On the aristocratic connotations of *bonus* and related words, see J. Hellegouarc'h, *Le vocabulaire latin des rélations et des partis politiques sous la république*: Publications de la Faculté des lettres et sciences humaines de l'Université de Lille 11 (Paris, 1963), pp. 484–500. Hellegouarc'h's attempt to distinguish ethical from social uses of such words is anachronistic: see C. de Meo, *Lingue tecniche del latino*, Testi e manuali per l'insegnamento universitario del latino 16 (Bologna, 1983), pp. 209–23

51. The texts of the inscriptions are conveniently arranged and analyzed by J. van Sickle, "The *Elogia* of the Cornelii Scipiones and the Origin of Epigram at Rome," *American Journal of Philology* 108 (1987): 41–55. See also A. Ernout, *Receuil des textes latins archaïques* (Paris, 1957), pp. 12–21, and F. Coarelli, "Il sepolcro degli Scipioni," *Dialoghi di archeologia* 6 (1972): 36–106.

52. On the aristocratic Roman funeral, see M. Durry, *Éloge funèbre d'une matrone romaine* (Paris, 1950); C. Nicolet, *The World of the Citizen in Republican Rome*, trans. P. S. Falla (Berkeley, 1980), chapter 9; W. Kierdorf, *Laudatio funebris*, Beiträge zur klassischen Philologie 106 (Meisenheim am Glan, 1980); also F. Dupont, *L'acteur-roi* (Paris, 1985). The key ancient text is Polybius 6.123.

53. On the inventiveness of the historiographical tradition, see C. Letta, "L'Italia dei mores romani nelle Origines di Catone," *Athenaeum* 62 (1984): 3–30 and 416–39; and R. E. Mitchell, *Patricians and Plebeians: The Origin of the Roman State* (Ithaca, N.Y., and London, 1990).

54. A. Appadurai, "The Past as Scarce Resource," *Man* n.s. 46 (1981): 201–19.

55. On the link between epinician and funeral laudation in Pindar, see Kurke, *The Traffic in Praise*, pp. 62ff. and 257ff.

56. Of course there is an element of theatricalization of aristocratic performance as early as Homer. For the continuing tension between theatrical and narratival authority in Roman culture more generally and Roman historiography in particular, see A. Feldherr, *Spectacle and Society in Livy* (Berkeley, 1997). S. Bartsch, *Actors in the Audience: Theatricality and Doublespeak from Nero to Trajan* (Cambridge, Mass., 1994), observes a similar tension but attributes it to a small group of emperors rather than to the structural dynamics of Roman society.

57. For a useful assessment of Terence's relationship to members of the Roman aristocracy, see Gruen, *Culture and National Identity*, pp. 183ff., with ample consideration of earlier views. I am generally in accord with Gruen's view of second century theater "as setting forth the articulation and propagation of aristocratic values" (p. 202).

58. On Terence and oratory, see Goldberg, *Understanding Terence*, pp. 40ff.

59. *Contaminatio* is often misinterpreted as referring to mixing or combining when in fact it refers to spoilage. For the correct interpretation of the term in a literary context, see Goldberg, *Understanding Terence*, pp. 91–122.

60. On the meaning of *populus*, see Hellegouarc'h, *Le vocabulaire latin des rélations et des partis politiques sous la république*, pp. 515–18; and Nicolet, *The World of the Citizen*, pp. 361–73. On the *populus* as audience of Roman theatrical productions, see Wiseman, *Remus*, p. 132n. 11. I have not encountered elsewhere the sociological interpretation of *Heaut.* 32 advanced in the text.

61. I rely on the report in Kauer and Lindsay's Oxford text.

62. The verse was already correctly interpreted by Lindenbruck in 1726: est autem locutio elegans, licet rarior, q.d. mores utriusque ex comparatione mutua aestimans, et de utriusque ex hac comparatione judicam.

63. D. Konstan, *Roman Comedy* (Ithaca, 1986), interprets the entire play as an ironic reading of the comic tradition.

64. Roman attitudes toward Greeks and Greek culture are treated by C. Gallini, "Che cosa intendere per ellenizzazione? Problemi di metodo," *Dialoghi di Archeologia* 7 (1973): 175–91, and P. Veyne, "The Hellenization of Rome and

the Question of Acculturations," *Diogenes* 106 (1979): 1–27, both of whom consider varietes of Hellenization; by N. Petrochilos, *Roman Attitudes to the Greeks*, National and Capodistrian University of Athens Faculty of Arts, S. Saripolos's Library 25 (Athens, 1974)—largely a catalogue of references; and by R. MacMullen, "Hellenizing the Romans (2nd Century B.C.)," *Historia* 40 (1991): 419–38—an insightful article, I although I am less inclined than is MacMullen to take Roman moralizing about sexual matters at face value.

65. For the Carneades episode, see Plutarch *Cato* 22.1–5, Cic. *Rep.* 3.9, Pliny *H.N.*. 7.112; discussion by Gruen, *Culture and National Identity*, p. 53. On Cato's familiarity with and interest in Greek literature and learning, see Letta, "L'Italia dei mores romani," and Gruen, *Culture and National Identity*, pp. 52–83.

66. On the controversy of 92 B.C.E., see Gruen, *Studies in Greek Culture and Roman Policy*, pp. 179–91, a study to be used with caution, since Gruen somewhat uncritically absorbs the elite perspective of the sources, referring to "vulgarizers who would cut [traditional education] adrift from its Hellenic moorings," "the humane tradition of Greek learning," (as opposed to Latin!), "the cultured intellectual L. Crassus," "the refined elite" (all quotations from pp. 190–91). For a different perspective on the controversy, see E. Narducci, "Le risonanze del potere," in *Lo spazio letterario di Roma antica*, ed. G. Cavallo et al. (Rome, 1989), vol. 2, pp. 533–77: Narducci argues that the *ludus* of the *rhetores Latini* would have made the socially and politically valuable rhetorical education available to a broader sector of the population than did home schooling by Greek preceptors and thus would have posed a potential threat to aristocratic hegemony. The strong-arm attempt to close the schools thus reflects what Narducci describes as "l'esigenza di conservare nelle mani del ceto dirigenti l'arma potentissima della parola." (p. 548) On Cicero's education, see the closing chapters of the *Brutus*. On his son's, see the opening of *De officiis*.

67. The classic discussion of symbolic capital is to be found in P. Bourdieu, *Outline of a Theory of Practice*, trans. R. Nice (Cambridge, 1977), pp. 177–83. But see also the less widely cited piece by Bourdieu entitled "Symbolic Power," a translation by R. Nice of a lecture delivered at Harvard in 1973 and printed as part of *Centre for Contemporary Cultural Studies, Stencilled Occasional Paper* 46 (University of Birmingham, 1977).

68. On sumptuary legislation see Kübler, article "sumptus" in *RE* 2.7.4A.1:901ff.; D. Daube, *Aspects of Roman Law* (Edinburgh, 1969), pp. 117–28; A. Astin, "Roman Government and Politics, 200–134 B.C." in *Cambridge Ancient History*, 2d ed., vol. 8: *Rome and the Mediterranean to 133 B.C.*, pp. 163–96 (esp. pp. 181–85); Meyer, "From a Turkish Village to Republican Rome" Ampolo, commentary on Meyer, "From a Turkish Village"; Gruen, *Culture and National Identity*, pp. 69–70. Ampolo resurrects L. Gernet's argument that legislation limiting funerary expenditures forces aristocrats to spend outside the clan. While this may be an indirect effect of such legislation, I find it difficult to relate this explanation to the series of sumptuary laws in the third through first centuries B.C.E. at Rome that set an absolute limit on expenditure.

69. See Kurke, *The Traffic in Praise*, pp. 225ff., who builds upon the analyses of M. I. Finley, *Studies in Land and Credit in Ancient Athens, 500 to 200 B.C.*

(New Brunswick, N.J., 1952); L. Gernet, *The Anthropology of Ancient Greece*, trans. J. Hamilton and B. Nagy (Baltimore, 1981), pp. 343–48; and V. Gabrielson, "Phanera and Aphanes Ousia in Classical Athens," *Classica et Mediaevalia* 37 (1986): 99–114.

70. For a brief discussion of the censorship and the census, see A. Drummond in *Cambridge Ancient History*, 2d ed., vol. 7, part 2 (Cambridge, 1989), pp. 197–98; also chapter 2 of Nicolet, *The World of the Citizen*. Cf. G. Pieri, *L'histoire du cens jusqu'à la fin de la république romaine*, Publications de l'Institut de Droit Romain de l'Université de Paris 25 (Paris, 1968).

71. On this strategy, see Z. Yavetz, "The Failure of Catiline's Conspiracy," *Historia* 12 (1963): 485–99 and chapter 3 in this volume.

72. E. J. Kenney, "Books and Readers in the Roman World," in *Cambridge History of Latin Literature*, ed. E. J. Kenney and W. V. Clausen (Cambridge, 1982), pp. 3–32; R. Starr, "The Circulation of Literary Texts in the Roman World," *Classical Quarterly* 81 (1987): 213–23; and G. Cavallo, "Testo, libro, lettura," in *Lo spazio letterario di Roma antica*, 5 vols., ed. G. Cavallo et al. (Roma, 1989), vol. 2, pp. 307–42.

73. W. Görler, "Zum Virtus-Fragment des Lucilius (1326–1338 Marx) und zur Geschichte der stoische Güterlehre," *Hermes* 112 (1984): 445–68; W. Raschke, "The Virtue of Lucilius," *Latomus* 49 (1990): 352–69.

74. Goldberg, *Understanding Terence*, pp. 10ff.

75. Letta, "L'Italia dei mores romani nelle *Origines* di Catone."

76. T. Habinek, "The Politics of Candor in Cicero's *De Amicitia*," *Apeiron* 23 (1990): 165–85; "Ideology for an Empire in the Prefaces to Cicero's Dialogues," in *Roman Literature and Ideology: Ramus Essays for J. P. Sullivan, ed.* A. J. Boyle (Berwick, 1994), pp. 55–67.

77. On representations of Greek vs. Roman modes of philosophizing, see T. Habinek, "Science and Tradition in *Aeneid* 6," *Harvard Studies in Classical Philology* 92 (1989): 223–55, esp. 247ff.

78. On *tutela*, see S. Dixon, "*Infirmitas sexus*: Womanly Weakness in Roman Law," *Tijdschrift voor Rechtgeschiedenis/ Legal History Review* 52 (1984): 343–71; and J. F. Gardner, *Women in Roman Law and Society* (London, 1986), pp. 5–30. Further discussion of Cicero's use of the term in relationship to Greek cultural wealth at Habinek, "Ideology for an Empire," pp. 58ff., esp. n. 10.

79. The prefaces to *De oratore, Tusculan Disputations, De finibus*, and *De officiis* are discussed in greater detail at Habinek, "Ideology for an Empire." On Cicero's attempt to create for an expanded Roman elite "una base comune di cultura e di idealità etico-politiche," see also Narducci, "Le risonanze del potere."

80. Bourdieu, *Outline of a Theory of Practice*, p. 177.

81. This is the position of T. P. Wiseman, *Catullus and His World: A Reappraisal* (Cambridge, 1985). On the chronologies more generally, see chapter 4 in this volume.

CHAPTER THREE
CICERO AND THE BANDITS

This chapter was first delivered as a lecture before the Southern Section of the California Classical Association in April 1990. During the spring of 1994, it was updated in preparation for publication in this volume. Since then, two important works on the Catilinarians have come to my attention: D. Konstan, "Rhetoric and the Crisis of Legitimacy in Cicero's Catilinarian Orations," in *Rethinking the History of Rhetoric*, ed. T. Poulakos (Boulder, Colorado, 1993), pp. 11–30, and W. Batstone, "Cicero's Construction of Consular *Ethos* in the *First Catilinarian*," *Transactions and Proceedings of the American Philological Association* 1994 (124): 211–66. Konstan shares my view of the Catilinarians as expressive of a "crisis of legitimation" and reads them as exemplary of political rhetoric's more general tendency to persuade not so much by argumentation as by making contested assumptions seem self-evident. Batstone analyzes the first speech in terms of traditional focus on "rhetorical problem" and concludes that the speech is chiefly concerned to "display Cicero, his passion and his reason, his wisdom and providence, his powers of oratory" (p. 217). Batstone summarizes his difference with Konstan, which he rightly describes as "a matter of degree," as follows: "Konstan's view . . . allows him to see a substantive contest of symbols and values; mine brings to light a more purely rhetorical effort to establish the authority of the consul's voice and *ethos*. . . . I believe that Cicero needed flexible authority supported by a range of symbolic associations more than he needed to establish the legitimacy of a particular symbolic system" (p. 218, n. 17). My position is that Cicero gets what Batstone says he wants (flexible authority) by doing what Konstan says he does (raising issues of legitimacy). As to the "reality" of the crisis of legitimacy, I am inclined to believe that Cicero's invocation of it is itself testimony to its existence. Viewed collectively, the historicizing tendencies of Konstan, Batstone, and myself represent a decided shift from earlier interest in ancient political orations as "eloquent expressions of basic human values" (C. Wooten, cited by Konstan, "Rhetoric and the Crisis of Legitimacy," p. 29).

1. The passage in the text is from Aug. *Civ. dei* 4.4, which is an elaboration of an anecdote in Cic. *Rep.* 3.24. These and the other passages cited in this paragraph are discussed by A. La Penna, "Il bandito e il re," *Maia* 31 (1979): 29–31.

2. Tac. *Ann.* 2.40.5; cf. Dio 57.16.4.

3. Dio 76 (77) 10.7.

4. On bandits in the ancient Mediterranean world, see P. Briant, "«Brigandage», Dissidence et Conquête en Asie Achéménide et Hellenistique," *Dialogues d'histoire ancienne* 21 (1976): 163–279; La Penna, "Il bandito e il re"; A. Milan, "Ricerche sul *latrocinium* in Livio I: *Latro* nelle fonti pre-augustee," *Atti dell'Istituto Veneto di Scienze, Lettere ed Arti*, Classe di scienze morali, lettere ed arti 138 (1979/80): 171–97; J. Burian, "*Latrones*: Ein Begriff in römischen literarischen und juristischen Quellen," *Eirene* 21 (1984): 17–23; and B. Shaw, "Bandits in the Roman Empire," *Past and Present* 105 (1984): 3–52. On bandits or banditry in relationship to the state, see in particular Caes. *B.G.* 7.38.8 and Sall. *Hist.* 4.69.23, where the Romans are describes as *latrones gentium*. N. Brown, "Brigands and State Building: The Invention of Banditry in Modern Egypt," *Comparative Studies in Society and History* 32 (1990): 258–81, discusses the close link between banditry and state building in nineteenth-century Egypt and Ottoman Cilicia; in the first case, the authorities "invented" banditry to justify the extension of the state security apparatus; in the second, the authorities "disinvented" banditry by offering bandit leaders "membership in the ruling

elite" (p. 280). See also P. Sant Cassia, "Banditry, Myth, and Terror in Cyprus and other Mediterranean Societies," *Comparative Studies in Society and History* 35 (1993): 773–95.

5. On bandits as a group, note the use of the collective *latrocinium*, in contrast to *grassator* (mugger) and *sicarius* (cutthroat) for which there is no collective noun. For bandit protocol, see Apul. *Met.* 4.21, 6.31, with discussion by T. Habinek in "Lucius' Rite of Passage," *Materiali e discussioni per analisi dei testi classici* 1990 (25): 40–69, esp. pp. 64–66, and the various passages discussed by J. Winkler, "Lollianos and the Desperadoes," *Journal of Hellenic Studies* 100 (1980): 155–81. That these texts are fictional is immaterial, since what concerns us here are representations of banditry and their deployment within certain rhetorical contexts. In addition, Aug. *Civ. dei.* 4.4 mentions procedures used by bandits for distributing booty among themselves.

6. Shaw, "Bandits in the Roman Empire."

7. For the history and context of the Catilinarian orations, see the items listed by A.Vasaly, *Representations: Images of the World in Ciceronian Oratory* (Berkeley, 1993), ch. 2, n. 16; also Batstone, "Cicero's Construction of Consular Ethos."

8. The passages cited in the text are from *Catil.*1.23, 1.27, 1.31, and 1.33, respectively. See also *Catil.* 2.1, 2.16, 2.24, and 3.17. In the fourth, Catilinarian references to bandits are dropped, although the imagery associated with banditry is not, as will be discussed in the text.

9. *Paradoxa Stoicorum* 27.

10. For a list of occurrences of this and other insults, see G. Achard, *Pratique rhétorique et idéologie politique dans les discours 'optimates' de Ciceron, Mnemosyme* Supplement 68 (Leiden, 1981). Catiline, Clodius, and Antonius are frequently targeted by Cicero as *latrones*, Gabinius once (*prov. cons.* 9): see Achard, *Pratique rhetorique*, p. 521. Clodius, Piso, Gabinius, and Antony are also described as pirates (*praedones* [Achard, p. 329]), figures regarded by the ancients as bandits of the sea. Achard notes that during the final years of Cicero's life the charge of *latrocinium* makes its way into the writing of Cicero's correspondents. A. Corbeill, *Controlling Laughter: Political Humor in the Late Republic* (Princeton, 1996), discusses other sorts of insults in Ciceronian oratory, especially those having to do with physical peculiarities, bodily functions, unusual names, and violations real or perceived of the Roman system of sex and gender.

11. Decrees not valid if passed at night: Liv. 44.20.1, Cic. *Att.* 1.17.9, Cic. *Phil.* 3.24, Aul. Gell. 14.7.8. See also P. Willems, *Le Sénat de la république romaine*, tome II: *Les attributions du Sénat* (Louvain and Berlin, 1883); and M. Bonneford-Coudry, *Le Sénat de la république romaine de la guerre d'Hannibal à Auguste: Pratiques délibératives et prise de décision*, Bibliothèque des écoles françaises d'Athènes et de Rome, 273 (Rome, 1989).

12. Boy sacrifice: Dio 37.30.3. On accusations of human sacrifice in antiquity, see the important discussion by J. B. Rives, "Human Sacrifice among Pagans and Christians," *Journal of Roman Studies* 85 (1995): 65–85. With respect to the story of human sacrifice by the Catilinarian conspirators, Rives observes: "The effect of the story was to 'barbarize' a Roman, to put the Catilinarian conspirators outside the pale of civilization as everyone in Rome, of whatever political inclinations, would define it."

13. Wall references at *Catil.* 1.10, 1.32, 2.17.

14. Wives against husbands: Appian *B.C.* 2.2.

15. Sons against fathers: Sall. *Catil.* 43.2; at least one father fought back: *Catil.* 39.5. Dio 37.36.4 refers to fathers who slew their sons.

16. Hilaria episode: Herodian 1.10f., a passage discussed at some length by Shaw, "Bandits in the Roman Empire," pp. 45–46. See also M. Gleason, "Festive Satire: Julian's *Misopogon* and the New Year at Antioch," *Journal of Roman Studies* 76 (1986): 106–19.

17. *Catil.* 3.10: quod Lentulo et aliis Saturnalibus caedem fieri atque urbem incendi placeret.

18. Cf. the definition of *res publica* offered at Cic. *Rep.* 1.39.

19. Milan, "Ricerche sul *latrocinium* in Livio I," reviews the pre-Augustan uses of the terms *latro* and *latrocinium*, but makes an unnecessary distinction between so-called political uses of the terms and references to brigandage. As the present chapter suggests, banditry always has the potential to be political or to be treated as political by representatives of the state. R. Nisbet, *M. Tulli Ciceronis In L. Calpurnium Pisonem Oratio* (Oxford, 1961), Appendix on Invective, categorizes accusations of *latrocinium* under "greed"; Achard, *Pratique rhétorique et idéologie politique*, pp. 329 and 340, attributes Cicero's use of the word to its association with violence. On the history of the term *latro*, see also Shaw, "Bandits in the Roman Empire," pp. 26ff.

20. Cf. the remark of Cato at Sallust *Catil.* 52 to the effect that the senators care more about their villas and art collections than about the "common wealth."

21. Z. Yavetz, "The Failure of Catiline's Conspiracy," *Historia* 12 (1963): 485–99.

22. Yavetz, "The Failure of Catiline's Conspiracy." Fear of freed slaves may also figure in Cicero's boast of avoiding a *tumultus*, since the declaration of a *tumultus* can involve the arming of slaves. See discussion in text, below.

23. J. Griffin, *Real Life and Latin Poetry* (Oxford, 1982), pp. 44–45, remarks, "Cicero is not trying to transport his audience into an ideal realm of exotic fictions, but to present recognisable and real people in a special way, to lead to decisive action."

24. qui magno in aere alieno maiores etiam possessiones habent, quarum amore adducti dissolvi nullo modo possunt. horum hominum species est honestissima (sunt enim locupletes), voluntas vero et causa inpudentissima: (*Catil.* 2.18).

25. ii sunt coloni, qui se in insperatis ac repentinis pecuniis sumptuosius insolentiusque iactarunt. Hi dum aedificant tamquam beati, dum praediis lectis, familiis magnis, conviviis apparatis delectantur, in tantum aes alienum inciderunt, ut, si salvi esse velint, Sulla sit iis ab inferis excitandus (*Catil.* 2.20).

26. Non vident id se cupere, quod si adepti sint, fugitivo alieni aut gladiatori concedi sit necesse? (*Catil.* 2.19).

27. qui partim inertia, partim male gerendo negotio, partim etiam sumptibus in vetere aere alieno vacillant, qui vadimoniis, iudiciis, proscriptione bonorum defetigati permulti et ex urbe et ex agris se in illa castra conferre dicuntur (*Catil* 2.21).

28. quintum genus est parricidarum, sicariorum, denique omnium facinerosorum (*Catil.* 2.22).

29. The passage in the text is a paraphrase of *Catil.* 2.26: vos quem ad modum iam antea dixi vestra tecta vigiliis custodiisque defendite; mihi, ut urbi sine vestro motu ac sine ullo tumultu satis esset praesidii, consultum atque provisum est. Coloni omnes municipesque vetri certiores a me facti de hac nocturna excursione Catilinae facile urbes suas finesque defendent.

30. On the meaning of *coniuratio* see *RE* 4.885, J. Hellegouarc'h, *Le vocabulaire latin des relations et des partis politiques sous la république*, Publications de la Faculté des lettres et sciences humaines de l'Université de Lille 11 (Paris, 1963).

31. For text, see A. Ernout, *Récueil des textes latins archaïques* (Paris, 1957), pp. 58ff.

32. This passage is ably discussed by A. Feldherr in his 1990 Berkeley dissertation, "Spectacle and Society in Livy's History," which is the basis of a forthcoming book of the same title (Berkeley, 1997). I am grateful to him for calling my attention to the passage and to the articles by Bleicken and Instinsky cited in the following note.

33. J. Bleicken, "*Coniuratio*: Die Schwurszene auf den Münzen und Gemmen der römischen Republik," *Jahrbuch für Numismatik und Geldgeschichte* 13 (1963): 51–69; H. Instinsky, "Schwurszene und *Coniuratio*," *Jahrbuch für Numismatik und Geldgeschichte* 14 (1964): 83–87.

34. Servius *Ad Aen.* 8.5: CONIVRAT nota de re bona coniurationem dici posse: nam coniuratio ton meson est.

35. Willems, *Le Sénat de la république romaine*, 2.253, n. 1.

36. On the meaning of *tumultus* and its use during the Republic, see *RE* 2.7.2.1344–5; Ch. Daremberg and E. Saglio, *Dictionnaire des antiquités grecques et romaines*, 5 vols. (Paris, 1877–1919), 5:532 (more useful); and E. Gabba, *Republican Rome, the Army and the Allies*, trans. P. J. Cuff (Berkeley, 1976), pp. 5, 8, and 24.

37. Dio 37.33.3 and 37.40.2 refers to the donning and removal of military garb but does not otherwise contradict Cicero's repeated claims concerning absence of tumult. Dio 37.29.4 also reports that Cicero wore a breastplate under his toga but made sure it was visible to observers: if true, this detail is further evidence of Cicero's construction of what I have called a tumult in abeyance.

38. Omnes adsunt omnium ordinum homines, omnium generum, omnium denique aetatum; plenum est forum, plena templa circum forum, pleni omnes aditus huius templi ac loci. Causa est enim post urbem conditam haec inventa sola, in qua omnes sentirent unum atque idem praeter eos, qui cum sibi viderent esse pereundum, cum omnibus potius quam soli perire voluerunt. (*Catil.* 4.14).

39. C. Nicolet, "*Consul togatus*: Remarques sur le vocabulaire politique de Cicéron et de Tite-Live," *Revue des études latines* 38 (1960): 236–63, and R. Seager, "*Iusta Catilinae*," *Historia* 22 (1973): 240–48, discuss the relationship between Cicero and Pompey at this time, especially as reflected in the speeches.

40. J. Scheid, "La spartizione sacrificiale di Roma," in *Sacrificio e società nel mondo antico*, ed. C. Grottanelli and N. Parisi (Roma–Bari 1988), pp. 267–92 (reprinted from *Studi Storici* 4 [1984]: 945–56).

41. Scheid, "La spartizione sacrificiale di Roma," p. 273.

42. With reference to Varro's handbook, see Gellius 14.7, especially the following: immolareque hostiam prius auspicarique debere, qui senatum habiturus

esset (Gell. 14.7.9). On the actions of the presiding magistrate at meetings of the Senate, see Willems, *Le sénat de la république romaine*, 2:173: "Avant d'entrer dans le local, le magistrat-président immole une victime et consulte les auspices. . . ." Willems cites Gell. 14.7.9, Serv. *Ad Aen.* 11.235, Suet *Caes.* 81, and other corroboratory passages.

43. On Cicero's choice of the temple of Jupiter Stator as the site of the meeting, see Vasaly, *Representations*, pp. 49ff. Vasaly argues that Romulus, in his connection with Jupiter Stator, symbolizes military leadership and the foundation of the city. In her view, the association with Romulus and the temple encourages the senators to think in terms of Sabine *hostes* and the original Palatine settlement of Rome. Her points are well taken, but it is worth noting that in the final section of the speech Cicero's description of the conspirators as *hostes patriae* precedes the climactic phrases *latrones Italiae scelerum foedere inter se ac nefaria societate coniunctos* (*Catil.* 1.33). On Romulus, see also discussion in text, below.

44. See, for example, Girard, *Le bouc émissaire* (Paris, 1982).

45. Hisce ominibus, Catilina . . . proficiscere ad impium bellum ac nefarium. Tu, Iuppiter, qui isdem quibus haec urbs auspiciis Romulo es constitutus . . . hunc et huius socios a tuis ceterisque templis, a tectis urbis ac moenibus, a vita fortunisque civium omnium arcebis et homines bonorum inimicos, hostis patriae, latrones Italiae scelerum foedere inter se ac nefaria societate coniunctos aeternis suppliciis vivos mortuosque mactabis (*Catil.* 1.33).

46. There is a similar assignment of responsibility for the outcome of the rivalry between Pompey and Caesar in Lucan's poem. See C. M. C. Green, "'The Necessary Murder': Myth, Ritual, and Civil War in Lucan, Book 3," *Classical Antiquity* 13 (1994): 203–33.

47. Livy 1.4.9, 1.5.3 describes Romulus and Remus as leaders of a shepherd gang that preys upon bandits (*latrones*). See also Eutropius 1.1–3. On the difficulty distinguishing between shepherds and bandits, see discussion in Shaw, "Bandits in the Roman Empire."

48. In a powerful and erudite discussion of the Remus story, T. P. Wiseman, *Remus: A Roman Myth* (Cambridge, 1995), argues that "the myth of Remus was begun, developed and essentially completed within a quite short and specific period of time—twenty years or so, at the end of the fourth and the beginning of the third centuries BC" (p. 158). He regards the duality of the founders of Rome as inextricably linked with the double nature—patrician and plebeian—of archaic Rome, and connects the death of Remus at the walls with the human sacrifice at the site of the temple of Victory in 296 B.C. J. D. Noonan, "Daunus/Faunus in Aeneid 12," *Classical Antiquity* 12 (1993): 111–25 (not discussed by Wiseman), attributes the split between Romulus and Remus to a linguistic duality in the Roman community, with a comparable split manifested in the doubleness of Daunus and Faunus. Noonan seems willing to place the creation of a dual founder as late as the fourth century B.C.E., like Wiseman. Even if the late dating of Remus's entry into the legend is correct—as it seems likely to be—Remus was clearly sufficiently well established in the legend and iconography of the founding of Rome for his absence in Cicero's speeches and in particular in his description of the statue struck by lightning to be worthy of note. As Wiseman puts it, "between 342 and 266 BC, a period coterminous with the Roman conquest of Italy

and the last stage of the 'struggle of the orders', a series of political events seems to have generated legendary analogues in the Remus and Romulus story, from the origin of the twins to the death of Remus and Romulus' rule as sole king. . . . Fabius Pictor at the end of the third century gave [the story] an authority that put all rival versions in the shade" (*Remus*, p. 128). Also important on Romulus-Remus is C. J. Classen, "Zur Herkunft der Sage von Romulus und Remus," *Historia* 12 (1963): 447–57.

49. Livy 1.12.6, *D.H.* 2.50.3, Ovid *Fasti* 6.793.

50. quoniam illum qui hanc urbem condidit, ad deos inmortalis benivolentia famaque sustulimus, esse apud vos posterosque vestros in honore debebit is qui eandem hanc urbem conditam amplificatamque servavit: (*Catil.* 3.2).

51. K. Toll, "The *Aeneid* as an Epic of National Identity: *Italiam Laeto Socii Clamore Salutant,*" *Helios* 18 (1991): 3–14.

52. G. B. Miles, *Livy: Reconstructing Early Rome* (Ithaca, N.Y., 1995), p. 102. But Miles may undestimate the complexity of Cicero's performance when he states that "Cicero is the first in this century for whom we can be certain of a favorable identification with Romulus," since it seems clear that Cicero, too, was aware of the dangers of associating himself too closely with the example of Romulus and sought in the Catilinarians to take advantage of Romulus's *auctoritas* while separating himself from more problematical aspects of his exemplum.

53. Vasaly, *Representations*, p. 81.

54. P. Rose, "Cicero and the Rhetoric of Imperialism: Putting the Politics Back into Political Rhetoric," *Rhetorica* 13 (1995): 359–400, is excellent on the need to "read the silences" in political oratory—indeed, in all literature.

55. On Remus as a foundation sacrifice, see Wiseman, *Remus*, pp. 117ff., citing Prop. 3.9.50 (caeso moenia firma Remo) and Florus 1.1.8 (prima certe victima fuit munitionemque urbis novae sanguine suo consecravit).

56. And indeed, the *Invectiva in Ciceronem* sometimes attributed to Sallust addresses Cicero as *Romule Arpinas* (*Inv.* 7). Catullus, too, used the connection with Romulus to Cicero's disadvantage at poem 49: *Disertissime Romuli nepotum. . . .*

57. D. Konstan, "Narrative and Ideology in Livy: Book 1," *Classical Antiquity* 5 (1986): 198–215.

58. See, in addition to passages on *tumultus* cited above, Cic. *Pis.* 73, which specifically describes the toga as the garb of peace, not of war or tumult.

CHAPTER FOUR
CULTURE WARS IN THE FIRST CENTURY B.C.E.

Among the few scholars to consider seriously the identity politics of the literature of the late Republic and/or early Principate are M. Sordi and her collaborators, known as the "Gruppo di Ricérca sulla propaganda antica," who discuss Propertius as a Tuscan poet in an essay entitled "L'integrazione dell'Italia nello Stato romano attraverso la poesia e la cultura proto-augustea," in *Contributi dell'istituto di storia antica*, ed. M. Sordi, Pubblicazioni della Università Cattolica del Sacro Cuore (Milan, 1972), vol. 1. pp. 146–75. Also important are the remarks of K. Toll, in "The *Aeneid* as an Epic of National Identity: *Italiam Laeto*

Socii Clamore Salutant," *Helios* 18 (1991): 3–14, specifically her argument that "the *Aeneid* is a poem of Italian national character, and examining it for any smaller if less difficult object can only do less than justice to its scope and its yearnings" (p. 3). Toll's attempt to shift the focus of ideological inquiry into the *Aeneid* "from Augustus to Italy" (p. 3) is the starting point for my own reflections here on the construction of national identity in a range of texts from classical Rome.

1. Besides *The Roman Revolution*, important works on relations between Rome and Italy in the first century B.C.E. include R. Syme, "Caesar, the Senate, and Italy," *Proceedings of the British School in Rome* 14 (1938): 1–31, reprinted in *Roman Papers*, ed. E. Badian (Oxford, 1978), vol. 1; P. Brunt, "Italian Aims at the Time of the Social War," *Journal of Roman Studies* 55 (1965): 90–109; G. Tibiletti, "*Italia Augustea*," in *Mélanges d'archéologie, d'épigraphie et d'histoire offerts à J. Carcopino* (Paris, 1966), pp. 917–26; E. Badian, "Roman Politics and the Italians 131–91 B.C.," *Dialoghi di Archeologia* 4/5 (1970/71): 373–421; F. de Martino, "Note sull'Italia Augustea," *Athenaeum* n.s. 53 (1975): 245–61; E. Gabba, *Republican Rome, the Army and the Allies*, trans. P. J. Cuff (Berkeley, 1976); E. T. Salmon, *The Making of Roman Italy* (London, 1982); A. Keaveney, *Rome and the Unification of Italy* (London and Sydney, 1987); S. Dyson, *Community and Society in Roman Italy* (Baltimore, 1992). On the various possible referents of the term *Italia*, see F. Klingner, "Italien. Name, Begriff und Idee im Altertum," *Die Antike* 17 (1941): 89ff., reprinted in *Römische Geisteswelt* (Suttgart, 1979), pp. 11–33; P. Catalano, "Appunti sopra il più antico concetta juridico di Italia," *AAT* 96 (1961/62): 198–228; G. Radke, "*Italia*: Beobachtungen zu der Geschichte eines Landenames," *Romanitas* 10 (1967); E. Gabba, "Il problema dell'unità dell'Italia romana," in *La Cultura Italica: Atti del Convegno della Società Italiana di Glottologia*, Orientamenti linguistici 5 (Pisa, 1978), pp. 11–28. I have not yet had the opportunity to consult J.-M. David, *La romanisation de l'Italie* (Paris, 1994).

2. Sordi et al., "L'integrazione dell'Italia."

3. C. Nicolet, *L'inventaire du monde: Géographie et politique aux origines de l'Empire romain* (Paris, 1988), pp. 181ff (translated as *Space, Geography, and Politics in the Early Roman Empire* [Ann Arbor, 1991]).

4. See the works cited in the headnote. In addition, A. Giardina, "L'identità incompiuta dell'Italia Romana," in *L'Italie d'Auguste à Dioclétien*, Collection de l'école française de Rome 198 (Rome, 1994), pp. 1–89, discusses in passing the varying representations of Italy in the works of Vergil, Livy, Horace, and Propertius.

5. Basic works on the dating of the late works of Horace (esp. *Odes* 4 and *Epistle* 2.1) include T. Mommsen, "Die Litteraturbriefe des Horaz," *Hermes* 15 (1885): 103–15, reprinted in *Gesammelte Schriften*, 7: 175–82; L. R. Taylor, *The Divinity of the Roman Emperor*: American Philological Association Philological Monographs 1 (Middletown, Connecticut, 1931), pp. 142–80; and C. O. Brink, *Horace on Poetry: Epistles Book II* (Cambridge, 1982). Recent scholarly consensus confirms the assignment of *Odes* 4 to 13 B.C.E. and *Epistle* 2.1 to 12. For *Odes* 4, see M. Santirocco, *Unity and Design in Horace's Odes* (Chapel Hill, 1986),

and M. Putnam, *Artifices of Eternity: Horace's Fourth Book of Odes*, Cornell Studies in Classical Philology 43 (Ithaca, 1986). For *Epistle* 2.1, see N. Rudd, *Horace, Epistles Book II and Epistle to the Pisones* (Cambridge, 1989), and R. Kilpatrick, *The Poetry of Criticism* (Edmonton, 1990). The exception to this consensus is G. Williams, *Horace, Greece and Rome*, New Series in the Classics 6 (Oxford, 1972). Williams's revised dating of *Odes* 4 to as late as 8 B.C.E. ignores two important *termini ante quem*: (1) Early 10 B.C.E., when the Senate voted to close the gates of the Temple of Janus but war broke out in Pannonia before the edict could be enforced. It seems highly unlikely that Horace would celebrate the closing of the temple in a prominent passage of *Odes* 4.15 (line 9) so soon after this embarrassment. (2) Drusus's sudden and unexpected death in 9 B.C.E. Would Horace's lyric celebrations of his victories have been appropriate so soon after his untimely demise? As for *Epistle* 2.1, Brink seems unnecessarily cautious with respect to the positive evidence adduced by Mommsen and Taylor for a date following the pontifical comitia and death of Agrippa, the former from 13 or 12 (on which see also G. Bowersock, "The Pontificate of Augustus," in *Between Republic and Empire: Interpretations of Augustus and His Principate*, ed. K. Raaflaub and M. Toher [Berkeley, 1990], pp. 380–94, esp. 382–83), the latter securely dated to March of 12. Taylor is surely right to connect the revised worship at the *compita* with the pontifical assemblies and to link both to *Ep.* 2.1.15–17. Brink's concern about the difference between *genius* and *numen* does not withstand careful reading of D. Fishwick, "*Genius* and *Numen*," *Harvard Theological Review* 62 (1969): 356–67, which makes it clear that the *genius Augusti* could be described as a *numen*. On a likely allusion to the recent death of Agrippa in 12 B.C.E., see note 11, below. As with *Odes* 4, so *Ep.* 2.1 has a *terminus ante quem* of 10 B.C.E. in the reference to the closing of the gates of the Temple of Janus (*Ep.* 2.1.255). Book 4 of the *Odes*, it should also be noted, has a clear *terminus post quem* in the Alpine victories of Drusus and Tiberius of 16–14 B.C.E. Since several poems speak of Augustus as still absent from Italy, early 13 emerges as the most likely date of publication. The publication of *Odes* 4 is itself a *terminus post quem* for *Ep.* 2.1, since lines 251–54 seem to refer to *Odes* 4.14 (E. Fraenkel, *Horace* [Oxford, 1957], p. 398; cf. Brink's refutation of Williams's misunderstanding of the verses); and in any event Augustus is described as at work in Italy (line 2). Finally, the sequence *Carmen Saeculare, Odes* 4, *Epistle* 2.1 is implied by a passage in the *Vita Horati* of Suetonius; see note 32, below. It is unclear to me why A. La Penna, *Saggi e studi su Orazio* (Florence, 1993), p. 220, attributes *Ep.* 2.1 to "14 o, al piu tardi del 13."

6. On Octavian's behavior toward Italian communities during the triumviral period, see Syme, *Roman Revolution*, pp. 98ff.; M. Volponi, *Lo sfondo italico della lotta triumvirale* (Genoa, 1975); Dyson, *Community and Society in Roman Italy*, pp. 89ff. On the Perusine War, see the account in Appian *B.C.* 5.32–49.

7. Appian *B.C.* 5.130–32.

8. See Dyson, *Community and Society in Roman Italy*, p. 95, for discussion and further bibliography.

9. P. Ceaucescu, "*Altera Roma*: Histoire d'une folie politique," *Historia* 25 (1976): 79–108; Nicolet, *L'inventaire du monde*, pp. 206ff.

10. I am not persuaded by O. Murray's attempt to interpret poem 15 as a

displaced introduction to the fourth book ("Symposium and Genre in the Poetry of Horace," *Journal of Roman Studies* 75 [1985]: 39–50, an otherwise compelling and important essay). On poem 1's fitness as a preamble, see T. Habinek, "The Marriageability of Maximus," *American Journal of Philology* 107 (1986): 407–16. Also, the verb *canemus* at the end of 4.15 points to the future of Horace's poetry and poetry like his; a similar phenomenon occurs at the end of *Epistles* 1 and the end of *Odes* 3. On 4.15 and early Roman symposia, see the brief reference in N. Zorzetti, "The *Carmina Convivalia*," in *Sympotica: A Symposium on the Symposion*, ed. O. Murray (Oxford, 1990), pp. 289–307.

11. Brink, *Horace on Poetry*, is overly cautious. The rhetoric of the lines clearly isolates and emphasizes the word *solus* prior to the tricolonic description of Augustus's labors. Moreover, Agrippa had assumed an important role in the management of Italy in the years immediately preceding his death; see Dio 54.24.5 and 54.28–29. For numismatic evidence of Agrippa's prominence in 13 B.C.E., see *The Roman Imperial Coinage*, ed. C. H. V. Sutherland and R. A. G. Carson (London, 1984), vol. 1, pp. 72–73.

12. Taylor, *The Divinity of the Roman Emperor*. On the *comitia*, see Bowersock, "The Pontificate of Augustus."

13. On the relationship between Augustus's activities and those attributed to Romulus, Liber, the Dioscuri, and Hercules, see Brink, *Horace on Poetry*, and Fraenkel, *Horace*, pp. 385–86. For the suspension of veteran settlements, see Dio 54.25.5–6, and L. Keppie, *Colonisation and Veteran Settlement in Italy 47–14* B.C. (London, 1983). On *Epistle* 2.1 more generally, see A. Barchiesi, "Insegnare ad Augusto" in *Materiali e discussioni per l'analisi dei testi classici* 31 (1993): 149–84, who discusses the poem together with Ovid *Tristia* 2 from the standpoint of "loro struttura insegnativa."

14. On Catullus's praise of Nepos as ironic, see J. P. Elder, "Catullus I, His Poetic Creed, and Nepos," *Harvard Studies in Classical Philology* 71 (1966): 141–49; F. Cairns, "Catullus I," *Mnemosyne* 22 (1969): 153–58. For the common ground between Nepos and Catullus, see L. Alfonsi, "Sulla Cronaca di Cornelio Nepote," *Rendiconti di Istituto Lombardo* 76 (1942/43): 331–40; M. Gigante, "Catullo, Cornelio, e Cicerone," *Giornale Italiana di Filologia* 20 (1967): 123–29; T. P. Wiseman, *Clio's Cosmetics: Three Studies in Greco-Roman Literature* (Leicester, 1979), pp. 143–82, and Wiseman, *Catullus and His World: A Reappraisal* (Cambridge, 1985), pp. 107ff, 197. F. Décreus, "Catulle *c.* 1, Cornelius Nepos e les *Aitia* de Callimaque," *Latomus* 43 (1984): 842–60, pushes the connection between Catullus, Nepos, and Apollodorus further than other scholars, perhaps further than the linguistic evidence permits. N. Horsfall, *Cornelius Nepos: A Selection, Including the Lives of Cato and Atticus* (Oxford, 1989), p. 116, considers the reasons for Catullus's admiration of Nepos "unclear."

15. Wiseman, *Catullus and His World*, p. 197.

16. Wissowa *RE* 4.1.1408–1418 on the Italian aspect; Alfonsi, "Sulla Cronaca di Cornelio Nepote, p. 333 ("si tratta quindi di una trasposizione su piano italico di tutta la storia") and Gigante, "Catullo, Cornelio e Cicerone," on the broad cultural aspect; Wiseman, *Clio's Cosmetics*, on the synchronisms between Italian or Roman and Greek affairs. In a sense, the Italianness of Nepos's *Chronica* is itself less important than what was made of it by Catullus (who called

attention to Nepos as Italian) and Atticus and Varro, whose chronologies were more Rome-centered. For the fragments of Nepos's *Chronica*, see H. Peter, *Historicorum Romanorum Reliquiae* (Leipzig, 1914), vol. 2, pp. xxxx-lvi, and A. Leopoldo, *Opere di Cornelio Nepote* (Turin, 1977).

17. On the Celts, see Wiseman, *Clio's Cosmetics*, p. 162.

18. The word *saeculum* can be used to describe the notional longest lifespan of a human being, with a new *saeculum* being celebrated when no one is still alive who celebrated the previous *saeculum*. Thus the celebration of the *saeculum* marks the continuity of the collective in opposition to the mortality of the individual. Décreus, "Catulle *c*. 1, Cornelius Nepos et les *Aitia* de Callimaque," pp. 850–51, seeks to relate the phrase *plus uno maneat perenne saeclum* to "Apollodorus" as reconstructed from Ps-Skymnos's dedication to Attalus II Philadelphus: το ς ἐν Περγ μει Βασιλε σιν ὧν ἡ δ ξα κα τεθνηκ των παρ π σιν ἥμ ν ζ σα δι παντ ς μ νει. If an allusion is operative here, then the contrast between Skymnos's vague δι παντ ς and Catullus's precise *plus uno . . . saeculo* is all the more productive of meaning.

19. Horsfall, *Cornelius Nepos: A Selection*, p. xvii: Nepos's *Chronica* "were shortly to be superseded by Atticus' *liber annalis*."

20. Décreus, "Catulle c. 1, Cornelius Nepos and les *Aitia* de Calimaque," notes the recurrence of the verb *explicare* in Nepos's descriptions of his own studies (*De exc. duc. ext. gent.* pr. 8; *Pelopidas* 1; *Hannibal* 1.34), but does not mention the passage from the *Brutus*. The word may be less a stylistic tic on Nepos's part than a description of a certain type of historical writing. On Atticus's achievement, see also Cic. *Brut.* 14: omnem rerum memoriam breviter et ut mihi quidem visum est perdiligenter complexus est.

21. F. Münzer, "Atticus als Geschichtsschreiber," *Hermes* 40 (1905): 50–100.

22. T. P. Wiseman, *Catullus and His World: A Reappraisal* (Cambridge, 1985), pp. 107ff., discusses the Italian origin of the transpadane colonists, many of whom were probably "veterans from Marius' and Catulus' armies and enterprising settlers from Italy." R. Syme, "*Transpadana Italia*," *Athenaeum* 73 (1985): 28–36, observes that in later periods "in certain contexts 'Italia' by itself denotes Transpadania" (p. 28).

23. See E. Badian, "Roman Politics and the Italians 131–91 B.C.," *Dialoghi di Archeologia* 4/5 (1970/71): 373–421, for the political status of these orators: "I think the conclusion must be that all these orators, wherever they came from, were citizens at the time they appeared in the Roman Forum—even if they came from allied Asculum and the Marsi. For Cicero they are all simply 'rustics' and by no means aliens" (p. 383).

24. In context the phrase *ad domum redeamus* seems to refer to the conclusion of both the brief digression on *urbanitas* at Athens and of the larger section on Italian orators lacking in Roman *urbanitas*. The phrase precedes discussion of Crassus and Antonius, the heroes of Cicero's earlier work, *De oratore*.

25. On the two speeches of Anchises and the significance of the contrast between them, see T. Habinek, "Science and Tradition in *Aeneid* 6," *Harvard Studies in Classical Philology* 92 (1989): 223–55. For the emphasis on Italy as source of military manpower, see also Giardina, "L'identità incompiuta."

26. On which, see the interesting remarks of N. Horsfall, "Virgil and Marcel-

lus' Education," *Classical Quarterly* 83 (1989): 266–67, who links the passage to Augustus's funeral *laudatio* for Marcellus.

27. See Toll, "The *Aeneid* as an Epic of National Identity."

28. On the connection between the expression *Romane memento* and the Sibylline oracle "produced for the Ludi Saeculares of May 31–June 3, 17 B.C.," see J. Zetzel, "*ROMANE MEMENTO*: Justice and Judgment in *Aeneid* 6," *Transactions and Proceedings of the American Philological Association* 119 (1989): 263–84, esp. pp. 278ff.

29. On the meaning of *tumultus*, see the discussion in chapter 3, above.

30. My translation of Polybius 2.23.8–14, following the Budé text.

31. A. La Penna, "Orazio, augusto, e la questione del teatro latino" *Annali della Scuola normale superiore di Pisa*, Cl. di lettere e filosofia 2 (1950) = *Orazio e l'ideologia del principato* (Turin, 1963), pp. 148–62. Despite the reference to ideology in his title, La Penna emphasizes narrowly literary reasons for Horace's rejection of theater (i.e., "Callimacheanism") without considering the array of cultural factors implied by the context, generic background, and language of the Epistle. See also R. F. Thomas, "New Comedy, Callimachus, and Roman Poetry," *Harvard Studies in Classical Philology* 83 (1979): 179–206. In *Saggi e studi su Orazio* (Florence, 1993), La Penna briefly returns to the question of *Ep.* 2.1 and theater, now stating that in the letter Horace avoids a frontal atack on theater, instead asserting the rights of literature designed for readers, especially aristocratic ones: "il gusto aristocratico rifiutava la letteratura 'popolare', e il rifiuto doveva restare uno dei principi base della poeticà classicista" (p. 220).

32. On Varro's *Imagines*, a picturebook on famous men, see Dahlmann (RE) 1935.1229; also Pliny *H.N.* 35.11, who calls attention to the potentially wide circulation of the work: "imaginum amorem flagrasse quondam testes sunt Atticus ille Ciceronis edito de iis volumine, M. Varro benignissimo invento insertis voluminum suorum fecunditati etiam septingentorum inlustrium aliquo modo imaginibus, non passus intercidere figuras aut vetustatem aevi contra homines valere, inventor muneris etiam dis invidiosi, quando immortalitatem non solum dedit, verum etiam *in omnes terras misit*, ut praesentes esse ubique ceu di possent. et hoc quidem alienis ille praestitit." I do not mean to say that Varro is nonelite in origin or ideology, but the audience for a work such as the *Imagines* need not have been as well-educated as the implied audience/readership of Horace's own writings. Cicero had snubbed Varro in the *Brutus*, according to F. della Corte, *La filologia latina* (Florence, 1954/1981), when he referred to him as an antiquarian even though he had written numerous orations. For aspects of Horace's disagreement with Varro not discussed in the present study, see C. O. Brink, "Horace and Varro," in *Varron, Entretiens* Fondation Hardt 9 (Genève-Vandoeuvres, 1963), pp. 173–200, and Brink, *Horace on Poetry*, pp. 85–86.

33. *Ep.* 2.1.15ff.

34. Nicolet, *L'inventaire du monde*, pp. 216ff.

35. Ibid. p. 221.

36. Suetonius Vita Horatii:

Scripta quidem eius usque adeo probavit mansuraque perpetuo opinatus est, ut non modo Saeculare carmen componendum iniunxerit sed et Vindelicam victoriam Tiberii Drusique, privignorum suorum, eumque coegerit propter hoc tribus Carminum libris ex longo intervallo quartum addere; post Sermones vero quosdam lectos nullam sui mentionem habitam ita sit questus: "irasci me tibi scito, quod non in plerisque ius modi scriptis mecum sit quod videaris familiaris nobis esse?' Expressitque eclogam ad se, cuius initium est: [there follows a quotation of the first four lines of Ep. 2.1].

37. Nicolet, *L'inventaire du monde*, p. 223: "elle ne sera plus guère qu'une province parmi d'autres."

38. Translation by C. MacLeod, *Horace: The Epistles, translated into English verse with brief comment*, Instrumentum litterarum 3 (Rome, 1986). The Latin expression *neque . . . nec* (*Ep.* 2.1.264, 266) introducing the possibilities of waxen images and shoddy verses suggests that they constitute two distinct insults to the poet's dignity; but the combination cannot fail to put the reader in mind of the picture books with verse epitaphs developed by Varro and Atticus in Horace's lifetime. On Varro's *Imagines*, see note 32, above; on Atticus's *Imagines*, see Nepos *Vita Attici* 18.5.

39. Note, for example, a title such as A. Kernan's *The Death of Literature* (New Haven, 1990). More optimistic is I. Illich, *In the Vineyard of the Text* (Chicago, 1994), who recognizes the diversity of relationships possible among reader, writer, and text, and regards the current crisis of the book as a crisis of scholasticism, not of writing or literature.

40. Giardina, "L'identità incompiuta dell'Italia romana," argues that a sense of local identity reemerges within a few generations of the Augustan settlement and proposes the creation of a catalogue of references in ancient literature to the characteristics of specific towns and cultures of Italy.

CHAPTER FIVE
WRITING AS SOCIAL PERFORMANCE

In recent years a number of Latinists have come to consider the interpretive implications of the contrast between written text and evocation of real or implied performance contexts that characterizes much of classical Latin literature. W. Fitzgerald, *Lyric Poetry and the Drama of Position: Catullan Provocations* (Berkeley, 1995), and D. Selden, "*Ceveat Lector*: Catullus and the Rhetoric of Performance" in *Innovations of Antiquity*, ed. R. Hexter and D. Selden (New York, 1992), pp. 461–512, explore this issue with respect to the poetry of Catullus while, F. Dupont, *L'invention de la littérature* (Paris, 1994), presents detailed analyses of poems of Catullus and passages from Apuleius's *Metamorphoses* within the context of a wideranging account of the movement in antiquity from literature as event to literature as text. Of the three, Selden is most interested in the political and social dimension of the literary performance and persuasively describes Catulus's self-representation throughout his poetry as an intervention in a late Republican discourse of *imagines*, or image making. My discussion here pursues Selden's lead into the social and political, but without sharing his assumption that differentiation from other types of performance necessarily implies resistance to or subversion of them. In addition, my remarks are designed to put the issue of performance versus text into a broader historical context, broader even than that offered by Dupont, by considering a wide range of Roman authors as well as drawing heavily on important recent research on the materialities of communication in the Roman world. Moreover, whereas Dupont discusses historical transition during antiquity (the subtitle of her book is *De l'ivresse grecque au livre romain*), I prefer to describe the tension between event and text as continuously open to negotiation by ancient authors and to consider the direction which many, but not all, of those negotations seem to take.

Among the works I rely on most heavily in discussing the material aspects of reading and writing are the essays gathered under the title *Literacy in the Roman World: Journal of Roman Archaeology*, Supplementary series 3 (Ann Arbor, 1991), including papers by Mary Beard, Alan Bowman, Mireille Corbier, Keith Hopkins, and Nicholas Horsfall referred to individually below. The volume in question, it should be noted, is itself designed as a response and supplement to W. V. Harris's groundbreaking study, *Ancient Literacy* (Cambridge, Mass., 1989). Other helpful works include the essays gathered in *Lo spazio letterario di Roma antica*, 5 vols., ed. G. Cavallo et al. (Roma-Bari, 1989)—see esp. vol. 2: *La circolazione del testo*, relevant essays cited individually below; J. E. G. Zetzel, *Latin Textual Criticism in Antiquity* (Salem, N. H. 1980, and New York, 1984); E. J. Kenney, "Books and Readers in the Roman World," in *Cambridge History of Latin Literature*, ed. E. J. Kenney and W. V. Clausen (Cambridge, 1982), pp. 3–32; P. Fedeli, "Autore, committente, pubblico in Roma," in *Oralità, scrittura, spettacolo*, ed. M. Vegeti (Torino, 1983), pp. 77–106; R. Starr, "The Circulation of Literary Texts in the Roman World," *Classical Quarterly* 81 (1987): 213–23; and N. Horsfall, "Rome without Spectacles," *Greece and Rome* 42 (1995): 49–56 (on professional readers in the Roman world). Still helpful on the social context of literary performance is A.-M. Guillemin, *Le public et la vie littéraire à Rome*, Collection d'études latines 13 (Paris, 1937), who, it should be noted, regards the elitism of the ancient context as a virtue; see also E. Fantham, *Roman Literary Culture* (Baltimore, 1996). I regret that I have not had the opportunity to read M. Citroni, *Poesia e lettori in Roma antica: Forme della communicazione letteraria* (Roma–Bari 1995).

1. Dio 40.54.
2. See Hor. *Ep.* 1.20, discussed by E. Oliensis, "Life after Publication: Horace, *Epistles* 1.20," *Arethusa* 28 (1995): 209–24. On *pumice* in Catullus 1, see W. Fitzgerald, "Catullus and the Reader: The Erotics of Poetry," *Arethusa* 25 (1992): 419–43. On Cynthia's waywardness, see, for example, Propertius 1.2.
3. E.g., Ovid *Tristia* 1.1, 1.7.23–24, 1.11, 2.1, 3.1, 3.14.19ff. Cf. discussion in chapter 8, below.
4. Quint. *Inst. Or.* 1 *praef.* 7.
5. Cato *ORF* 8.173, a fragment of the speech entitled *De sumptu suo*.
6. Pliny *Ep.* 2.3.8 with discussion by F. Dupont, "*Recitatio* and the reorganization of the space of public discourse" in *The Roman Cultural Revolution*, ed. T. Habinek and A. Schiesaro (Cambridge, 1998), pp. 44–60.

7. Tac. *Dial.* 10.2: ut semel vidit, transit et contentus est, ut si picturam aliquam vel statuam vidisset.

8. The story is told by Livy at 5.41.8–9. The point is not, as has been suggested, that the aristocratic Roman is uptight and impassive, but rather that he keeps his vital energy restrained, ready (in this case, too ready) to release it at the slightest insult to his dignity.

9. On the circulation of texts, see the works listed in the headnote above. On profitability (or not), see also E. T. Sage, "The Publication of Martial's Poems," *Transactions and Proceedings of the American Philological Association* 50 (1919): 168–76; F. R. Cowell, "Book Production in Ancient Rome," *History Today* 24 (1974): 794–98.

10. T. P. Wiseman, "*Pete nobilos amicos*: Poets and Patrons in Late Republican Rome," in *Literary and Artistic Patronage in Ancient Rome*, ed. B. K. Gold (Austin, Texas, 1982), pp. 28–49. On the goods and services exchanged between poet and patron, see P. White, *Promised Verse: Poets in the Society of Augustan Rome* (Cambridge, Mass., 1993).

11. Tac. *Dial.* 9.5

12. Juvenal 1.134, 7.74–97.

13. Tac. *Dial.* 10.1.

14. Pliny *Ep.* 11.2.

15. Martial 2.8.3–4: non meus est error, nocuit librarius illis / dum properat versus annumerare tibi.

16. Martial 1.117.

17. Martial 13.3.3–4: quattuor est nimium? poterit constare duobus, / et faciet lucrum bybliopola Tryphon.

18. H.-I. Marrou, *A History of Education in Antiquity*, trans. G. Lamb (London, 1956); S. F. Bonner, *Roman Education* (Berkeley, 1986).

19. Suet. *gram.* 16.

20. N. Horsfall, "Empty Shelves on the Palatine," *Greece & Rome* 40 (1993): 58–67. Cf. R. Fehrle, *Das Bibliothekwesen im alten Rom*, Schriften der Universitätsbibliothek Freiburg I. Br. 10 (Wiesbaden, 1986), who also discusses the tendency to place Greek and Latin libraries in symmetrical structures.

21. *Milesiaka* in Crassus's camp: Plut. *Crassus* 32.

22. Martial 12.1.

23. Catullus 68.36.

24. Trevor Murphy, unpubl. paper on the circulation of Cicero's writings in his lifetime, collects what little evidence there is for Cicero's circulation of his own texts, especially the *philosophica*. On the related topic of the decision not to publish some texts (in this case orations), see J. Crawford, *M. Tullius Cicero: The Lost and Unpublished Orations*, Hypomnemata 80 (Göttingen, 1984).

25. Pliny *Ep.* 4.7.7. See also *Ep.* 4.2.

26. See A. Dalzell, "C. Asinius Pollio and the Early History of Public Recitation at Rome," *Hermathena* 86 (1955): 20–28; O. A. W. Dilke, *Roman Books and Their Impact* (Leeds, 1977); E. Léfèvre, "Die römische Literatur zwischen Mündlichkeit und Schriftlichkeit," in *Strukturen der Mündlichkeit in der römischen Literatur*, ed. G. Vogt-Spira (Tübingen, 1990), pp. 1–15; and F. Dupont,

"*Recitatio* and the Reorganization of the Space of Public Discourse." The section on *recitatio* in G. Williams, *Change and Decline: Roman Literature in the Early Empire* (Berkeley, 1978), is misleading.

27. Sen. Elder *Contr.* 4 *praef.* 2

28. On the social origins of the declaimers and Seneca's role in their promotion, see W. M. Bloomer, "A preface to the history of declamation," in *The Roman Cultural Revolution*, ed. T. Habinek and A. Schiesaro (Cambridge, 1997), pp. 199–215.

29. Aper speaks of the fame associated with recitation (*Dial.* 10.1), albeit only to disparage it.

30. Plut. *Lucullus* 42.

31. On Pollio's library, see Fehrle, *Das Bibliothekwesen*, pp. 58–65.

32. On the characteristics of popular justice, see H. Usener, "Italische Volkjustiz," *Kleine Schriften* (Stuttgart 1912/13), vol. 4, pp. 356–82; E. Fraenkel, "Two Poems of Catullus," *Journal of Roman Studies* 51 (1961): 46–53; and A. Lintott, *Violence in Republican Rome* (Oxford, 1968). For the view that various aspects of legal discourse constitute an extension to the public sphere of such "private" forms of retribution, see A. A. Kelly, "Damaging Voice: Language of Aggression for the Athenian Trial" (Ph.D. diss., University of California, Berkeley, 1994). On written propaganda during the Roman civil wars, see P. Jal, *La guerre civile à Rome: Étude littéraire et morale*, Publications de la Faculté des lettres et sciences humaines de Paris, Série "Recherches" 6 (Paris, 1963), pp. 72–213, esp. 152ff.

33. See J. Hallett, "*Perusinae Glandes* and the Changing Image of Augustus," *American Journal of Ancient History* 2 (1977): 151–71; cf. *Ephemeris Epigraphica*, vol. 6, ed. C. Zangemeister (Rome and Berlin, 1885), for texts inscribed on bullets.

34. Tac. *Hist.* 2.48.2: libellos epistulasque studio erga se aut in Vitellium contumeliis insignis abolet.

35. Cicero describes the incident at *ad Att.* 16.5.2: commutatus est totus et scriptis meis quibusdam quae in manibus habebam et adsiduitate orationis et praeceptis.

36. Tac. *Ann.* 4.27.1: mox positis propalam libellis ad libertatem vocabat agrestia.

37. Kenney, "Books and Readers," pp. 14–15. Cf. the similar remarks by Moses Finley cited in P. Fedeli, "I sistemi di produzione e diffusione," in *Lo Spazio letterario di Roma antica*, vol. 2, p. 348.

38. E. Gellner, *Nations and Nationalism* (Oxford, 1983), p. 34.

39. In describing grammarians and other teachers as "guardians of identity" I am deliberately expanding the range of significance implied in the title of R. Kaster's work on the grammarians in late antiquity, *Guardians of Language: The Grammarian and Society in Late Antiquity* (Berkeley, 1988). Although the time frame of Kaster's important study is later than mine, his work is suggestive in the present context for its clear demonstration of the mediocre social position of the grammarian as "as far above the common people in the city and its hinterland as he was below the men who directed the central and provincial administra-

tion of the empire" (p. 133), occupying a position of "genteel obscurity and dependence . . . in his relations with patrons and the state" (p. 134).

40. Suet. *gram.* 1.

41. Horace *Ep.* 2.1.69ff.

42. Suet. *gram.* 8. For the Ennius revival during the Empire, see Guillemin, *Le public et la vie littéraire à Rome*, pp. 71–72.

43. By inference from Suet. *gram.* 2.

44. Ibid., 2.

45. Ibid., 13.

46. Ibid., 17.

47. Ibid., 23.

48. Imperial and patronal largess continued into the later period; see Kaster, *Guardians of Language*, pp. 116ff.

49. Suet. *rhet.* 1.2 and Gell. 15.11.1. E. Gruen, *Studies in Greek Culture and Roman Policy*, Cincinnati Classical Studies (Leiden, 1990), pp. 170–79, questions the enforceability of such measures without recognizing that laws can constrain or deter behavior in the absence of strict or universal enforcement.

50. Suet. *rhet.* 1.1 and Gell. 15.11.2.

51. See the classic discussion of R. MacMullen, *Enemies of the Roman Order: Treason, Unrest, and Alienation in the Empire* (Cambridge, Mass., 1966).

52. On the sociology of inscriptional writing, see G. Sanders, "Texte et monument: L'arbitrage du musée épigraphique," in *Il museo epigrafico*, ed. A. Donati, (Faenza, 1984), pp. 85–118, and M. Corbier, "L'écriture dans l'espace public romain," in *L'Urbs: Espace urbaine et histoire 1er siècle avant J.-C.–IIIe siècle aprés J.-C.: Actes du colloque international organisé par le Centre national de la recherche scientifique et l'École française de Rome*, Collection de l'École française de Rome 98 (Rome, 1987), pp. 27–60.

53. E.g., *CIL* 10.4643. Further examples at Sanders, "Texte et monument," p. 100.

54. On inscriptions and the human voice, see J. Svenbro, *Phrasikleia: Anthropologie de la lecture en grèce ancienne* (Paris, 1988), published in English as *Phrasikleia: An Anthropology of Reading in Ancient Greece*, trans. J. Lloyd (Ithaca, N.Y., 1993); and F. Dupont, *L'invention de la littérature*, pp. 76ff., 233ff. Dupont rightly differentiates inscriptional writing from literary on the grounds that inscriptions frequently require the reader to be the subject of the utterance and not the interpreter of the text.

55. For interpretation and translation of this verse, see D. Korzeniewski, "*Exegi monumentum*: Hor. *carm.* 3.30 und die Topik der Grabgedichte," *Gymnasium* 79 (1972): 380–88.

56. M. Jaeger, "The Poetics of Place: The Augustan Writers and the Urban Landscape of Rome" (Ph.D. diss., University of California, Berkeley, 1990).

57. Corbier, "L'écriture dans l'espace public romain," p. 31, with remarks to this effect by ancient authors.

58. For the theme of the distance between place of birth and place of death, see P. Cugusi, *Aspetti letterari dei Carmina Latina Epigraphica: Testi e manuali per l'insegnamento universitario del latino* (Bologna, 1985), pp. 200–217.

59. *CIL* 5.1027 (*CLE* 406.1) Ereptus fato est Aquileiae, Tiburi natus / frater defunctum uoluit uenerare sepulchro.

60. *CLE* 418: Roma mihi tellus genus inde, sed hospita sedes: from a tombstone in Satala, in Armenia, marking the grave of "una donna nativa di Roma, morta in Armenia" (Cugusi, *Aspetti letterari*, p. 209).

61. Mantua me genuit, Calabri rapuere, tenet nunc Parthenope: cecini pascua rura duces. Discussed by Cugusi, *Aspetti letterari*, pp. 212ff., and M. Bettini, "L'epitaffio di Virgilio, Silio Italico, e un modo di intendere la letteratura," *Dialoghi di Archeologia* 9/10 (1976/77): 439–48.

62. Corbier, "L'écriture dans l'espace public romain," p. 31.

63. *CIL* 4.2360 (*CLE* 45), *CIL* 4.4008 (*CLE* 1864), *CIL* 4.1798, *CIL* 13.10017.40, discussed by B. Forsmann, "ANNEMOTA in einer dorischen Gefassinschrift," *Münchener Studien zur Sprachwissenschaft* 34 (1976): 39–46; followed by Svenbro, *Phrasikleia*, pp. 207ff.

64. For polished books, see Martial 1.117.16; for statues, see Lucretius 5.1451: carmina picturas et daedala signa polire.

65. E. Norden, *Agnostos Theos: Untersuchungen zur Formengeschichte religiöser Rede* (Stuttgart, 1923).

66. M. Beard, "Writing and Religion: *Ancient Literacy* and the Function of the Written Word in Roman Religion," in *Literacy in the Roman World*, pp. 35–58.

67. A. Appadurai, *The Social Life of Things* (Cambridge, 1986).

68. *Libellus* eventually was coopted as the term for a book of carefully crafted poetry, but its extraliterary meaning remained available for activation at any time.

69. For *libelli* as ephemera, see *OLD* s.v. *libellus* 1b, 2, and 4.

70. The distinction between "private" and "public" writing is made by Corbier, "L'écriture dans l'espace public romain." One aim of the present discussion is to modify Corbier's attempt to mark a sharp distinction between the two types.

71. Lucretius 3.830ff.

72. Verg. *Aen.* 6.664, discussed by T. Habinek, "Science and Tradition in *Aeneid* 6," *Harvard Studies in Classical Philology* 92 (1989): 223–55.

73. E. Hobsbawm, *Nations and Nationalism since 1780* (Cambridge, 1990), pp. 37–38.

74. Hor. *Ep.* 2.1.264–270.

75. Plut. *Quaestiones Romanae* 59; *Oxford Classical Dictionary*, s.v. "Carvilius."

76. Suet. *gram.* 1.

77. For the early history of textual criticism at Rome, see Zetzel, *Latin Textual Criticism in Antiquity*, pp. 10–26.

78. H.-I. Marrou, *A History of Education in Antiquity.*

79. On theater troupes in Rome, see E. Jory, "Associations of Actors in Rome," *Hermes* 98 (1970): 224–53. On the *Dionysou technitai*, see F. Poland, "Technitae," *RE* VA2.2473–2538. J. E. G. Zetzel, "Religion, Rhetoric, and Editorial Technique," in *Palimpsest: Editorial Theory in the Humanities*, ed. G. Bornstein and R. Williams (Ann Arbor, 1993), pp. 99–120, discusses the origins of the Plautine manuscript tradition in "actors' versions" (p. 112). See also

C. Questa and R. Raffaelli, "Dalla Rappresentazione alla lettura," in *Lo spazio letterario*, vol. 3, pp. 139–215.

80. H. B. Mattingly, "The Date of Livius Andronicus," *CQ* n.s. 7 (1957): 159–63 proposes an unlikely interpretation of Livy's expression *illa tempestate* (27.37). Yet Mattingly is right to note that on the orthodox chronology Livius Andronicus would have been extremely old in 207 B.C. Moreover, Livy's account states that the hymn used in 207 was composed by Andronicus, not that it was commissioned or composed for that occasion. Mattingly may also be correct in his interpretation of the phrase *patrum memoria* (31.72), which is used to describe the precedent that prompted a hymnic commission for P. Licinius Tegula in 200 B.C. If the Senate had just made such a commission seven years earlier, would the pointed expression *patrum memoria* be necessary or appropriate?

81. Suet. *gram.* 2. See Zetzel, *Latin Textual Criticism in Antiquity*, pp. 10ff.

82. Suet. *gram.* 2: ac legendo commentandoque etiam ceteris not facerent Cf. ut postea Q. Vargunteius Annales Ennii, quos certis diebus in magna frequentia pronuntiabat (also Suet. *gram.* 2).

83. Aulus Gellius, Probus, Servius Auctus, Macrobius, Lactantius, Nonius, and Priscian all refer to a text of Naevius divided into books.

84. Isid. *Orig.* 6.5.1 (Romae primus librorum copia advexit Aemilius Paulus, Perse Macedonum rege devicto; deinde Lucullus e Pontica praeda), discussed by Fehrle, *Das antike Bibliothekwesen*, pp. 15ff. Also relevant is Plutarch's *Life of Aemilius Paulus*, in which the books are made to seem insignificant in comparison to the booty Aemilius might have assigned his sons had he been a less responsible father.

85. Fehrle, *Das antike Bibliothekwesen*, p. 15.

86. R. Pfeiffer, *History of Classical Scholarship* (Oxford, 1968), pp. 98ff.; P. Fraser, *Ptolemaic Alexandria* (Oxford, 1972) vol. 1, 305ff.; Horsfall, "Empty Shelves on the Palatine." Fedeli, "Autore, committente, pubblico in Roma," suggests that libraries would have constituted the chief clientele for copyists.

87. E.g., 368–72 Warmington (=351, 352–55 Marx); 377–79W=364–66M. Note also the visual metaphor in 84–85W=84–85M.

88. Lucilius 1013W=1085M.

89. Lucilius 1014W=1084M.

90. On roll versus codex, see T. Birt, *Das antike Buchwesen in seinem Verhältnis zur Literatur* (Berlin, 1882); W. Schubart, *Das Buch bei den Griechen und Römern* (Berlin, 1907); Guillemin, *Le public et la vie littéraire à Rome*, pp. 65ff.; F. Kenyon, *Books and Readers in Ancient Greece and Rome*, 2d edition (Oxford, 1951), pp. 87–120; C. H. Roberts, "The Codex," *Proceedings of the British Academy* 40 (1954): 169–204; G. Cavallo, *Libro e publico alla fine del mondo antico* (1975); O. A. W. Dilke, *Roman Books and Their Impact* (Leeds, 1977); E. G. Turner, *The Typology of the Early Codex* (Philadelphia, 1977); Kenney, "Books and Readers in the Roman World"; and Fedeli, "Autore, committente, pubblico in Roma."

91. Kenyon, *Books and Readers*; Roberts, "The Codex" (expense of papyrus); T. C. Skeat, "The Length of the Standard Papyrus and the Cost-Advantage of the Codex," *ZPE* 45 (1982): 169–76; Fedeli, "Autore, commitente, pubblico."

92. Kenyon, *Books and Readers*; G. Cavallo, "Testo, libro, lettura," in *Lo spazio letterario di Roma antica*, vol. 2, pp. 307–42, esp. pp. 327ff.

93. Turner, *Typology of the Early Codex*, p. 40.

94. Kenyon, *Books and Readers*; Roberts, "The Codex"; Turner, *Typology of the Early Codex*, p. 40; Fedeli, "Autore, committente, pubblico."

95. For example, Roberts, "The Codex," p. 195, writing about third-century codices, states: "These are omnibus volumes of a poverty-stricken age in which fewer and fewer people would be able to build and maintain private libraries." But it is equally possible that the circulation of cheap codices enabled more and more people to gain access to books, or at least enabled different people to gain access to books in different ways. On the need to develop a more sophisticated typology of early writing materials, see A. Bowman, "Literacy in the Roman Empire: Mass and Mode," in *Literacy in the Roman World*, pp. 119–32.

96. Catullus 42.

97. Pliny *H. N.* 13.68: cum chartae usu maxime humanitas vitae constet, certe memoria.

98. Martial 14.1–5, discussed by Kenyon, *Books and Readers*, pp. 92–94; Turner, *Typology of the Early Codex*, pp. 37ff.; Cavallo, "Testo, libro, lettura," pp. 325–26; and J. P. Sullivan, *Martial: The Unexpected Classic* (Cambridge, 1991), pp. 12–15.

99. Kenyon, *Books and Readers*, p. 90.

100. Bowman, "Literacy in the Roman Empire," p. 128.

101. Ibid.

102. Turner, *Typology of the Early Codex*, pp. 89–101.

103. R.W. Müller, *Rhetorische und syntaktische Interpunktion: Untersuchungen zur Pausenbezeichnung im antiken Latein* (Ph.D. diss., University of Tübingen, 1964); T. Habinek, *The Colometry of Latin Prose* (Berkeley, 1985), pp. 42–88; J. N. Adams, "The Language of the Vindolanda Writing Tablets: An Interim Report," *Journal of Roman Studies* 85 (1995): 86–135.

104. T. Veblen, *The Theory of the Leisure Class* (New York, 1934). Of course luxury codices could also be produced. Cowell, "Book Production in Ancient Rome," uses the price list on Diocletian's Edict to estimate the cost of a deluxe codex of Vergil at 2500 denarii, in contrast to the 150 denarii limit set on the daily wages of a figure painter. Cf. Fedeli, "Autore, committente, pubblico."

105. Martial 14.1–5 (see n. 94, above).

106. See N. Horsfall, "Statistics or States of Mind?" in *Literacy in the Roman World*, pp. 59–76, for a fuller discussion of the issue.

107. Fehrle, *Das antike Bibliothekwesen*; P. Fedeli, "Biblioteche private e pubbliche à Roma nel mondo antico" in *Le biblioteche nel mondo antico e medievale*, ed. G. Cavallo (Roma–Bari, 1989), pp. 31–53.

108. See works cited in headnote, above.

109. Bowman, "Literacy in the Roman Empire," p. 123.

110. For entrepeneurs, see the satirical portrait in Petronius's *Cena Trimalchionis*.

111. M. K. Hopkins, "Conquest by Book," in *Literacy in the Roman Empire*, pp. 133–59.

112. Horsfall, "Statistics or States of Mind?"; Hopkins, "Conquest by Book."

113. G. Susini, *The Roman Stonecutter: An Introduction to Latin Epigraphy*, ed. with an intro. by E. Badian, trans. A. M. Dabrowski (Totowa, New Jersey, 1973).

114. See the inscriptions quoted in M. Lefkowitz and M. Fant, *Women in Greece and Rome* (Toronto, 1977).

115. On the status of early Christians, see R. Lane Fox, *Pagans and Christians* (New York, 1987), pp. 265ff.

116. Hopkins, "Conquest by Book," p. 145, n. 33. Cf. Cavallo, "Testo, libro, lettura," pp. 329ff., on the association of papyrus rolls with the accoutrements of *otium*.

117. My discussion of Coptic is drawn from Hopkins, "Conquest by Book," pp. 144–48. He cites P. E. Kahle, *Bala'izah* 1 (Oxford, 1954), pp. 193ff. We might also note Cavallo's remarks ("Testo, libro, lettura," p. 336) on the ancient Roman's ability to choose between reading silently and reading aloud.

118. Hopkins, "Conquest by Book," p. 146.

119. Ibid., p. 147.

120. Ibid., p. 145.

CHAPTER SIX

ROMAN WOMEN'S USELESS KNOWLEDGE

Amy Richlin, in her article "Sulpicia the Satirist," *Classical World* 86 (1992): 125–40, calls attention to the puzzling scarcity of women writers in the Roman world. She lists the surviving texts from pre-Christian Rome as "six or eight poems by Sulpicia the elegist, two spurious letters of Cornelia, a Greek version of a speech by Hortensia, a mutilated letter from a frontier fort in northern Britain" (p. 125). On writing by ancient women, see also J. Snyder, *The Woman and the Lyre* (Carbondale, Illinois, 1989); M. Lefkowitz, "Did Ancient Women Write Novels?" in *Women Like This: New Perspectives on Jewish Women in the Greco-Roman World*, ed. A.-J. Levine (Atlanta, 1991), pp. 199–220; and R. S. Kraemer, "Women's Authorship of Jewish and Christian Literature in the Greco-Roman Period," in *Women Like This*, pp. 221–42. On women and literacy, see the sources listed in M. Lefkowitz and M. Fant, *Women in Greece and Rome* (Toronto, 1977); also S. B. Pomeroy, *"Technikai kai Mousikai," American Journal of Ancient History* 2 (1977): 51–68; and S. G. Cole, "Could Greek Women Read and Write?" in *Reflections of Women in Antiquity*, ed. H. Foley (New York, 1981), pp. 219–46. For a view of the gender dynamics of Latin love poetry comparable to that developed here, see K. Gutzwiller and A. N. Michelini, "Women and Other Strangers: Feminist Perspectives in Classical Literature," in *(En)Gendering Knowledge: Feminists in Academe*, ed. J. E. Hartman and E. Messer-Davidow (Knoxville, Tennessee, 1991), pp. 66–84, who suggest that "by using the subversive strain of the Hellenistic to effect a covert reversion to the masculine ethos, Roman love poets found ways of reasserting traditional male dominance in matters of sex" (p. 76). B. K. Gold, " 'But Ariadne Was Never There:' Looking for Roman Women in Latin Love Poetry," in *Feminist Theory and the Classics*, ed. N. Rabinowitz and A. Richlin (New York, 1993), cites the article by Gutzwiller and Michelini but contends that love poetry such as that of Propertius creates a space for the questioning of traditional male ethos without, however, pointing to any traces of such questioning in the historical record of the period. I agree that love elegy participates in a transformation of Roman discourse concerning sexuality and gender but regard that transformation as more complex than a simple transition from acceptance of patriarchy to rejection of patriarchy. See my paper "The Invention of Sexuality in the World-City of Rome," in *The Roman Cultural Revolution*, ed. T. Habinek and A. Schiesaro (Cambridge, 1997), pp. 23–43.

1. Richlin, "Sulpicia the Satirist," p. 125.
2. J. E. G. Zetzel, *Latin Textual Criticism in Antiquity* (Salem, N.H., 1980, and New York, 1984), p. 237.
3. On Roman education, see H.-I. Marrou, *A History of Education in Antiquity*, trans. G. Lamb (London, 1956), and S. Bonner, *Education in Ancient Rome* (Berkeley, 1977).
4. Ennius *Annales* 268–86 (Skutsch). For discussion, see chapter 2, above; also T. Habinek, "Towards a History of Friendly Advice: The Politics of Candor in Cicero's *De Amicitia*," *Apeiron* 23 (1990): 165–85.
5. Catullus 65.2, Ovid *Ars* 2.425, etc.
6. *Aen.* 6.292.
7. Propertius 1.7.11, 2.11.6, 2.13.11; Ovid *Am.* 2.4.17; Tibullus 3.12.1.
8. *Tr.* 3.7.31.
9. Martial 2.90.9.
10. *CIL* I².1214.2, Sallust *Catil.* 25.2, Pliny *Ep.* 1.16.6, Statius *Silvae* 2.7.83.
11. Probus Verg. *buc.* 6.31p.336 (cited by Skutsch) refers to *Aen.* 6.724. On Anchises as a paradigm of Roman learning, see T. Habinek, "Science and Tradition in *Aeneid* 6," *Harvard Studies in Classical Philology* 92 (1989): 223–55.
12. *Thesaurus Linguae Latinae* vol. 5, pt. 1, col. 1751ff.
13. The *locus classicus* is the pair of letters by Seneca, numbers 94 and 95, on which see M. Bellincioni, *Educazione alla sapientia in Seneca*, Antichità classica e cristiana 17 (Brescia, 1977); Habinek, "Science and Tradition in *Aeneid* 6"; and chapter 7, below. On writing in Latin versus writing in Greek, see J. André, *La philosophie à Rome* (Paris, 1977), pp. 60–61.
14. Cic. *Brut.* 181ff., esp. 184–85. See also 198–200, 320.
15. Virtually the entire *Brutus* consists of evaluation of past orators. For exhortation concerning the present and future, see 330ff.
16. Vergil *Aen.* 6.292: et ni docta comes tenuis sine corpore vitas/ admoneat volitare cava sub imagine formae. Translation in text by Robert Fitzgerald. Norden's comment ad loc., "*doctus* stehendes Epitheton der Seher, z.B. Ovid fast. 1, 499 met. 3,322," is instructive but does not explain why the word is appropriate as a characteristic of a seer (E. Norden, *P. Vergilius Maro Aeneis Buch VI* [Stuttgart, 1926]).
17. Suet. *Nero* 23.
18. On *doctus* used of poets, see, for example, Lucretius 2.600, Propertius 2.34b.89, 3.21.28, Ovid *Am.* 3.9.62, Statius *Silvae* 2.7.76, Claudian 23.11, in addition to the passages discussed in the text.
19. On Hortensia, see Val. Max. 7.3, Quintil. 1.1.6, Appian 4.32.34.

20. Thus, O. Murray, "Symposium and Genre in the Poetry of Horace," *Journal of Roman Studies* 75 (1985): 35–50, remarks, "But in Italy from the Etruscan period women seem often to have been present as equals" (p. 40). The whole issue of women's involvement in symposia would probably benefit from careful reconsideration.

21. On homosociality in Catullus, see W. Fitzgerald, *Catullan Provocations: Lyric Poetry and the Drama of Position* (Berkeley, 1995).

22. The poem of Sappho is #31LP. The relationship between Sappho and Catullus is discussed most recently by D. O'Higgins, in "Sappho's Splintered Tongue: Silence in Sappho 31 and Catullus 51," *American Journal of Philology* 111 (1990): 156–67, which does not, however, refer to Catullus 35.

23. I read 2.13A and 2.13B as a connected text. For a recent discussion positing a lacuna within a single unified poem, see S. J. Heyworth, "Propertius 2.13," *Mnemosyne* 45 (1992): 45–59.

24. Propertius 2.13.57–58: sed frustra mutos revocabis, Cynthia, Manis:/ nam mea quod poterunt ossa minuta loqui? I translate *revoco* in accordance with meaning 4a in the *Oxford Latin Dictionary*, viz, "return the summons of, issue a counterchallenge." Cynthia's voice here exists only as counterpart to Propertius's. His muteness (*mutos Manis*) guarantees the inefficacy (*frustra*) of her speech. In line 58 my translation is based on the reading *qui* not *quid*.

25. See Cic. *In Pisonem* 99, where the orator proclaims his success in reducing Piso to a creature *sine voce*. My thanks to Andrew Kelly for calling this important passage to my attention.

26. Elizabeth D. Harvey, "Ventriloquizing Sappho: Ovid, Donne, and the Erotics of the Feminine Voice," *Criticism* 31 (1989): 115–38 (quotation from pp. 129–30). See also E. Harvey, *Ventriloquized Voices: Feminist Theory and English Renaissance Texts* (London, 1992).

27. On the importance of aristocratic display and literary performance, see F. Dupont, "*Recitatio* and the reorganization of the Space of Public Discourse," in *The Roman Cultural Revolution*, ed. T. Habinek and A. Schiesaro (Cambridge, 1997), pp. 44–60.

28. non sunt longa quibus nihil est quod demere possis (Martial 2.77.7).

29. See Gutzwiller and Michelini, "Women and Other Strangers"; Habinek, "The Invention of Sexuality," esp. pp. 29–30 and 37–38; and M. K. Gamel, "*Non sine caede*: Abortion Politics and Poetics in Ovid's *Amores*," *Helios* 16 (1989); 183–206.

30.   en ego, cum caream patria vobisque domoque,
            raptaque sint, adimi quae potuere mihi,
        ingenio tamen ipse meo comitorque fruorque:
            Caesar in hoc potuit iuris habere nihil.
        quilibet hanc saevo vitam mihi finiat ense,
            me tamen extincto fama superstes erit,
        dumque suis victrix omnem de montibus orbem
            prospiciet domitum Martia Roma, legar.

                                    (Ovid, *Tr.* 3.7.45–52)

CHAPTER SEVEN
AN ARISTOCRACY OF VIRTUE

An earlier version of this chapter appeared under the title "An Aristocracy of Virtue: Seneca on the Beginnings of Wisdom" in a collection dedicated to the study of beginnings in classical literature (*Yale Classical Studies* 29 [1992]) edited by F. M. Dunn and T. Cole. Although it was composed for that volume, it builds upon earlier work of mine on exhortation as a literary and cultural phenomenon in the Roman world, specifically "Science and Tradition in *Aeneid* 6," *Harvard Studies in Classical Philology* 92 (1989): 222–55, and "Greeks and Romans in Book 12 of Quintilian," *Ramus* 16 (1987): 192–202. Since the publication of those papers and of the earlier version of this chapter, I have had the opportunity to study the growing bibliography on literature as performance (see chapter 5) and to incorporate into this chapter some remarks on exhortation as the performative context recreated by Seneca's philosophical letters and treatises. My concern with performance—and with the social implications thereof—is the source of my reservations about M. Nussbaum's otherwise compelling rehabilitation of Seneca as a philosopher in her study *The Therapy of Desire: Theory and Practice of Hellenistic Ethics* (Princeton, 1994). Nussbaum rightly calls attention to the language of therapy that pervades writings in the Hellenistic philosophical tradition, including Seneca, and seeks to differentiate philosophy as therapy from other major types of philosophical discourse, ancient as well as modern. My own sense, largely formed prior to reading Nussbaum's work, is that the role of doctor or therapist is but one of many Seneca subsumes into his mega-performance (to borrow R. Martin's term in "The Seven Sages as Performers of Wisdom," in *Cultural Poetics of Archaic Greece*, ed. C. Dougherty and L. Kurke [Cambridge, 1993], pp. 108–28) as moral exhorter, one that derives its authority as much from cultural models of paternal responsibility, friendly advice, and patriotic exemplum as from what the Romans tended to regard as the highly specialized and rather low-status skills of doctoring and philosophizing. On the relationship between general and specific expertises in Roman culture there is now a very helpful discussion by A. Wallace-Hadrill, in "*Mutatio Morum*: The Idea of a Cultural Revolution," in *The Roman Cultural Revolution*, ed. T. Habinek and A. Schiesaro (Cambridge, 1997), pp. 3–22. Wallace-Hadrill discusses the disintegration of aristocratic authority as specialized expertises come into play in the late republic and the efforts of Julius and especially Augustus Caesar to coordinate the work of specialists in fields like time, law, and language to the advantage of the Roman state. My reading of Seneca presents him as very much a latter-day Augustus, eager to align the authority of various experts to his own expansive personal and cultural project. For more conventional accounts of the place of Seneca as a thinker within the intellectual history of the ancient world, see A. A. Long, *Hellenistic Philosophy* (New York, 1974), and M. Colish, *The Stoic Tradition from Antiquity to the Early Middle Ages*, 2 vols., Studies in the History of Christian Thought 34 and 35 (Leiden, 1985). On Seneca as a figure within Roman culture, still helpful is S. Dill, *Roman Society from Nero to Marcus Aurelius* (London, 1904). M. T. Griffin, *Seneca: A Philosopher in Politics* (Oxford, 1976), resolves many particular problems with respect to Seneca's career but presents little over-all sense of the ideological grounding and significance of his surviving writings.

1. *Brev.* 3.5; *Ep.* 13.16–17; 23.9–10. Related to the idea of beginning to live is the claim that we are not born wise or innocent, but make ourselves so, e.g., *Clem.* 1.6.4; *Ira* 2.10.

2. W. V. Harris, *Ancient Literacy* (Cambridge, Mass., 1989), pp. 175–284; with modification and expansion in *Literacy in the Roman World, Journal of Roman Archaeology*, Supplementary Series 3 (Ann Arbor, 1991).

3. Quint. 10.1.126. Tac. *Ann.* 12.8 offers general confirmation of Seneca's popularity.

4. Griffin, *Seneca*, describes Lucilius, Seneca's most frequent addressee, as a "self-made *eques*" (p. 91) and, more tentatively, Aebutius Liberalis, addressee of *De beneficiis*, as "a provincial who rose through the ranks quickly" (p. 456). Other addresses include Annaeus Serenus, who served as praefectus vigilum; Seneca's brother Novatus, of senatorial rank; Seneca's father-in-law, Pompeius Paulinus, who reached the rank of praefectus annonae; his mother, Helvia; Marcia, the daughter of the senatorial historian Cremutius Cordus; Polybius, the freedman of Claudius; and the young emperor Nero. The addressees were no doubt of loftier status than the average reader, but the latter would almost certainly have been a member of the educated, propertied, urban elites.

5. I know of no single comprehensive work on the Roman tradition of exhortation. Helpful on aspects of the topic are the following: J. André, *La philosophie à Rome* (Paris, 1977), pp. 40ff.; H. Cancik, *Untersuchungen zu Senecas epistulae morales*, Spudasmata 18 (Hildesheim, 1967); A. Guillemin, *Pline et la vie littéraire de son temps*, Collection des études latines 4 (Paris, 1929), chap. 1; I. Hadot, *Seneca und die griechisch-römische Tradition der Seelenleitung*, Quellen und Studien zur Geschichte der Philosophie 13 (Berlin, 1969); as well as works by Dill and Habinek cited in the headnote to this chapter.

6. On which see the useful collection of essays *Mega nepios: Il destinatario nell'epos didascalico/ The Addressee in Didactic Epic*, ed. A. Schiesaro, P. Mitsis, and J. S. Clay, Materiali e discussioni per analisi dei testi classici 31 (Pisa, 1993).

7. See, for example, the parainetic oratory of the Aztecs, discussed by D. Abbott, "The Ancient Word: Rhetoric in Aztec Culture," *Rhetorica* 5 (1987): 251–64. L. Kurke, "Pindar's Sixth *Pythian* and the Tradition of Advice Poetry," *Transactions and Proceedings of the American Philological Association* 120 (1990): 85–108, traces a genre of *hypothēkai*, or precepts, in Greek literature to at least as early as the fifth century B.C.E.

8. Nussbaum, *Therapy of Desire*, pp. 45–46 and throughout, recognizes the importance of effect as a measure of therapeutic argumentation more generally.

9. *Ep.* 20.9; cf. *Ep.* 62.3.

10. deinde plus habiturum me auctoritatis non dubitabam ad excitandam te, si prior ipse consurrexissem (*Helv.* 1.1).

11. An old feature of aristocratic culture. See Habinek, "Science and Tradition," and chapter 2, above.

12. *Ep.* 21. Throughout the early letters Seneca calls attention to Epicurus as

a way of assimilating the philosopher's influence to his own as well as a means of signaling a generic competition with antiquity's most famous writer of philosophical letters. On Seneca's assimilation of Epicurus's teaching and authority, the bibliography is extensive. Particularly helpful is W. Schmid, "Eine falsche Epikurdeutung Senecas und seine Praxis erbauenden Lesung," *Acme* 8 (1955): 119–29. Seneca's attempted assimilation of Epicurus is probably not simply of antiquarian or aesthetic interest, but a part of Roman Stoicism's attempt to insist on the totality of its own explanatory (and hence political) power. For the extent of Epicureanism in the Principate, see P. Innocenti, "Per una storia dell'epicureismo nei primi secoli dell'era volgare: temi e problemi," *Rivista critica di storia della filosofia* 27 (1972): 123–47. On the connection between explanatory and political power, see B. D. Shaw, "The Divine Economy: Stoicism as Ideology," *Latomus* 44 (1985): 16–54.

13. Seneca's references to Demetrius are extensive, but consist chiefly of brief citations or allusions. He treats him as something of a freak whose distance from normal Roman social behavior is emphasized in order to keep the logical consequences of carrying out Seneca's teaching from becoming apparent.

14. At *Ep.* 21.44–45. Seneca contrasts by implication the true glory he offers Lucilius with the political glory sought by Cicero. At *Ep.* 23.1 and *Ep.* 67.1 he criticizes epistolary commonplaces of the sort found in Cicero's letters. At *Ep.* 97 he quotes an extensive passage of *Ad Atticum* 1.16.5 as evidence of the corruption of the times, and at *Ep.* 118.2 he specifically objects to Cicero's tendency to write whatever pops into his head (actually, mouth: quod in buccam venerit). The allusions to Cicero would have been especially functional as part of a campaign of self-glorification if the letters to Atticus had just become widely available. For publication in the Neronian period, see D. R. Shackleton Bailey, *Cicero's Letters to Atticus* (Cambridge, 1965) vol. 1, pp. 59–73; opposed by A. Setaioli, "On the Date of Publication of Cicero's Letters to Atticus," *Symbolae Osloenses* 51 (1976): 105–20.

15. In *Ep.* 94 and 95 Seneca expressly takes issue with what he represents as Aristo's representation of exhortation as derivative of dogma, and therefore dispensable. For discussion, see Habinek, "Science and Tradition," esp. pp. 241ff.

16. Wallace-Hadrill, reference in headnote above.

17. A. Traina, *Lo stile 'drammatico' del filosofo Seneca* (Bologna, 1978); M. Bellincioni, *Educazione alla sapientia in Seneca* (Brescia, 1977). My disagreement with Traina's description of a dramatic conflict between good and evil is not meant to deny the strongly theatrical element in Seneca's writing. But this theatricality is due, in my view, to the performative genre Seneca seeks to recreate and its strong association with aristocratic dominance.

18. E. Said, *Beginnings: Intention and Method* (New York, 1985), p. 34.

19. Virtue available to all: *Ep.* 44.3, 66.3; *Vit. beat.* 24.3; *Ben.* 3.18.1, 3.28.1–3.

20. *Brev.* 1.1–4, where the greater part of mortals is said to include even noble men (clarorum virorum) and the philosopher Aristotle.

21. Vivere, Gallio frater, omnes beate volunt, sed ad providendum quid sit quod beatam vitam efficiat caligant (*Vit. beat.* 1.1).

22. argumentum pessimi turba est (*Vit. beat.* 2.1).

23. On theatricality as an important element of the political life under the Roman emperors, see S. Bartsch, *Actors in the Audience: Theatricality and Doublespeak from Nero to Hadrian* (Cambridge, 1994). While Bartsch is right to see that theatricality becomes problematized in interesting ways during the period in question, its importance as an expression of aristocratic authority is much older than her study allows for.

24. E.g. *Ep.* 40, *Ep.* 52.14, *Ep.* 114. Note the paradoxical expression at *Ep.* 100.4: oratio sollicita philosophum non decet; how can one achieve decorum (the implication of *decet*) without being to some degree *sollicitus*, i.e., attentive?

25. On decorum as a process of exclusion, see E. Oliensis, "Canidia, Canicula, and the Decorum of Horace's Epodes," *Arethusa* 24 (1991): 107–38.

26. This quotation and those that follow are from *De ira* 1.1.2–4.

27. The role of exhortation in friendship is implied by the very setting of the *Laelius*. More particularly, see sections 17 and 88, as well as discussion by, T. Habinek, "Towards a History of Friendly Advice: The Politics of Candor in Cicero's *De Amicitia*," in *The Poetics of Therapy*, ed. M. C. Nussbaum, *Apeiron* 23 (1990): 165–85.

28. E. Cantarella, *Secondo natura: La bisessualità nel mondo antico*, Nuova biblioteca di cultura 289 (Rome, 1988), 129ff. (= *Bisexuality in the Ancient World*, trans. C. O. Cuilléanáin [New Haven 1992]). This division between the sexually entitled and the sexually available seems to have persisted despite other important developments in the Roman system of sex and gender during the principate. On the latter, see T. Habinek, "The Invention of Sexuality in the World-City of Rome," in *The Roman Cultural Revolution* (Cambridge, 1998), pp. 23–43.

29. Sen. *Contr.* 4pr10; cf. the discussion by A. Richlin, *The Garden of Priapus* (New Haven, 1983; reissue with new introduction, New York, 1992), pp. 220–26, esp. n. 11.

30. E.g., Tigellinus, as described at Tac. *Hist.* 1.72. This motive is imputed to Messalina's "husband" Silius at Tac. *Ann.* 11.28. Caligula is said to have seduced Ennia Naevia in order to have influence over her husband (Suet. *Cal.* 12). Mnester seems to have gained influence over Caligula this way (Suet. *Cal.* 36 and 55). Strategic seduction figured in the careers of Sejanus (Dio 57.19.5 and Tac. *Ann.* 4.1.2, 4.3.2f.) and perhaps Seneca (cf. the charges of adultery with Agrippina).

31. E. Cantarella, *Pandora's Daughters*, trans. M. Fant (Baltimore and London, 1987), pp. 135ff. While Roman women played an important role in the politics of the late republic, the elevation of a single household to supreme power expanded the opportunities for influence on the part of aristocratic women.

32. The charges are scattered throughout the accounts of the period by Dio, Suetonius, and Tacitus. For analysis of the political implications of the emperors' untraditional sexual behavior, see M. Cazenave and R. Auguet, *Les empereurs fous* (Paris, 1979), who argue among other things for a differentiation between emperors who seek to appeal to the populace, and thus are criticized savagely by a proelite historiographical tradition, and the so-called good emperors who are presented as such because they have made their peace with the aristocracy.

33. See Habinek, "The Invention of Sexuality in the World-City of Rome," drawing in particular on D. Milligan, *Sex-Life* (London, 1993), for the relationship between sexuality and cities, and on C. Barton, *The Sorrows of the Ancient*

Romans (Princeton, 1993), and D. Cohen, "The Augustan Law on Adultery: The Social and Cultural Context," in *The Family in Italy*, ed. R. Kertzer and D. Saller (New Haven, 1991), pp. 109–26, for the place of honor and shame in Roman society.

34. On the behavior expected of *cinaedi*, see J. Colin, "Juvenal, les baladins et les retiaires d'après le manuscrit d'Oxford," *Atti della Accademia delle Scienze di Torino, Classe di scienze morali, storiche e filologiche* 87 (1952–53): 315–85. A. Richlin, "Not before Homosexuality: The Materiality of the *Cinaedus* and the Roman Law against Love between Men," *Journal of the History of Sexuality* 3 (1993): 523–73, has argued that the *cinaedi* of ancient Rome represent a subculture comparable to male homosexuals in contemporary society. Her argument is part of a broader essentializing tendency of scholars who seek to locate forerunners of contemporary sexual categories in the ancient world. For my reservations about the approach and disagreements about aspects of the specific argument concerning homosexuality, please see my essay "The Invention of Sexuality in the World-City of Rome."

35. On the shame associated with being penetrated, and worse, with enjoying it, see the evidence collected by W. A. Krenkel, "Fellatio and irrumatio," *Wissenschaftliche Zeitschrift der Wilhelm-Pieck-Universität Rostock* 29 (1980): 77–88.

36. For the connotation of *grande*, cf. *Ep.* 92.35, where Maecenas is said to have had a genius that was *grande et virile*—if only prosperity hadn't unbelted him: *habuit enim ingenium et grande et virile, nisi illud secunda discinxisset*.

37. On reading and penetration, see J. Svenbro, *Phrasikleia: anthropologie de la lecture en Grèce ancienne* (Paris 1988) (= *An Anthropology of Reading in Ancient Greece*, trans. J. Lloyd [Ithaca, NY 1993]); also B. Forssmann, "ANNEMOTA in einer dorischen Gefassinschrift," *Münchener Studien zur Sprachwissenschaf* 34 (1976): 39–46.

38. Cf. the comments of Shaw, "The Divine Economy," p. 54, concerning Stoicism generally: "The doctrine faced the listener and reader, even the occasional one, with the fearsome and challenging possibility of the whole world being explicable by an idea that systematically excluded, even threatened, other interpretations of it. On the other hand, the enticement was that you actually knew what you were doing and knew that it was right."

39. On lyric apostrophe, see J. Culler, "Apostrophe," in *The Pursuit of Signs* (Ithaca, New York, 1981); on hymnic apostrophe, see A. L. T. Bergren, "Sacred Apostrophe: Re-presentation and Imitation in the Homeric Hymns," *Arethusa* 15 (1982): 83–108.

40. I follow the text of F. Haase in the Teubner edition (Leipzig, 1852).

41. The textual corruption makes it impossible to say that Seneca does not specify the basis for selection; but the lacuna/e cannot be lengthy because of the reference to the addressee (always early in Seneca) and the close rhetorical and grammatical connection between *nihil* and the clause beginning *quod*.

42. P. Bourdieu, "Symbolic Power," translation by R. Nice of a lecture given at Harvard in 1973; printed as part of Centre for Contemporary Cultural Studies, *Stencilled Occasional Paper*, no. 46 (University of Birmingham, 1977), quotation from p. 2.

43. Quotations from Shaw, "The Divine Economy," pp. 36, 37, 48.

44. On Seneca's encounter with Posidonius in this letter and the letters surrounding it, see A. D. Leeman, *Mnemosyne* 4 (1951): 175–81; 5 (1952): 57–78; 6 (1953): 307–13; 7 (1954): 233–40.

45. The word *subrepens* describes the action of snakes. For the erotic implication, see W. Krenkel, "Tonguing," *Wissenschaftliche Zeitschrift der Wilhelm-Pieck-Universität Rostock* 30 (1981): 37–54, esp. 41–42. For the erotic significance of *inrumpo*, see Krenkel, "Fellatio and irrumatio." The imagery of snakes figures prominently in Nussbaum's interpretation of Seneca's *Medea*, chapter 12 of *The Therapy of Desire*.

CHAPTER EIGHT

PANNONIA DOMANDA EST

Important recent studies of Ovid's exile poetry include F. Millar, "Ovid and the *Domus Augusta*: Rome seen from Tomoi," *Journal of Roman Studies* 83 (1993): 1–17; P. Green, "Ovid in Exile," *Southern Humanities Review* 28 (1994): 29–41; and G. Williams, *Banished Voices: Readings in Ovid's Exile Poetry* (Cambridge, 1994), with a thorough and up-to-date bibliography. Also useful are H. B. Evans, *Publica Carmina: Ovid's Books from Exile* (Lincoln and London, 1983), and B. R. Nagle, *The Poetics of Exile: Program and Polemic in the Tristia and Epistulae ex Ponto of Ovid*, Collection Latomus 170 (Brussels, 1980). Closest to my approach is M. Labate, "Elegia triste ed elegia lieta. Un caso di riconversione letteraria," *Materiali e discussioni per analisi dei testi classici* 19 (1987): 91–129. In the second half of his article Labate discusses Ovid's negotiation of the revised protocols of friendship prompted by his isolation from Rome; my focus is on Ovid's construction of relations within the elite and between elite and subordinate populations as enabling conditions for new strategies of pacification. For the historical context of the exile poetry, see in particular volume 10 of the revised *Cambridge Ancient History* (Cambridge, 1996), especially chapters by E. S. Gruen, "The Expansion of the Empire under Augustus," pp. 147–97; M. Crawford, "Italy and Rome from Sulla to Augustus," pp. 414–33; and J. J. Wilkes, "The Danubian and Balkan Provinces," pp. 545–85. For more detail on Tomis and its surroundings I have relied on N. Ehrhardt, *Milet und seine Kolonien*, Europäische Hochschulschriften, 3. Reihe Geschichte und ihre Hilfswissenschaften, Bd. 206 (Frankfurt am Main, 1983), as well as specialized articles and studies listed in the notes below. Useful works on colonialism in other periods of history, and especially the relationship between literature and colonialism, include S. Greenblatt, *Marvelous Possessions: The Wonder of the New World* (Chicago, 1991), and A. Grafton, *New Worlds, Ancient Texts: The Power of Tradition and the Shock of Discovery* (Cambridge, Mass., 1992), on European encounters with the Americas in the fifteenth through seventeenth centuries; S. Gruzinski, *The Conquest of Mexico*, trans. E. Corrigan (Cambridge, 1993), on Spanish-Aztec interactions in early colonial Mexico; M. L. Pratt, *Imperial Eyes: Travel Writing and Transculturation* (New York, 1992), and E. W. Said, *Culture and Imperialism* (New York, 1993), chiefly on nineteenth- and early twentieth-century European approaches to Latin America, Africa, and India; and C. Dougherty, *The Poetics of Colonization in Archaic Greece* (Oxford, 1993). More conventionally historical works include F. Jenkins, *The Invasion of America* (Chapel Hill, 1975), on the Puritans in New England, and D. K. Fieldhouse's comparative study, *The Colonial Empires: A Comparative Survey from the Eighteenth Century* (Frankfurt am Main, 1965; repr. New York, 1991).

The text of Ovid used throughout this chapter is the Oxford text of S. G. Owen. There is a new translation of the exile poetry, together with extensive notes, by P. Green in the Penguin Classics series (London, 1994). The epigraph for the chapter is cited, without specific attribution, by Said at *Culture and Imperialism*, p. 13.

1. On the mutually constructing relationship of periphery and center, see Pratt, *Imperial Eyes*, esp. pp. 4–6. Pratt is also the source of the expression "contact zone," introduced above.

2. The key ancient sources on the period are Velleius 2.111, Dio 55.34, and Pliny *H.N.* 7.149. For a modern evaluation, see chapter 12 of the revised *Cambridge Ancient History*.

3. Dio provides an especially vivid account of turmoil at Rome prompted by the extreme measures (heavy taxation, extraordinary military levies, etc.) required in the suppression of the Pannonian revolt at 55.22–27.

4. The term *sodalis* occurs at *Tr.* 1.51., 1.7.10, 3.8.9, 4.5.1, 4.645, 4.8.11, 4.10.46; *P.* 1.8.25, 2.4.33, 2.6.5, 3.6.1, 4.13.1. On the sympotic connotations of the word, see chapter 2, above. Labate, "Elegia triste e elegia lieta," discusses Ovid's thematization of the requirements of friendship in the poetry from exile. Cf. E. Block, "Poetics in Exile: An Analysis of *Epistulae ex Ponto* 3.9," *Classical Antiquity* 1 (1982): 18–27.

5. Editors disagree whether *Tr.* 5.7.25 commences a new elegy or not. See the recent discussion in Williams, *Banished Voices*, pp. 20–26.

6. See the discussion in chapter 2, above.

7. For the application of the adjective to Ovid's poetry, see *Tr.* 3.1.10.

8. P. Hardie, "Questions of Authority," in *The Roman Cultural Revolution*, ed. T. Habinek and A. Schiesaro (Cambridge, 1997). With respect to *Tristia 2*, addressed to Augustus, see the sensible remark of A. Barchiesi, "Insegnare ad Augusto: Orazio, Epistole 2, 1 e Ovidio, Tristia II," *Materiali e discussioni, per analisi dei testi classici* 31 (1993): 149–84: "Con le fonti che abbiamo, non possiamo neppure immaginare cosa volesse dire essere 'contro Augusto,'" (given our sources, we cannot even imagine what it would mean to be "anti-Augustan") (p. 151).

9. On the "unreality" of the exile poetry, see Williams, *Banished Voices*, pp. 3–49, and Green, "Ovid in Exile." The argument that Ovid never went into exile has been forcefully advanced by A. D. Fitton Brown, "The Unreality of Ovid's Tomitan Exile," *Liverpool Classical Monthly* 10.2 (February 1985): 18–22. Cf. the rebuttal by D. Little, "Ovid's Last Poems: Cry of Pain from Exile or Literary Frolic in Rome?" *Prudentia* 22 (1990): 23–39. Throughout this essay I have written as if Ovid did in fact go to Tomis, but the ideological force of his depiction of the Tomitans and of himself would not be categorically different if the whole project were fictitious. I believe that the modern fascination with the exile poetry stems in large part from an underlying conviction that the exile took place. J.-M. Claassen, "Ovid's Poems from Exile: The Creation of a Myth and the Triumph of

Poetry," *Antike und Abendland* 34 (1988): 158–69, refers to the "myth" of exile as a way of circumventing the reality/unreality debate. But her discussion does not consider the significant social and ideological functions that myth serves, in antiquity as in the present day.

10. On the close connection between *Tristia* 2 and Horace *Epistle* 2.1, see also Barchiesi, "Insegnare ad Augusto."

11. D. Adamasteanu, "Sopra il 'Geticum libellum,' " in *Ovidiana*, ed. N. I. Herescu (Paris, 1958), pp. 391–95.

12. The Getic poem, its content, and its context are discussed by Ovid at *Epistulae Ex Ponto* 4.13.17ff. For discussion, see D. Adamasteanu, "Sopra il 'Geticum libellum,' " E. Lozovan, "Ovide et le bilingualisme," and N. I. Herescu, "Poeta Getes," all in *Ovidiana*, ed. N. I. Herescu (Paris, 1958), pp. 391–95, 396–403, and 404–5 respectively. Millar, "Ovid and the *Domus Augusta*," connects the content of Ovid's laudation to other descriptions of the transfer of power between Augustus and Tiberius, including *Fasti* 1.529–36 and the oath of loyalty from Palaipaphos in Cyprus (*Supplementum Epigraphicum Graecum* 18.578). For a sense of the uncertainties prompted by the death of Augustus, at home and abroad, one need look no further than the vivid account in book 1 of Tacitus's *Annales*.

13. See, for example, E. Hall, *Inventing the Barbarian: Greek Self-Definition through Tragedy* (Oxford, 1989).

14. On the restriction of the vendetta, see C. Barton, "All Things Become the Victor: Paradoxes of Masculinity in Early Imperial Rome" (lecture delivered at Princeton University, March, 1993).

15. On evidence for Greek institutions and civic culture in Tomis, see C. Danoff, "Tomis" *RE* suppl.-bd. 9.1397f.; S. Lambrino, "Tomes, cité géto-grecque, chez Ovide," in *Ovidiana*, 379–90; E. Lozovan, "Realités pontiques et necessités littéraires chez Ovide," in *Atti del Convegno Internazionale Ovidiana, Sulmona, maggio 1959* (Rome, 1959), vol. 2, pp. 355–70 and "Ovide, Agnothète de Tomes," *Revue des études latines* 39 (1961): 172–81; D. M. Pippidi, "Tomis, cité géto-grecque à l'époque d'Ovide," *Athenaeum* 65 (1977): 250–56; Ehrhardt, *Milet und sein Kolonien*, passim; and Green, "Ovid in Exile." Millar's remarks at "Ovid and the *Domus Augusta*," p. 10, are typical of the trend of research: "Ovid may mislead his readers into forgetting that Tomis, far from being 'Getic,' was a long-established Greek city, which will have had much the same diplomatic relations to governors and emperors as any others." On Roman presence in Tomis and the other cities of the Dobrudja, see Wilkes, "The Danubian and Balkan Provinces," esp. pp. 568–69.

16. Williams, *Banished Voices*, pp. 8ff., following F. Hartog, *The Mirror of Herodotus: The Representation of the Other in the Writing of History* (Berkeley, 1988), and R. F. Thomas, *Lands and People in Roman Poetry: The Ethnographical Tradition* Proceedings of the Cambridge Philological Society, suppl. vol. 7 (Cambridge, 1982).

17. Greenblatt, *Marvelous Possessions*.

18. Williams, *Banished Voices*, p. 7.

19. Compare Ovid's formulation to Tacitus *Annales* 1.9.5, where those who praise Augustus at the time of his death do so in part because he has set secure

boundaries for the empire and left the various military assets well coordinated with one another: mari Oceano aut amnibus longinquis saeptum imperium; legiones provincias classes, cuncta inter se conexa.

20. See Dougherty, *The Poetics of Colonization*, p. 23, where she dicusses Plutarch's version of the colonization of Syracuse as "part of a larger pattern of colonial representation dating back to the Homeric poems—one that omits mention of the bloodshed inherent in colonizing foreign lands and substitutes for it stories of Greek colonists as murderers in exile."

21. On the identity and significance of Ovid's addressees, see especially R. Syme, *History in Ovid* (Oxford, 1978).

22. *P.* 4.14.53–56.

23. Lozovan, "Ovide, agnothète de Tomes."

24. See note 30, below.

25. Pippidi, "Tomis, cité géto-grecque à l'époque d'Ovide."

26. For language as a mark of elite status in the Roman world and in particular the struggles over Latinity in the early principate, see W. M. Bloomer, *Latinity and Literary Society at Rome* (Philadelphia, 1997).

27. Plowing as metaphor for sexual intercourse: P. duBois, *Sowing the Body* (Chicago, 1988), p. 65, with a long list of primary sources in note 1. See also J. N. Adams, *The Latin Sexual Vocabulary* (Baltimore, 1982), pp. 24, 154–55. On writing and sexual intercourse, see J. Svenbro, *Phrasikleia: An Anthropology of Reading in Ancient Greece*, trans. J. Lloyd (Ithaca, 1993), pp. 187ff., also discussing Roman material.

28. On the meaning of *opus* and other sexual metaphors in Ovid's description of his elegies, see D. Kennedy, *The Arts of Love* (Cambridge, 1993), pp. 46–63.

29. Fieldhouse, *The Colonial Empires*, p. 103.

30. The Conrad reference is from Said, *Culture and Imperialism*, p. 68. On the general transformation of Roman imperialism during the reign of Augustus, see the judicious discussion of Gruen, "The Expansion of the Empire." With respect to the year 10 C.E., in the aftermath of the Pannonian revolt, Gruen writes, "[t]he process of consolidation and organization lay in the future. But the conquest was complete" (p. 178). His remarks are remarkably consistent with the position of Ovid discussed throughout this chapter.

31. The quotations in this paragraph are all from Green, "Ovid in Exile," pp. 36, 38, 33, and 34, respectively.

32. Williams, *Banished Voices*, pp. 154ff., esp. pp 182–84. Gruen also misconstrues the force of the gerundive when he writes, "Even in the poems from exile, late in Augustus' reign, Ovid's praise of the princeps places stress upon victory, the garnering of military laurels, the conquest of Pannonia, Raetia, and Thrace." My interpretation is more in accord with Peter Green's note on the passage in his Penguin translation: "The topical allusions are followed by a flashback" (p. 227).

33. T. Weidemann, "The Political Background to Ovid's *Tristia* 2," *Classical Quarterly* 25 (1975): 264–71, provides an insightful analysis of the vulnerability of the princeps prior to and during the early years of Ovid's relegation, referring to domestic disturbances and to political maneuvering among the elites over control of Augustus's would-be heirs. But he ventures into unnecessary speculation

when he suggests that Ovid did not intend for Augustus to read *Tristia* 2 and that he was "unable to hide his bitterness towards Augustus" (p. 271) in the poem. Pointing out contradictions between Augustus's treatment of Ovid and his handling of other cultural matters hardly seems an inappropriate or intemperate tack to take with respect to the emperor. Read purely in terms of Ovid's practical goal of gaining relief from the conditions of relegation, the poem might better be said to seek support wherever Ovid can find it.

34. The most useful discussion of the ideology of the arena is Erik Gunderson's article of the same title in *Classical Antiquity* 15 (1996): 113–51. The paper modifies in important ways the discussions of Carlin Barton in "The Scandal of the Arena," *Representations* 27 (1989): 1–36, and in *The Sorrows of the Ancient Romans: The Gladiator and the Monster* (Princeton, 1993).

35. D. Kennedy, "'Augustan' and 'Anti-Augustan': Reflections on Terms of Reference," in A. Powell, ed., *Roman Poetry and Propaganda in the Age of Augustus* (Bristol, 1992), pp. 59–82.

36. Said, *Culture and Imperialism*, p. 67.

37. Pratt, *Imperial Eyes*, pp. 124ff.

38. Ibid., p. 18.

39. J. I. Sanchez, *The Spanish Black Legend: Origins of Anti-Hispanic Stereotypes* (Albuquerque, N.M., 1990); D. J. Weber, *The Spanish Frontier in North America* (New Haven, 1992), pp. 336ff.

40. Pratt, *Imperial Eyes*, pp. 244ff.

41. G. B. Conte, "The Inventory of the World: Form of Nature and Encyclopedic Project in the Work of Pliny the Elder," in *Genres and Readers*, trans. by G. W. Most with a foreword by C. Segal (Baltimore, 1994), pp. 67–104.

42. While my critique has focused on contemporary scholarly receptions of the exile poetry, it could easily be extended to include recent poetry, artistic renderings, and especially novels. D. Malouf, *An Imaginary Life* (New York, 1978) presents an Ovid revitalized by the discovery of a "wild boy" raised completely apart from human company; C. Ransmayr, *The Last World* (New York, 1990), translation of *Die letzte Welt* (Nordlingen, 1988) by J. E. Woods, describes Cotta's quest for Ovid in a version of Tomi that combines contemporary and historical features. P. G. Christensen's study, "The Metamorphosis of Ovid in Christoph Ransmayr's *The Last World*," *Classical and Modern Literature* 12 (1992): 139–51 also refers to Vintila Horia, *God Was Born in Exile* (New York, 1961).

INDEX OF PASSAGES CITED

GENERAL INDEX

acculturation, 45, 54, 137, 184–85
Actium, battle of, 91
Aelia Galla, 130–31
Aelius Stilo, 51
Aeneas, 157
aestimatio. See *existimatio*
agriculture, 47
Agrippa (Marcus Vipsanius Agrippa), consul, 90, 92, 110–11, 198
Agrippa Postumus, 69
Alcaeus, 54
Alexander the Great, 30, 35, 69, 169
Alexandria, 91, 110; Museum at, 116
Alexandrianism, 63, 126–27
ambiguity, literary, 165–66
American Philological Association, 9
amicitia, 10–11, 186; in Ennius, 50–51
Anchises, 96–97, 124–25, 139
Anderson, Benedict, 6–7, 100
anti-Semitism, 30
Antony (Marcus Antonius), triumvir, 13, 157
Apollinaris, 131–32
Apollo, 40, 157
Appadurai, A., 54
Archilochus, 54
Aristo, 214
aristocracy, 12, 135, 141; in Cicero, 66, 69–70; characteristics of, 61–62, 134, 141–42, 202; in conflict with other sectors, 48, 53, 59, 106, 142–43; in Propertius, 129; in Seneca, 137–38, 150
aristocrats: acculturation of, 45; and *existimatio*, 45–60, 126–27; as performers, 103; as reliant on past, 45, 51–52; women as, 127, 130–35. *See also* birth
Aristotle, 169
Atticism, 63
Atticus (Titus Pomponius Atticus), 67, 94–6
Atrium Libertatis, 107
Augustus (Gaius Iulius Caesar Octavianus), emperor, 109, 199; in Horace, 92–93, 99–102; and imperial frontier, 88, 91–93, 153; and Italy, 88–89, 91–93, 98–100;

monuments of, 98, 110–11; in Ovid, 135, 151, 155–56, 161, 164–65; as pontifex, 93, 99–100; and Roman culture, 140, 151, 212; vulnerability of, 220
authority: ascribed vs. achieved, 185; as reorganized by Augustus, 140, 212; tradition as basis of, 46, 114
Aztecs, 45, 213

Badian, Ernst, 199
Bacchanals, 41, 76
bandits: in ancient history, 69–72, 75; in ideology, 69–70, 86; post-classical, 190–91. *See also* latro
Barchiesi, Alessandro, 9
Bartsch, Shadi, 214
Batstone, William, 190
Beard, Mary, 112
Berlin, University of, 17, 167
Bernal, Martin, 15, 21, 30, 173–74
birth, 137–38, 142, 148, 150
Blake, William, 151
Bolivar, Simon, 168
bonus/boni, 51, 56, 83, 141, 150
books: circulation of, 103, 107, 114, 116–17, 121, 137, 154; price of, 106
Bourdieu, Pierre, 66–67, 148
bulla, 143
Bulla Felix, 69

Caecilius, 127–28
Caecilius Epirota, 106–7
Caligula (Gaius Iulius Caesar Germanicus), emperor, 143
Calvus (Gaius Licinius Calvus Macer), 128–32
Campanile, E., 42
Campus Martius, 110
canons, literary, 94–98
Carneades, 60–61
carmina, 38–39; 49, 97–98
Carnochan, W. B., 171
Catholicism, 15, 22, 24, 27
Catilinarian Conspiracy, 70–75, 76–78, 80–81, 85–86

About the Author

THOMAS N. HABINEK is Professor of Classics at
the University of Southern California and author of
The Colometry of Latin Prose.